BoardFree

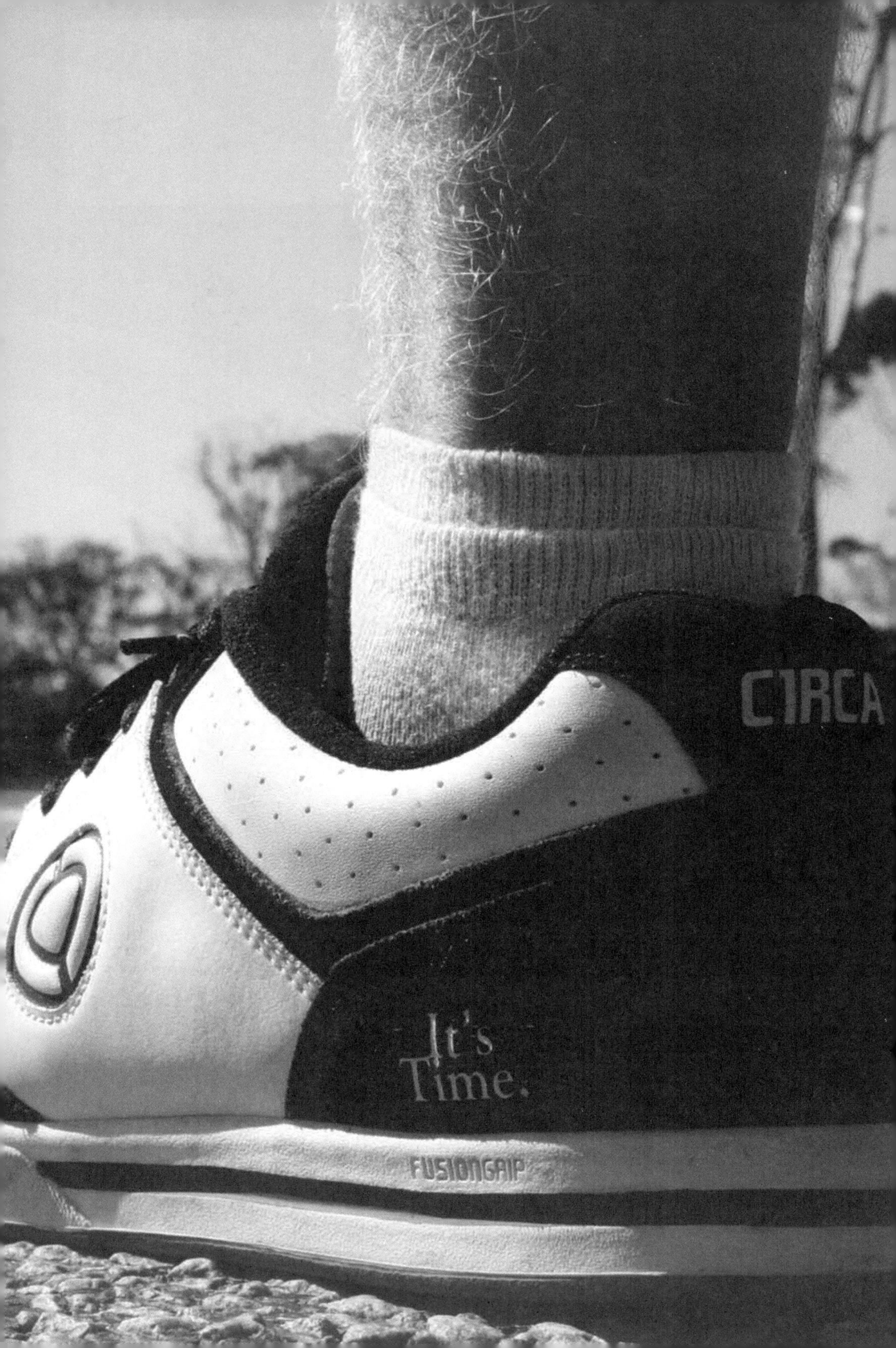
C1RCA
It's
Time.
FUSIONGRIP

BoardFree

The Story of an Incredible Skateboard
Journey across Australia

Dave Cornthwaite

PORTICO

First published in the United Kingdom in 2007 by
Portico
10 Southcombe Street
London
W14 0RA

An imprint of Anova Books Company Ltd

ISBN 10: 1 90603 219 X
ISBN 13: 9781906032197

A CIP catalogue record for this book is available from the British Library.

10 9 8 7 6 5 4 3 2 1

Reproduction by Spectrum Colour Ltd, UK
Typeset by SX Composing DTP, Rayleigh, Essex
Printed and bound by CT Printing Ltd, Hong Kong

This book can be ordered direct from the publisher.
Contact the marketing department, but try your bookshop first.

www.anovabooks.com

Contents

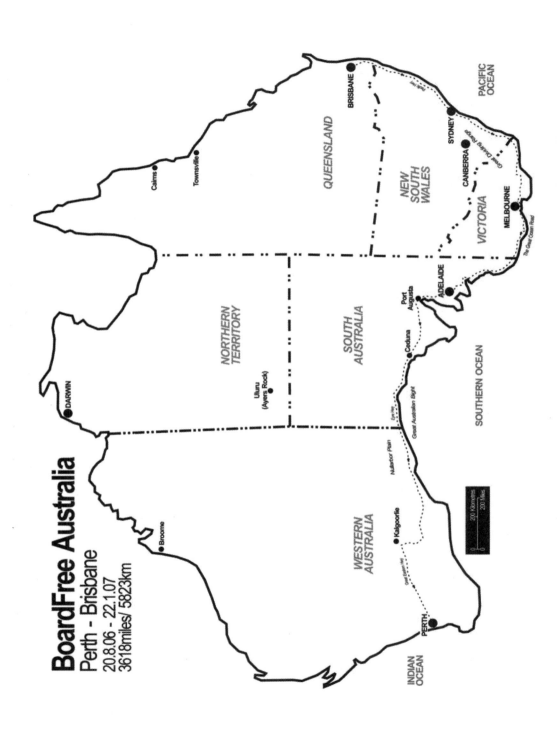

BoardFree Australia
Perth - Brisbane
20.8.06 - 22.1.07
3618miles/ 5823km

For Pauline, Peter and Andy Cornthwaite, whose unwavering support made the difficult times just that little bit easier. And for Kate, who despite everything stuck by me to the bitter end.

A Letter

4 August 2006

Hilarious man,

You have no idea what you are getting yourself into. And neither do any of the people spurring you on in this message board. My recommendation is bring a lot of hard core sunscreen bro you'll bloody need it. I'll be amazed if you make it through one full day without collapsing from exposure to the sun let alone get across the country. Half the Brits that turn up on on Bondi beach keel over after a day in the sun. To think that you can brave one of the harshest environments on the planet for the length of time you are planning with that pastey skin of yours is just laughable.

To give you an idea of what you are in for . . .

In the day time think Death Valley, Think Sahara. At night think snakes, goannas, poisonous spiders and scorpions crawling into your shoes and sleeping bag for warmth. And that's without mentioning speed crazed truckies driving by in giant articulated road trains full of cattle tossing up massive clouds of choking bull dust in their wake and that's just if it doesn't hit you. You will know what I mean when you see how one of those trucks can reduce a 7 foot red Kangaroo to a 30 foot long red smear in about a tenth of a second. They have a stopping distance of a half kilometre once they are up to speed and you don't wanna get in the way of one.

You had better get some all terrain wheels for that board too cos the road across the Nullarbor (which means no trees hence no shade by the way) isn't some rural English back road where the biggest obstacle is a cow pat. Those hard urathane wheels won't cut it unless you want to be the first person to carry a skateboard across Australia.

Oh and by the way it is dead flat and straight for hundreds and hundreds of kilometres so I hope you have been working out hard on your pushing leg.

My mates and I are taking bets on what day you will end up in hospital from dehydration, sunstroke or third degree sunburn. I am finding it hard to get someone to take anything beyond day 4 in the pool. Right now you probably think I am a wanker but in reality I am trying to save your life.

Good luck mate
You'll need it.

Steve Furness

That's the thing about Australians. They can shatter your hopes and dreams in an instant, but are still friendly enough to call you 'mate' once they're done. I stared at the screen for a little while, double-checking everything just in case I'd missed the general gist of Mr Furness's argument. Then, deciding that yep, this chap wasn't too keen on my little Australian plan, I took a sip of water and realised just how much I was shaking.

You see, this wasn't the first message of its kind that I'd received in the past year. I thought I'd got used to receiving them, but I hadn't. I probably never would. And perhaps it was time to accept that. But I was still trembling nevertheless and no matter what I told myself the reason was plain and simple. Because it hurt. I had dreamed a dream and I was pursuing it with plenty of gusto, but I didn't need obstacles like this. Little snipes from strangers. Verbal batterings from people around the world. I was trying to do something good, for God's sake, it wasn't like I'd set up a website declaring war on babies. But still they came, these messages, and this one cut deep. I'd never been to Australia before, and Steve Furness obviously had because he'd called me *mate*, but that's not the point. The point is, I'd never been to Oz, he had, and he was telling me that with all his knowledge of that vast, red, empty country, he wouldn't do what I was about to attempt. Which was, in short, a journey across Australia, on a skateboard. I shut my computer down, pondering the situation. Was this guy for real? Did he know something I didn't? Was he trying to save my life? Or, as he'd laid the option open to me, was he just a wanker? I picked up my board, Elsa, and decided that yes, he was a wanker. And no, he wasn't going to stop me. And that in his own little way he'd just made me more determined, which was a dangerous way to dissuade me from doing anything in the first place.

And then I went for a skate, because I was in training. And in nine days I was flying to Perth, Western Australia, because that was where my journey was starting. And I'd booked my tickets already, so even though Steve Furness had just scared the crap out of me I had to go. It was too late now. There was no backing out. So thanks for everything Steve, see you on the other side.

2 That Morning: Part One
Mid-April 2005

I woke to a deep rumbling that shook my pillow to its core. There was a degree of pressure on my forehead, not quite enough to force me downwards but enough to warrant some concern. So I opened my eyes to find out just what was happening, and there was the unmistakable shape of a cat's head obscuring my vision. 'Morning Kiwa,' I said, trying to feign sprightliness, because she's not happy when I'm grumpy.

My father's parents spent much of the sixties in East Africa. My dad was born in Tanzania and his sister schooled in Kenya, but without question the Cornthwaite's African legacy was to emerge through an unlikely lineage, cats. Almost every cat to have graced the doormat of a Cornthwaite home since the Amin era was given multiple Swahili names. The first was always *Paka*, which means, simply, 'cat'. *Paka* was always followed by something descriptive, like *kidogo*, describing the starting shape of my parents' cat, which was always rather small. Ironically, *Paka Kidogo* is now the prodigious holder of the title 'UK's fattest domestic cat', even though my mum insists it's on an eternal diet. My dad's sister, Auntie Ann, felt it necessary to label her new kitten *Paka*

Mukubwa, which in simple terms means 'large cat'. I never liked the thing, and that says a lot as I will always be a cat person, but it spent much of its time brooding beneath a stool or coffee table and you only realised it was there once you had prised two paws-full of extended claws out of your bleeding ankle.

Sometime in Spring 2004 I was finally handed the chance to add my own touch of novelty to the Cornthwaite's feline Swahili-naming tradition. I was working when the phone rang. It was Emily, my girlfriend's sister's partner. Long story.

'Dave,' said Emily sternly, 'do you want a cat?'

'Ummm, I'm not sure,' I answered glumly. I was struggling with the idea of gathering commitments; I was 24 years old and already had a house, a job and a long-term girlfriend. A cat would seal the deal and ensure that my youth was over. But I loved cats, and I couldn't resist, so I pushed my twenties aside and went for the kitten. 'I'll need to talk to Nat first, bring it over tonight and we'll see how it goes.'

When I got home Emily was on the sofa and Natalie clutched at four large paws. I poked around in her hands, trying to find out whether there was a kitten in there somewhere, and when I found it I lifted it up and my heart melted. This dark tortoiseshell, crying in high-pitched tweets, the largest paws you will ever see on a young cat. I was in love. 'You're not going anywhere, are you?' I said, without discussing anything with Nat. 'So what are we going to call you? Em, where did you find her?'

The tale of a house full of drug dealers unravelled and how they had left their house in Penlan under mysterious circumstances. A neighbour had peered over the fence and seen a small shape cowering in the long grass. A kitten! A call was placed, and then another, and the story ends here.

For the kitten had found a home, and it was to be named *Kiwa*, for *Kiwa* means 'abandoned' in the ancient language of Swahili.

*   *   *

Now, I was saying earlier that Kiwa had just woken me up by tapping my head. She customarily did this every morning because, I cynically assumed, she wanted feeding. But she did it so gently, so *softly*, as though she didn't want me to believe that food was the reason behind all of her show of affection. She actually loved me, and that I fed her was a pure, blissful bonus. This morning, however, seemed different. Her wide green eyes were burning into me, questioning with some urgency what we were doing here, again, another early morning in a lifetime of early mornings. At least, that's what I took from her stare.

'How you doing, girl?' I asked her.

She purred.

'Forty-five minutes until I have to be in work. Reckon I can make it?'

She purred.

'Why am I doing this Keys? I don't even want to go to work. I don't even like work.'

She purred.

'Look at you. You're what, two years old? You're never going to work, how's that fair? And you're perfectly happy with life aren't you, Kiwa? Tapping my head in the morning, getting fed. Curling up in a ball until I come home and feed you again. You lie on my bed all day, don't you? What a life.'

Kiwa cocked her head a little, pretending in her little cat way to hear something far away so she didn't have to listen to me anymore. By now she was sat neatly on my chest. She was always a very neat cat, paws all in order, side by side and not a millimetre out of place. She stared at me. Purring.

'But seriously Kiwa, if you don't have to go work, why should I? Seriously!'

She looked at me, alarmed that I was raising my voice. I felt sheepish after that, and just before I turned over and pushed my way to the side of the mattress I said one last thing to her, because I knew that as soon as I made my move she would be down the stairs and by the food bowl quicker than I could say . . .

'This sucks, doesn't it?'

And she nodded. I *swear* she nodded.

3 Rewind Three Weeks
Mid- to Late March 2005

Nat and I met in the first week of July 2002. I had begun what was to be an eighteen-month full-time post as editor of Swansea University's student newspaper, and she was a sabbatical officer for the Students' Union. At the end of that first week we had staff drinks. By the following Wednesday we were living together as a couple. Time went on and eventually our posts at the Union ran out. Nat and I moved from her place to mine, we began new jobs, we began to see less and less of each other. We were in our early twenties and lived like a married couple; a warm body nearby at night-time seemed to be just the trick. I loved her, she loved me, we loved what we had together but we didn't love where we were heading. We were young, changing, growing apart and avoiding the issue through pure comfort.

Facing up to reality wasn't easy. For three years Nat and I had shared each other's souls and I loved her desperately, but I wasn't happy. I knew she wasn't either but we never talked about it. We both knew that chat we needed to have would be the end of things – an agreement that yes we love each other, yes, we'd love it to work but no, it can't go on anymore. Mutual respect means saying goodbye and going our separate ways.

I found myself thinking, is this it? Do we continue to tiptoe around the subject in a hope that things would ignite again? I was scared. Everything in my life was about chasing an objective, making things work. Except at home. I didn't have the guts to deal with that.

One last throw of the dice. Come on holiday with my family, I ask her, hoping a week in the mountains would make our lives less stagnant and put things in perspective. She agrees. We buy heavy padded coats and gloves. I buy a beanie hat with a fluffy beaver's head sticking out of it. Let's go and play in the snow.

*   *   *

I sit on a flimsy plastic chair in Grenoble Airport. Milling around is an eclectic group with whom we had shared a chalet. Nat walks around a shop looking at cheap trinkets and souvenirs; she'd had a good time but preferred the après-ski to the ski. I was the opposite. Feet anchored to a snowboard, I had spent the week flat on my back, neck-deep in snow and failing miserably in a quest to be good at a sport I really enjoyed. Seven years had passed since my last stint on a snowboard. I hadn't retained much skill in that time and now, heading home, I had a very real pang of disappointment. I've never liked to waste time and I was suffering from the unquestionable reality that the last week had been bloody brilliant and now it was over. I live in Swansea, South Wales. There is no snow in Swansea, there's not even a dry ski slope. Which means no snowboarding. Which means despite the obvious benefits of a holiday filled with fresh air and exercise I had just wasted a week.

I loved snowboarding, it was liberating and difficult and fast and every run left me full of hope, so the last thing I wanted was to return to the mountains next year having to spend yet another week as a beginner, wasting six days and several hundred pounds into the bargain. I started to wonder exactly how I could refine my snowboarding skills at home. Maybe surfing is the answer; God knows I need something new in my life. I stare around the airport at the array of faces. For some a holiday is ending, for others one is just beginning. For me, what is there to look forward to? My job is monotonous and dead-ended; my relationship with Nat wasn't exactly seaworthy. Great holiday. Let's go home.

My brother hands me an open magazine stuffed with articles about gadgets, an advert grabs my attention: *Tierney Rides T-Board: A longboard that rides like a snowboard, but on tarmac.* There is a picture of a green skateboard but it doesn't look like a skateboard. It's longer, and it only has two wheels. Big wheels, about the size of a fist, one at the front and one at the back. We're called to the gate and as we shuffle through customs I make a pact with myself: I'm going to get a T-Board.

Two days later. Back in the office. I stare at the Tierney Rides website, looking in amazement at videos of people carving down roads; tarmac pistes! How the hell had I missed this? Snowboarding on roads! The T-Board was £150, just about affordable, but I had other ideas. Part of my job was to compile, edit and design a newspaper called *HadOne*, which featured discount vouchers to be claimed in local shops and bars as well as feature content aimed at Swansea's youth, anyone from 13 to 35. Just what the paper needed, I proposed to myself – as I was, in fact, the editorial board – was a fortnightly section about extreme and alternative sports. I wrote to Tierney Rides, promising a full-page review in exchange for two boards, one to test and one to give away, and they replied before the day was out. Yes, they said, we accept your proposal.

*   *   *

Sunday morning. We returned from the snowboarding holiday one week ago. Nat is in town, the library or something. Lunch with a friend. Or something. I sit in the study; wooden floorboards and giant beanbags. I play a computer game, I fiddle with a website. I hear the front door open and shut, footsteps gently on the stairs. They sound different. Something is different.

> *I love her. She pushes upon the door.*
> *I love her.*
> *'We need to talk,' she says.*
> *I love her. I'm shaking.*
> *She stares at the floor.*
> *I stare at her. Numb.*
> *She sits.*
> *'I'm leaving you. We have to split up.'*
> *I stare at her, my head tumbling with emotion.*
> *Kiwa walks in. 'What about this one?' I ask.*
> *'She should stay here,' Nat says.*
> *We hug. I feel the love draining out of us.*
> *She stands and walks to the door.*
> *I stare at her.*

She doesn't look back.
I hear the front door open and shut.
She's gone.

* * *

Tuesday afternoon. A van pulls into a lay-by on the street below. Two heads peer through an oval window three floors above. One is mine; the other belongs to Neil, a friend and colleague. Neil and I have been waiting for this van and its contents every day for a week. Eleven days earlier I had read about the T-Board in Grenoble Airport and now I was preparing to sign for one. The deliveryman lugs out a package, it is actually longboard-shaped, wheels and everything. Neil and I get very excited.

We sit on the sofas in the foyer. I tentatively unwrap the board and then set it down on the carpet. I've never ridden any type of skateboard before and this T-Board, with its two parallel wheels, looks daunting. I have no idea what to do with it so I just look, touch, hold it. Spin its wheels. Little did I know it, but that board was going to change my life.

I cycle home with the board under my arm. Don a t-shirt, three-quarter-length trousers, socks, trainers and head out the door. At the bottom of my street there is a construction site where the old marina is being reinvigorated. It's relatively flat but there are a couple of sloping roads and I pause at the top of one of these, board at my feet, pulse racing. The T-Board's two-wheel set-up means it behaves somewhat like a bicycle, gaining stability as it gains speed. But speed wasn't something I was overly keen to discover on this first run; I just wanted a sign that I could ride the thing. With my right foot on the ground, just level with the centre of the board, I positioned my left at the front of the deck, directly over the front wheel but with my foot at a right angle across the board. It felt like the most unnatural thing in the world but I went with common sense and tried to keep my weight as central as possible. Then a final glance to check no one was around – this first run wasn't for anyone's eyes but mine – and I pushed off, lifting my pushing foot to the back of the deck, struggling to maintain balance as the board and I picked up speed, rolling downhill for all of ten seconds before the road bent gently to the left and levelled out. Thirty metres down the road I ran off the board, whooping with joy. My first ever hill, and no broken teeth. And then I swept up my board and ran to the top of the hill and did it again and again and again.

The next morning I skated to work, stumbling a few times, landing on my backside once when I misjudged the size of a stone. For five years I had been walking and cycling these boring, average streets and now, in one fell swoop, they had turned into a wonderland. Every pavement and curb was a roller coaster, every small hill a challenge, every lamppost an obstacle to carve around. A place I thought I knew so well was now full of fresh possibility and opportunity. My perspective had changed in an instant and I gave my board a name to reflect this. I searched for a Swahili word that would do the board proud, and decided to christen my T-Board *Uhuru*, which means 'freedom'.

The next issue of *HadOne* featured a double-page spread on the T-Board. Written with beginners in mind, through the eyes of a beginner, the article was well-received. A lady from the Gower Peninsula sent an email saying how much she had enjoyed the article and how keen she was to have a go on the T-Board. Another email, this time from a surfer, read: 'Dear Dave, I enjoyed the article. Will you be featuring more longboards in the future?'

I leant back in my chair considering the question. The whole process had seemed so easy. Tierney Rides had given me a board, why wouldn't other companies? Do I really want to start focusing on longboards every issue? It was a silly question, of course I do. This newspaper is just about the only thing that keeps me happy in this job so let's make it enjoyable, let's have a longboarding section.

I start to research the sport. Websites and forums full of longboard reviews, videos and pictures. I write to manufacturers and distributors, getting dragged into this new world full of words like carve and flow and stoke. There is nothing aggressive about this sport, it seems like everyone involved is cool and at ease with life. And although the 'cool' was still a bit beyond me, I was feeling energised by the enthusiasm that came with longboarding and its community. I wanted to be a part of it. I was *ready* to be a part of it.

4 That Morning: Part Two

Mid–April 2005

In the space of two weeks I had lost a partner and gained a hobby. I'd never go quite as far as to say I'd directly replaced Nat with a longboard, but I suppose, in a way, I had. Even in my condition of mild, convenient depression I could see that we weren't in an ideal state. I had gone to great lengths not to rock the boat where Nat was concerned and my complete lack of willingness to deal with the situation had effectively numbed me from everyday life. I was going through the motions, digging myself deeper and deeper into what I defined as a quarter-life crisis, but I knew my existence was drifting ever closer to the coastline of worthlessness. I was sick of myself.

I had held out my hand and counted my commitments, the things that anchored me to this deplorable position. Job. Girlfriend. House. Cat. Everything else was give and take, but these things formed a security blanket, a bubble, and to some extent a ball and chain. Thank God Natalie left me: not only did it free up one of my fingers, it made me realise that I probably shouldn't be seeing a woman who had bigger balls than me anyway. But I still had a Job. A House. A Cat.

Now, I don't want anybody to think I'm being ungrateful. I'm not, I'm really not, but this is how I was thinking about things. For some reason I just wasn't happy at work. I had a lovely little terraced house which was more than most people had when they were 25, but it wasn't anything without a mortgage and Uncle Halifax made sure he paid my bank account a visit every month. And then the Cat. Kiwa. I love the little ball of fluff, but if I go away I have to find someone to feed her, and I need to pay for that food, and the vet's bills. At least she was a cat, a nice, independent, occasionally aloof cat. And speaking of cats, I was telling you about the time when Kiwa *nodded* at me . . .

*   *   *

She was still there, paws together, perched upon my chest, staring intently. Just me and her in the house, broken gas timer clicking away like clockwork downstairs, a whistle of water through next door's pipes, swooshing eerily behind my wall. I was unhappy. Twenty-five years old and unhappy. It's just not right. I needed something to aim for, a chink of light at the end of it all, not just this end-of-month paper chase which was going to be spent and saved in unequal measure. So, I settled on logic to get me out of this mess. Forty minutes until work, let's think quickly. Kiwa helped me here, I imagined, and the questions she asked me are below, as the questions I *wanted* her to ask me, if you see what I mean.

'*What do you really want to do, Dave? If designing papers and websites isn't enough, what is?*'

'I want to travel. I've wanted to for a while. But with a difference. No more random backpacking, done that already. Travel with a difference. Maybe a job abroad? Maybe a journey with a purpose?'

'*OK, good.*' Kiwa continued to stare, and I convinced myself her eyes were wide with bemusement at the fact that for the first time in her short life, she was speaking English out loud. She continued, in her silent, purry way, '*So let's find a purpose. What do you want to do, what do you enjoy?*'

'Err, well . . . I like longboarding,' I said, and my heart started to beat faster. 'I really do like longboarding, I'm looking forward to the skate to work today, and the skate home, just not the bit in between.'

A surge of excitement bolted through me. My cat had asked me two very basic questions and I'd answered them with complete honestly. That's the benefit of talking about deep things with your pet, you can tell the truth without the weight of the world on your shoulders. I'd answered Kiwa's two questions and that was enough. I was going to put the two of them together, and I knew what was coming. I'd been single for less than a month and from that desperate, mournful position of having nowhere to go and no plan of attack, an idea was forming that was so completely ridiculous and brilliant at the same time that it had me gasping for air. And what's more, it had taken barely a minute's conversation with my cat, *with a cat*! Kiwa stared at me with concern, wondering why I was smiling so much, why I was breathing so heavily.

'*What's wrong with you?*' she asked, and I replied out loud, beaming.

'I'm going to go on a journey, on my board. I'm going to skate a really long way.'

I was out of bed in a flash and down the corridor into the study, where the wooden floorboards were always chilly in the morning. I hopped around a bit until I found my slippers in the corner, then unfurled my world map, laid it down on the desk, straightened it out, shivered, and looked at the world. My oyster. I can skate to work and then beyond. But where to? An imaginary line drew itself instantly. It started in Swansea, at home, here. Then went east. All the way to London. Not far enough. Carried on, across the Channel. Lille, not far enough. Brussels, not far enough. More, more! The line continued, appearing faster and faster, straight across Germany, into the Czech Republic, Slovakia, perhaps Poland. Then the Ukraine. Where the hell was I skating to? Into Russia. Ooooh, Russia. And I moved north a little and stopped on Moscow, and in an instant decided that no, Moscow wasn't the place to be, so my finger moved on and continued east as far as it could go until it hit water, and this little section from Moscow to the east coast took a fair bit of time, as you can imagine. And then I hunted for a major city where I could finish up, because after all of that time I'd want to treat myself to all the things a major city could offer, like showers, and I traced south down the coast, traced the border with North Korea but never went over it, they've got enough problems without me skating around. And I dabbed my finger at Beijing, then stopped looking, because inexplicably it felt right. Swansea to Beijing, a distance of 12,000 miles or so.

Then I folded up the map, popped it back on the shelf and did what I usually did on a workday morning. Only this time, as I skated the two miles to work I had something to skate for. To be excited about. To aim for. To live for. A journey on my board. I had purpose, and it felt brilliant.

*   *   *

I wasn't sure what to do with myself that morning. I wasn't about to rush into things and start telling people about it, but the planning phase had started already. What kind of rucksack would I have? I asked myself as I turned my computer on. How long could I honestly take to do this? How far would it be exactly? Has anyone done anything like this before? Would my journey be a world record? What board would I ride on? The questions flooded in and I grinned as Neil came in.

'What's up, mate?' he asked, customarily.

'Same old, same old,' I said, lying like a dog.

5 Losing Russia
Early May 2005

I'd only been skating for fifteen days but that didn't matter. The enormity of the challenge I'd just set myself didn't really occur to me, the fact that it was such a long way was part of the appeal. To succeed in this was going to mean determination, dedication and passion, and passion was precisely what I needed in my life. I wasn't about to shrug off a challenge just because it was going to be difficult. This journey, this idea, was a turning point I was going to take at very high speed. I'd been on the straight and narrow for far too long and it was time for a change.

Bursting at the seams, I was dying to tell people about my idea, but first I wanted to make sure I knew what I was doing. I had a suspicion that undertaking a long-distance skateboard journey would almost certainly mean giving up my job, so I needed a very solid base from which to launch this project. I didn't just want to flunk off and become a skateboarding gypsy, I wanted to achieve and create something worthwhile. A grotty backpack and a spare pair of socks wasn't going to cut it and very quickly I realised that the logistical side of the journey would create a new world I could dive headfirst into, so I laid the groundwork with one, simple aim. Lying in bed that morning with Kiwa I had said out loud, 'journey with a purpose', and by that I had meant more than just a journey on an unusual form of transport. This trip was going to be enormous, a very long way, and I thought that it might attract some attention. But what would I need attention for unless I had somewhere to direct it? It was instantly clichéd, but charity was the answer. For years I had been involved with charity projects, often unusual ones, and this was going to be no different. A long-distance skateboard journey *for charity*. Now we have an idea.

*   *   *

During my second year at university I managed to get involved with a fundraising event called the Morocco Hitch, an annual hitchhike between the UK and Morocco carried out by hundreds of students every Easter, each raising at least £200 for the event's organisers, Link Community Development. Link's main work is carried out in South Africa, Ghana and Uganda, where they work with local communities to improve education systems, focusing on implementing sustainable leadership and teaching skills. The proceeds from the Morocco Hitch made a big different to Link's work in the Sub-Sahara, and the event itself sounded ingenious.

A few weeks after signing up for the Hitch I walked onto the road leading out of Swansea, stuck my thumb in the air and travelled to North Africa in little more than five days, on a budget of barely five quid. This, I told myself, was something every student should do before they leave university. So I wrote to Bobby Russell, Link's Events Officer, and offered my services as a Morocco Hitch Rep for Swansea University. I got the gig and remained in charge of the Hitch until my final year at university, having encouraged over one hundred and fifty students to descend, thumbs aloft, upon Morocco. I wouldn't have been involved with the Hitch had I not believed in Link Community Development's work and they were a natural choice to be the first charity to benefit from my upcoming skateboard journey. Link's current Events Officer was Helen Thomas, who I'd worked with during my final two seasons as Hitch rep, and I dropped her a line to let her know about my plans. She responded immediately: 'Wow! What can I say? It sounds amazing, crazy and hilarious! Obviously from our point of view we'd love it, thanks so much for offering to include us in this.'

*   *   *

I had never travelled in Asia and was uncomfortably aware that the route I had chosen had been selected at random with no forethought or planning. God, I didn't even know whether there were roads all the way across Russia! Who the hell was I going to ask about that? I typed off some emails to the British embassies in Moscow and St Petersburg, explaining my plans and asking for advice, signing off with a sincere question: 'Would the British Embassy in Moscow recommend that I embark on this journey through the Russian Federation?'

I continued to write about longboarding in *HadOne* and used the paper's section to guide my decisions about a title for the project. I knew something was going to hit me right between the eyes but again my impatience had me thinking *too* hard, so I went back to basics as I had done on that first morning with Kiwa. *Let's put everything on the table; it's a journey on a board. What do I want to achieve with this journey?* I want to raise funds and awareness for charity. *Fine, what else?* I'd like to encourage people to do what I'm doing, get into board sports, break the mould, take a risk, live the dream. *All right, so it could be some kind of initiative. What's the personal incentive behind this?* In a nutshell, I want freedom.

And again, in a few simple steps, the old back-to-basics technique had got the job done. In essence, this journey was all about freedom. My own, but also the potential it had to inspire others to achieve their own freedom. To create freedom for the children and adults supported by Link Community Development and any other charities that the project helped. The freedom was all down to my new love, the board.

I ran my next longboarding article under the heading which was to become the hallmark of my journey, a new word, a brand even, that I hoped would become recognised far and wide as news of my long-distance skate spread. The section was called 'BoardFree', and ran with the endlessly cheesy by-line, 'Board With Peace, Ride With Soul'. I was really getting into this thing.

*   *   *

An email jumped into my inbox. It was from the Consular Section in Moscow and didn't carry good news. I got the impression several eyebrows had been raised at my email, and the response outlined the difficulty of getting private visas for anything more than three months. I'd need a lot longer than that to skate across the Russian Federation, but as there are always ways to get around visas that didn't put me off. Neither did the cursory warnings about safety:

> *I am afraid it would be difficult to give a straightforward reply re: safety of travelling on a skateboard through Russia. Most of the*

Russian territory is considered safe for travelling but you never know what might happen, since it's a vast territory. A foreigner travelling on a skateboard through never-ending Russian valleys and villages will definitely arouse interest and suspicion of local population (and militia, or Russian police). Unfortunately, militia's abuse of power has become a typical everyday practice in Russia, foreign tourists being their common target. One thing is definite: it will be safer to travel accompanied by a group (not alone), it is always safer to travel with other people.

Despite this, I knew that logistically there were more pressing issues to worry about than over-perky local militia. Travelling on a longboard meant I was largely dependent on road quality, and when the email outlined the wide-scale dearth of funding for road maintenance and the sheer lack of sealed roads in desolate areas, especially Siberia, my heart dropped like a stone. Swansea to Beijing was in real jeopardy. My pride deflated like a cheap balloon and I went out for a skate, telling myself that this wasn't the end of the world. There were other countries, new roads to travel along.

6 Finding Australia

Late May 2005

On the outskirts of Winchester, deep in the pristine old stone suburbia nestled at the very end of a narrow lane in St Cross, a little house named Brookside backs onto a river lined with water meadows and old, sagging trees. This house and its beautifully tended garden is, without question, my favourite place in the UK, yet strangely I haven't spent much time here. This is my third visit, and I'm here because it is the home of Alice, one of my first true friends.

Alice and I met on 18 January 1999, in the departure lounge at Heathrow Airport. Eighteen months before that I had been suffering from a fairly large lack of self-confidence brought on by an unhappy period at school, and had decided I needed a change. For all my youthful naivety I knew at least one thing, that I was too young to decide what university course I wanted to apply for and rather than make a snap decision to get the careers adviser off my back I was going to do the right thing by me. Which was, I felt, to do something that was going to give me a good hard lesson in life. I needed to grow up and it wasn't a career path that was going to help me out, it was travel. So I opted to take a gap year teaching in Uganda, East Africa. Having heard enough about the place from my father and grandfather – who had both lived there before Idi Amin's true infamy took hold – it was time to see it for myself.

So, there I was in Heathrow Airport, early 1999, my mother asking me whether I needed some condoms from the pharmacy. 'You never know when they might be useful, darling,' she added caringly, waving a pack of twenty above her head, which would have been fine had I been in the pharmacy with her. But I wasn't. I was twenty metres away, saying my first hellos to some of the other teenagers with whom I was to share the next six months in Africa. Complete and utter shame doesn't come close, but my fellow gappers accepted me into the fold despite awkward glances at my excited mother and my newly crew-cutted head, which had gained a new style days earlier when I thought I'd do a DIY job and take all the hair off because, well you know, it's hot in Africa. Alice was among that first group, and during early conversations on the flight to Nairobi and during our orientation beside the idyllic Lake Naivasha in the Great Rift Valley, it so turned out we were to be living in the same area in eastern Uganda, our respective schools separated by a five-minute walk through the bush. I lived in a four-room concrete block with a soon-to-be-medical-student named Tom, and Alice shared her equally squalid house with Luisa, who was obsessed with monkeys, and the four of us made ourselves at home and quickly became friends, eating together each evening and clinking copious bottles of Nile Special at the Nabweyo trading post not far down the main road towards Mbale.

One year on from that first stint in East Africa I again found myself travelling in Uganda, a little more grown up and this time with plenty more hair, and I laid the foundations for a two-week holiday for Alice and her family, who had decided that the Pearl of Africa would be a great place for a fortnight of adventuring. Later I was invited to their home near Winchester for some style of drunken event and I fell in love with the place; travel books lining bookshelves on all corners, the peaceful rush of water from the bottom of the garden, photos on the toilet wall showing a family who found much pleasure in their globetrotting. There were kindred spirits here, and it felt like home.

May 2005 came round, Alice had organised a fundraiser for the Hikkaduwa Aid Information Centre, which her brother Jack had set up in Sri Lanka after the 2004 Tsunami, and as usual she was rushing around Brookside making sure everyone felt at home, at the same time as worrying about getting everything ready on time. I leant against the doorway to her bedroom as Alice had her hair moulded into some extreme shape by Kara, a university friend of Al's who had coincidentally followed us to Uganda on the same gap year scheme, only a few months later.

'So what's new Dave?' she asked.

'You're going to like the news this time.' I grinned. 'I've decided to travel a long way on a skateboard.'

Kara looked at me sideways for a moment as though I didn't have a head, and Alice giggled before saying, 'For some reason, and I don't know why because it sounds ridiculous, but I'm just not surprised.' There was a little silence, and she thought aloud, 'I didn't even know you could skateboard, and where are you going for this journey of yours?'

'Well I've only been skating for a few weeks, and I was going to go from Swansea to Beijing, but that fell through so I'm still looking for a route. Any ideas?'

We all laughed for a bit after that, and came up with absolutely no ideas at all, but once everyone's hair had been meticulously tousled the subject of a long-distance journey on a skateboard reverberated around the party all night. I started to become restless: talking about a journey without a set destination was getting frustrating. The disappointment of resigning the Swansea to Beijing challenge had now been replaced with the excitement of possibility. I was eager to make an educated choice and start building a plan of action.

The next morning, head spinning from the night before, I took a break from the army-like process of collecting empty bottles, cleaning up spilt food and marquee dismantling to spend a few minutes with the travel books in the lounge. I pondered on a book about Canada for a while but moved back along the shelf. A guide to Chile with a vibrant red cover was asking to be picked up. I'd spent a good deal of time on a Chilean bus in 2000 and knew that the road infrastructure was half decent, although the endless mounds of rocks and flowers at the roadside were a poor advert for the quality of driving. I pulled the book from the shelf and another book came out with it and dropped onto my foot. I put the Chile guide straight back onto the shelf and picked up the book from the floor. I looked at the front, it was a slightly tatty *Lonely Planet Guide to Australia*. I opened it up and beneath the inside sleeve was a two-page folding map to the country.

I had never been to Australia; I was fascinated by its size and diversity and the undividable passion for his home that Steve Irwin had expressed during various TV programmes, but still, I'd never seriously considered a visit because it was English-speaking and well developed, not to mention bloody far away. I stared at the map, tracing a route with my finger. When reading a book, if a born and bred Englishman, you start from the left and work right. So I began on the west coast in the largest city there, which was in fact, the only city there, Perth. It looked like there was a road leading east, although I wondered whether it could be a train track, then plumped for luck and started dragging my finger across the desert, a terrifyingly empty space named the Nullarbor Plain. It scared the shit out of me just reading those two words, *Nullarbor Plain*, but my finger continued, reaching a place called Port Augusta. There, I had a choice. It seemed sensible, if starting on the west coast, to go all the way to the east coast, there would be a certain sense of satisfaction from crossing the entire width of the country. But the major Australian cities all had a romantic feeling about them, Adelaide, Melbourne, Sydney. I wanted to go through them all. So from Port Augusta my finger headed south to Adelaide, and as Melbourne was a few hundred miles further on around the coast that's where my finger went, and on and on, hugging the coastline until it reached Sydney. And there I paused, because Sydney is iconic, what a place to finish. And then, for reasons I would never come to comprehend, I thought to myself, nah, that's not far enough, and my finger cranked on up the east coast to Brisbane, which was prodded happily with my chubby right index. I stared at the map a little longer, retracing the route with my eyes, and then, whisking from Perth to Brisbane and then into the centre of the map where the word AUSTRALIA sat large and proud, I shrugged my shoulders and said out loud, 'Perth to Brisbane on a skateboard, that'll do.' The book went back on the shelf and I went back outside to help with the clear-up.

'I'm going to skate across Australia,' I said to Alice matter-of-factly.

'It's a beautiful country,' she said, her head in a bin bag.

And then she looked at me, thoughtfully.

'It's a very big country too, Dave,' she said, 'you know that, don't you?'

I put on a thoughtful face, nodding at the same time.

'Yep, I know, but it's not Wales to China, is it.'

And she agreed with me. Australia it is, then.

7 June

June 2005

During the week Neil and I would take our lunch breaks in the canteen and discuss how I was going to keep my longboarding plans a secret from the managers at work. 'I need the money, mate,' I told him. 'I'll work for as long as I can before heading off.'

'But they're going to find out at some point, mate,' Neil said.

'I know, I just have to work out the best way to tell them.'

Almost as quickly as I'd decided to raise funds and awareness for Link Community Development, I'd made a decision to support another charity. I wrote to my cousin Kate, who had lived and worked in Sydney for several years and was the only person I knew in Australia. 'Cuz', I wrote, 'I want BoardFree Australia to have a local benefit, do you know of any Aussie charities that would benefit from the media coverage and a few thousand extra dollars?' She had no doubts at all about promoting a charity to me. 'I'm a volunteer for a charity called Sailability,' she told me, explaining that the charity was based in clubs all around Australia and gave people with mental and physical disabilities the opportunity to sail. 'It's not just about giving our members the chance to take part in sport,' she continued, 'they sail side by side with able-bodied people, which creates a mutual respect that breaks down the simple fact that disability exists. Sailability provides an education to everyone involved, we'd love you to support us.' I researched Sailability's work for a couple of days, noting that most of their clubs sat around the south coast, very much along the route I was planning to skate, and then replied to my cousin, confirming BoardFree's support of Sailability.

Meanwhile, my search for the right board to travel on was in full flow as I put Google through its paces. Not many stood out from the pack but I started to gain an idea of which factors would make an ideal long-distance companion. I needed something light yet strong, incredibly well-built and engineered to incorporate a lower than average deck. Most boards sit fairly high, usually on a par with or even above the top of the wheels, but on these the standing leg would be bent at the knee and pushing effectively over a lengthy period would become tiresome, not to mention painful. Wheels also had to be a big consideration; I was going to be spending an awful lot of time pushing through remote areas where, I supposed, there wouldn't be regular road maintenance. The smaller the wheel the harder each push would be, so I was aiming big.

There was one website I kept going back to, one board that was always on my mind. It was called a rollsrolls. Not only were they manufactured in Germany, they stood out from other boards for a number of reasons, but the first, most noticeable difference was right there on the front page of www.rollsrolls.com. There was an image of three men pushing hard down a suburban road, legs raised mid-stride with traffic overtaking up close, and the men were riding these bizarre-looking bright yellow boards which had what looked like mudguards, I was enraptured. It wasn't the best photo in the world but it meant something to me. Above the image were the words, 'Two world records in Summer 2003', and underneath the image read, '3,000 miles across the USA. 4 riders on rollsrolls boards . . .'

Well, the first time I saw that I was blown away. These boards had been ridden for hundreds of miles, they'd broken world records, and they had mudguards! I called Neil up and asked him to come and take a look. 'How cool for those guys to have their picture there on the front of that website,' I said as Neil peered over my shoulder. 'What do you reckon mate?' I asked him.

'Look a bit odd, don't they,' he said, and scurried back down the corridor before The Boss got back from a fag break. I typed out a quick email to Peter Sanftenberg, the owner of rollsrolls, and without mentioning my intentions to skate an awfully long way asked him kindly if I could test out one of his boards. He wrote back that same afternoon, saying that there was a rollsrolls board in London and he'd instruct for it to be sent over to me, immediately. I liked that word, *immediately*. Very German, very efficient.

Deep down inside I was pretty sure that I'd found the right board, even before stepping onto one. But I wanted a second opinion, and who better to give it than the men who had ridden the boards further than anyone else. I wrote to one of the four Americans who had taken pride of place on the front of the rollsrolls website. Between them, these four men had relayed across the United States in 2003, taking 21 days to cross from Newport, Oregon to Williamsburg, Virginia. The journey had been carried out to raise the profile of Lowe Syndrome, an incurable children's disease that affects the brain, eyes, kidneys, bones and muscles. The disease had taken the life of a fourteen-year-old boy named Jack Jr and prompted by his son's death, Jack Smith, having skated across America twice before, in 1976 and 1984, decided to retrace his skate tracks one last time. So he organised Skate Across America: On Board for Lowe Syndrome, found three other riders to join him on the record-breaking journey, and sure enough they crossed America in three weeks, a new record. I emailed Jack, humbled by his achievement and not really expecting a reply, asking whether he could recommend the rollsrolls board and offer any advice to someone planning a long-distance skate journey.

The next day I switched on my computer to find this message in my inbox:

Dear Dave,

Your trek sounds like an amazing adventure. I'm sure you have researched road conditions, what have you found? Do you have sponsors lined up? The rollsrolls is the only board to use, nothing else comes close.

Please feel free to contact me at anytime with questions, I'll be happy to help in anyway I can.

All the best, Jack

I couldn't believe it! Jack Smith, world record-holding long-distance skateboarder, no, world record-holding long-distance skateboarding *legend*, had written to me. Me! And he seemed to hold the rollsrolls in very high regard.

Well, if Jack was happy with it that was enough for me. And he had offered to help where he could, so I typed out another email full of questions.

> *Dear Jack,*
>
> *Many thanks for writing back. I am working out my route across Australia, but in the meantime I want to get to grips with the basic things, like how to train for such a journey, what kind of roads would be best to travel on and how to keep the rollsrolls maintained during the trip. How long did you and the other guys train for the SAA trip before you set off? And did you always have a support van alongside as you went along, or did you carry everything between the four of you?*
>
> *I'd like to raise awareness and funds for some charities. Your most recent journey across the US has inspired me to go for this and I'd really like to support Lowe Syndrome. Would this be OK with you?*
>
> *Finally, for the time being, after the 21 days across the States, do you think could you have gone much further?!*
>
> *Kind regards, Dave*

It was all getting rather exciting. Very soon I was expecting to take delivery of a bright yellow carbon-fibre longboard with mudguards and I was swapping emails with a world record-holder. This didn't happen everyday! I'd also decided to support another charity, one helping Lowe Syndrome, which made more sense to me than almost anything else I'd ever done. This charity was inextricably linked to long-distance skateboarding and it was now my turn to carry the baton, what a privilege! Also, the selection of a third charity had settled me somewhat, because three, I thought, was enough. After a morning's research, I decided it would make sense to support the UK-based Lowe Syndrome Trust, rather than the US-based Lowe Syndrome Association, so I sent off an email to Lorraine Thomas, the Chair of the LST, to let her know.

Then, just as I had pressed Send, my computer beeped and another email jumped into my inbox. It was from Jack Smith.

Dear Dave,

I changed wheels once, not from wear, but from lost resiliency due to heat. Rode the same deck, trucks and bearings the whole way.

The Australia trek sounds great, I have actually thought about doing that myself. Would you mind if I joined you for a section?

As for benefiting the Lowe Syndrome Association, I would be honoured!

All the best, Jack

Blimey, I thought. Lucky that Jack was happy with my supporting Lowe Syndrome, if he hadn't been I would have had some explaining to do to Lorraine Thomas. But all is well – no, better than well, because Jack wants to join me for a section of the journey. Amazing! Good advice about the board parts, too. What a guy!

*   *   *

It was a Friday, always the best day of a working week. The sun was shining brightly and Swansea basked in almost Mediterranean-like warmth. That was the thing about Swansea, when the sun was out it was a beautiful city to be in. People were smiling; the buildings looked less shabby, the saltiness of the sea filled the air and seagull-calls echoed around town. I skated to work and propped my board up against the wall of my office.

'Parcel for you, Dave. Looks like another longboard.' Neil stood at the door, a familiar-shaped box resting vertically in front of him. 'Think this is the rollsrolls?'

'I think it is mate,' I said, wrestling it across the room, 'this could be the one.'

'The one you do the journey on?'

'Maybe.'

'Got to be honest mate, not sure you're going to need mudguards in Australia. It doesn't rain much there.'

'They're not really mudguards, doofus,' I muttered despairingly, 'they're just risen wheel wells, they need to be there because . . .' but Neil was already halfway down the corridor; he didn't care quite as much as I did about the varying builds of longboards. Nonplussed, I tore open the box and carefully raised the board away from its packaging. It was, as expected, the rollsrolls. Bright yellow deck, large black wheels, the familiar woven greeny-yellow pattern of carbon fibre on the underside. It was, by some distance, the strangest-looking longboard I had ever seen. It was going to be at least two hours before I could take it outside, and, believe it or not, there was work to be done. First though, I brought the board up to my eye level, took it all in, spun a wheel and watched it rotate for all of two minutes. And then it struck me: *this* could be the board, the very board that takes me across Australia. I had been pretty sure for a while that I'd choose a rollsrolls, but it hadn't quite occurred to me that the test board Peter Sanftenberg had so efficiently sent over to me would be *the board*. So right there and then, even before I'd stepped upon her, I decided that we were going to be spending so much time together that I needed to give this very special board a name. It was different, majestic even, and it was definitely, most certainly, female. A Swahili name didn't come to mind immediately, but my thoughts settled in Africa. Then I remembered the story of *Born Free*, of the Kenyan lioness and her siblings who were rescued as orphans by the Adamsons. This board was about to embark on quite a journey for BoardFree, and it seemed almost fitting to have a link to *Born Free*, another, albeit somewhat different story of freedom. My decision was made. Lifting her up again, I stroked a wheel well lovingly.

'I'm going to call you Elsa,' I told her. 'Are you ready for the journey of a lifetime?'

8 Quitting the Job
Mid-July 2005

I sat on my hands, kept my head down at work and did my hours. I began to train twice daily, pushing Elsa along the six-mile cycle path that borders the northern edges of Swansea Bay between the town and Mumbles. I'd wake at six, giving myself plenty of time to throw on some clothes, grab my board and be back as soon after eight as possible, in time to shower, eat and skate to work.

When I wasn't skating, I sat at my computer in the evenings and started to build a website for BoardFree. I'd always found it relaxing creating new designs, writing the copy and publishing the pages where the world could see them. But this was a different process; there was some real content here. There were hundreds of things I could put on this website: pictures, diaries, videos. At last, a real website! With a biro sticking out of the corner of my mouth I started with the basics – a description of BoardFree and early plans for the Australian journey. New ideas came along and BoardFree developed with this process, but I was bound not to publish the site to the web until I had told the people at work that I was undertaking this project. The larger the site became, the more I thought about quitting my job, but I knew this journey was going to come with a big financial cost. BoardFree kept me going at work, creating a light at the end of the tunnel. But as July wore on the desire to settle the situation and make BoardFree official kept me up at night, I couldn't keep this a secret any longer.

I probably wouldn't have decided to skateboard a long way had I truly been happy in my job. Let's face it, if I had been satisfied designing newspapers that nobody reads I would have continued to do so, smiling now and then at The Boss as he appeared in the doorway to check what I was doing. More often than not there would be a website about longboards on the screen when he came into the room, but sneakily I'd made a point in the last furniture reshuffle that my screen could only be seen by me, not from the door, and certainly not by The Boss if he was stood at the door. 'I get better lighting on my desk if it's this way,' I had told him, and because I was a designer he accepted that little bit of zen.

But as time went on I realised that my heart wasn't in this place, in this job that was relatively menial and without realistic goals. I longed to nurture my own ambition and make a break for it, because deep down I knew that although I was a half-decent employee, I just wasn't very good at working for somebody else. Now my escape plan was forming I knew I was only here for the money, and that when I finally did leave it may well be the last time I walk out of someone else's door. So I pretended to like my job for as long as I could, and then when I couldn't do that anymore I called a meeting. It was time to tell them about my plan.

They came into my office and sat down. The Boss and his Sidekick. The ones who made the decisions. At this point I was still unsure about saying goodbye to a regular wage and wasn't overly keen on eating into my savings, so I had formulated a cunning plan. I would ask for a sabbatical. For about six or seven months. To skateboard across Australia. This way, I argued with myself, I might be able to live with the job because the end was in sight. Maybe, just maybe, this would work. I told them everything; that I needed a bit of a break, that I wanted to go on a long journey, on a skateboard, that it would help me get refreshed and love my job more when I came back. But please realise that when I just said I told them everything, I didn't, actually, tell them everything. I missed out the bit where I was planning to skateboard a long way and then not return to the job. But I figured if I told them that then they would probably ask me to leave. Straightaway. And then I'd have no money. So it was a cunning plan. And they fell for it. And they agreed. And for one whole week everything was OK.

One week later, a man named Michael visited Swansea for a business dinner. I liked Michael, he was a friendly man who worked for his dad in a printing business, and Michael dealt with our company where printing was concerned. Shortly before my request for a Skateboard Sabbatical I had been elevated to position of Print Manager, as well as Design Manager. This was a big step for The Boss and his Sidekick, who were always quite protective over the company, and I honestly appreciated the extra responsibility, although in truth I hadn't so much received a promotion as just a new job title. Before I go on, I feel that I need to explain something. Although I spent a little bit of every day looking at websites about long skateboards, I was still very good at what I did. I was efficient and productive and made some money for the company and this, I suppose, is why they gave me some more responsibility.

So, as the new Print Manager, I was invited to a business dinner with The Boss, his Sidekick and Michael from the printing business. The food was nice, the drinks flowed, jokes were made and chuckled at, and after the fourth bottle of wine was quaffed we moved on to a pub around the corner. And it was at this pub where poor Michael was crowded into a corner, I felt, by The Boss and his Sidekick and a good deal of alcohol, on some business matter of sorts. Now, I have mentioned before that The Boss and his Sidekick had a monopoly on decision-making in the company, and because of this I hadn't been briefed on any particular plan of attack for the business dinner. I had assumed that we were just bonding as friends in order to make the future pleasant for all parties. I couldn't have been more wrong.

I had returned from the toilet and was perched on a rather uncomfortable wooden bench feeling decidedly giddy, a state I blamed entirely on the bottle of beer which inexplicably wobbled on the table in front of me, and then The Boss directed a question at me: 'What do you think, Dave?'

I hadn't been concentrating entirely on the conversation, mainly because I had been in the toilet, but it may have been the same conversation from before my toilet break, one I hadn't been involved in it at any point and had centred on what I thought was a rather bizarre plan by The Boss and his Sidekick to make Michael pay for everything they wanted to do in life. But I pulled myself into an upright position and offered my thoughts. Now, I might be a bit hazy on the exact conversation but I remember enough to know that when The Boss spoke to me I was feeling a bit uncomfortable for poor Michael, who was being badgered to put up some money for an idea that didn't seem feasible. So, ad-libbing a bit, I replied with something along the lines of, 'I'm not sure that the plan would be that simple to action, and honestly I don't think we should be asking Michael to sign off on anything with the amount of beer and wine we've been through.'

I could hear the sound of thunder, which was odd as it was a nice, balmy summer night, for Wales. I quickly realised that the thunder was actually more of a growl, and that The Boss and his Sidekick were glaring at me with eyes like saucers. And I'm sure they were holding daggers under the table and were ready to use them on me. I glanced at Michael, who I thought looked a bit bemused by the whole situation, and then I realised that I'd said the wrong thing because The Boss snarled, 'I'll remember that.' Oh dear, I thought, he's not happy.

We left the pub soon after and The Boss appeared to my left. 'What are you doing?' he rasped. 'We were close to sealing the deal, you're supposed to be on our side.'

I looked at him apologetically. 'I had no idea there was a deal to seal, you didn't tell me about it.'

'That's not the point, you're supposed to be on our side.' He stomped off, a bit moody, and I followed sheepishly, wondering how it had all become so heated. At Michael's hotel The Boss and his Sidekick left early; Michael and I stayed with drinks in our hands and we talked about travelling in the developing world, something we'd both done in the past, and then I wandered home across the river having completely forgotten about the little tiff in the pub which involved alcohol and being on the right side.

The next morning I arrived at work and sat in the foyer with a glass of water, chatting to Neil about something, which probably involved a long skateboard.

The Boss and his Sidekick appeared. 'Dave. Office. Now.' Apparently sentences weren't on the agenda this morning. I stood up, followed The Boss into the office, and the door shut behind me.

The Sidekick took a chair, I took a sofa, The Boss stood and paced. It was a hot day and he was sweating quite profusely, I remember his underarm wet patches looking a little like shadows, and I was staring at these when he launched into a verbal rampage about my conduct, how he and the Sidekick were furious with my lack of compliance the night before and generally what a bad man I was. As this went on I nursed my glass of water, glancing occasionally at the Sidekick who was nodding like a donkey. Then the boss did something he shouldn't have done. He *clicked* his fingers.

He *clicked* his fingers! Loudly! Thumb and middle finger snapped apart and the sound echoed around the room. Just before the *click* he had been perched edgily on the corner of his desk, there was complete silence apart from a good deal of heavy breathing. And then he spoke, staring at me straight, 'You know,

Dave,' he spat, 'we could replace you like that.' And on the 'that' he had *clicked* his fingers, swinging his right arm as he did it for maximum effect, as though he was trying to shoot me. *Click.* Ooof. I'm dead. At least how he thought it should have gone. But it didn't.

I was leaning back on the sofa, probably appearing a little too relaxed for my own good, but the whole clicking thing had really hit a nerve and I knew I was about to have one of those moments that working people all over the world dream about on a daily basis. It was almost *Matrix*-like. In slow motion I leant to the side and dodged the flying bullet of The Boss's *click*, and limbo-ing gracefully on the sofa as his bullet flew past my ear I thought about what he had said and how unbearably rude he had been. Replace. Me. Like That? *Click.* Ridiculous. Good luck with that, mate. And then, as his *click* bullet ripped into the cushions behind me I spoke for the first time since being ushered into the office.

'Well,' I said, 'I guess you're just going to have to replace me.' I breathed deeply, sucking in the air to summon the energy for the final, glorious culmination of this, *my* moment. 'Replace me like *that*!' and I raised my right hand so it hung in front of my face, snapped my fingers sharply and issued my very own *click* bullet, which shot straight across the room and made a very clean hole in the middle of his forehead.

Somehow, considering he had just suffered what was clearly a lethal injury, he managed to speak as I walked out. 'Get out of my sight,' he snarled, but I already was, storming down the corridor. Keys on the desk. Bag on my back. Elsa under my arm. Out the door. Down the stairs. Onto the street. Sun on my face. I stood there, outside the giant double doors, which would have been fit to secure a medieval castle but which were remarkably easy to leave through. I looked left. I looked right. I looked up at the clear, blue sky and sucked in clean summer air through my nose. I grinned, bade a mental 'cheerio' to my old job and skated down the street.

*   *   *

In truth, it had all come as a bit of a shock. Had I known I was going to do the spectacular quitting thing I wouldn't have bothered to devise the cunning Skate Sabbatical plan, I could have just stayed in bed one morning and never gone to work again. But I guess you can't plan these things, and as I skated home my heartbeat returned to its usual rate and I started to figure out what I was going to do next. Now I wasn't tied up with a nine-to-five anymore I had plenty of time to plan a skateboard journey and everything that was involved with that. But first I decided that I'd sit in my garden and have a tuna sandwich.

9 Summer Into Spring

July – December 2005

BoardFree had just taken on an entirely new meaning. Free from the shackles of a day job, I felt liberated. The only drawback was money, but I calculated that as long as I could do the occasional web design job, three years of savings would see me through to the end of the Australian journey. It wouldn't leave much over, but I wasn't about to bin it all over the small matter of cash flow. Biscuits for lunch until 2007, then.

At long last I uploaded the BoardFree website to the Internet, then sent an email to the local newspaper, the *South Wales Evening Post*. A couple of hours later I got a call from a journalist called Geraint Thomas, who seemed stoically amused by my story. We had a chat and met up a few hours later on the Sail Bridge, a new, sweeping structure crossing the River Tawe. Geraint had brought along a photographer, who proceeded to line me up for my first BoardFree photo shoot.

'Smile!' he shouted at me, 'Smile!' I tried my best but couldn't help wishing I'd cut my hair and appeared a little more presentable. The camera kept clicking, and the man behind it started to get a little carried away, I felt. 'They're not going to give any money to a miserable git, SMILE!'

'So how long have you been skating for, Dave?' Geraint asked me.

'Umm, about three and a half months,' I said.

Journalist and photographer looked at me with furrowed brows.

'Did you say months, or years?' said Geraint.

You know damn well I said months.

'Months,' I said.

'You've got balls, mate,' said the photographer.

I hoped that wasn't going to be the headline.

*   *   *

The next morning I trotted down to the newsagents and picked up an *Evening Post*. BoardFree had pride of place on page 3! I wrote a quick email to thank Geraint for the article. He replied straight away:

> *No worries . . . a guy called Arthur Hendey called me to say you*
> *have inspired him to take up skateboarding . . . at the age of 70!!*
> *His number is 53****, he wanted to talk to you. If you do give him*
> *a lesson let us know and we can do a story!*

Seventy! This guy sounded mad. I dialled the number and went through to his answer phone. It was then that I knew this wasn't your everyday seventy-year-old: 'Hello,' said the voice of a weary old man, 'you've reached Arthur's telephone. I'm afraid I'm not in right now, but I assure you that your cheque is in the post, and you'll get it very soon.'

And that was the first time I heard Arthur Hendey's voice. I chuckled, what a star! I waited for the beep, and spoke: 'Hello Arthur, this is Dave Cornthwaite. I'm the fella from the paper who wants to skateboard across Australia. Geraint Thomas tells me you'd like a lesson, and I'd like to let you know that it would be my pleasure. Give me a call back and we'll arrange a time.'

Then I went out for a skate. When I came home there was a message waiting. I pressed play: 'Hello Dave, Arthur Hendey here. You left a message before, ahhh yeah, I'd be interested in learning to skateboard. I don't know whether Geraint Thomas told you, but I'm seventy years old, OK, I'm as mad as a hatter . . . and I'm glad to say that you're as mad as a hatter, as well. Anyway, if you'd care to phone back I'm in now for the rest of the day. Bye now.'

I called him back and we chatted for a while. Arthur told me he'd tried stilt walking and liked winter swimming, which involves swimming in the sea in winter, and I knew then that however mad he thought I was, I was no match for him. We arranged to meet a few days later and I put the phone down wondering just how I'd roped myself into teaching a seventy-year-old to skateboard.

*   *   *

I trained each evening before sunset, sucking in the smell of newly cut grass through my nostrils, staring out over Swansea Bay wondering if Australia would look anything like this. I pushed on, mile by mile, imagining I was on the Nullarbor Plain; trying to flatten out the landscape, blow back the sea, take away the trees and push hard with my head down, on and on. But I picked up my head, saw the bay path before me, breathed hard and felt my legs burn. And then I pushed on some more.

As the days went on the twelve-mile run became easier, but not once did I forget what was coming. When it was hot I left the house at noon, the temperatures up into the mid-twenties, the sun beating down and draining my water bottles so much faster than on a cool, dark morning. It was laughable, how I was training to skate across Australian desert in the pleasant heat of a West Glamorgan June, and I giggled to myself that I had to start somewhere. I took my mind to other places, trying to focus on the distance and how I was going to deal with it, knowing that while I could happily push 24, even 36 miles to and fro around Swansea Bay, the glassy-smooth surfaces of the cycle path were going to turn to rocks and mud, the heat was going to be stifling, and the seagulls were going to turn into snakes. And I wasn't going to be able to skate home every twelve miles and pour myself a nice cold glass of water and slump into a beanbag. 'Just get yourself fit, Dave,' I told myself. 'You'll deal with the rest as it comes.'

*   *   *

A friend of mine named John, who I'd met at Swansea University, had recently set up a small company called Gower Graphics. The *Evening Post* and ITV Wales had both said they'd come along to film my first lesson with the irrepressible pensioner Arthur Hendey, and I thought it would be a nice touch to present him with a present. John kindly printed up a t-shirt bearing the slogan 'BoardFree: Never Too Old to Roll', and I rolled it up and popped it into my backpack.

At 1 p.m. on Monday 25 July 2005 I skated to the War Memorial on the seafront and shook hands with a reporter and cameraman from ITV. Geraint Thomas ambled up and while we waited for Arthur the men from ITV made jokes about how big my right leg was going to be after Australia.

'You'll be walking round in circles by the end of it!' Chuckled the cameraman, very satisfied with himself.

'Only if his legs work by then,' said the reporter. Which I didn't think was very funny. And then, thankfully, a man strode towards us, bearing more than a passing resemblance to Captain Birdseye. Arthur Hendey had a big white beard and a very wide smile. He pumped my arm up and down.

'It truly is good to meet you,' he said to me, and then he waved at everyone else, apart from Geraint, who he'd already spoken to on the phone, so he shook his hand.

'Before we get started I'd like to give you a t-shirt Arthur,' I said, handing over his prize. He pulled it on over his hooded top and it looked great. I told him so, he thanked me, and we began our lesson.

Hoping that the TV and newspaper reports of this session would encourage more people to take up skating, I was quite terrified that poor Arthur would take a dramatic tumble in front of the lenses that were aiming at him. And I could tell, mainly by the crossed fingers the cameraman held behind his back, that they were here for precisely that reason. I wasn't going to let it happen, for Arthur's sake, and stood beside him as I showed him where to put his feet, how to push and how to bring his pushing leg up onto the board. With hindsight, maybe I was a bit too protective of him, and Arthur's first piece to camera involved a little frustration at his lack of progress, but by the end of the lesson he was rolling along quite happily. Sure, his arms were flapping wildly above his head as he tried to regain his balance, but not once did he fall off, much to the disappointment of the media present. Before saying goodbye, I promised Arthur as many lessons as he wanted in the future, and from the glint in his eye I knew he was going to take me up on them.

'What about money?' he asked me.

'Ah I'm not going to charge you, Arthur,' I said.

'You're a true sport and the Aussies will love you. I spent a couple of years over there and they're always up for a nutcase.'

I had to laugh. 'You're a star now Arthur,' I ribbed, 'don't forget to watch the news tonight.'

'Don't worry,' he told me, 'I'll be there, resting my aching limbs.'

That night, sure enough, there we were on TV. Arthur was indeed the star of the show, starting his interview with, 'I thought it was a lunatic thing to do, and fortunately I'm still a lunatic at heart, so here I am.'

I was interviewed too, and complimented Arthur on his attempts. When quizzed about my feelings about the Australian journey I said the first thing that came into my head: 'It's going to be gruelling, it's going to be tough, but

I'm confident I'm going to make it and I'm fully prepared to go all the way and break any pain barriers that I might have to.' Even then, with over a year to go until I stepped into the unknown, I had no doubt that skating across Australia would be difficult, yet was equally sure that the journey was possible. But Australia wasn't really on my mind that day. At seventy years old, Arthur Hendey was a perfect example of someone who lived his life to the full. Unlike many people who were getting on a bit – and I assure you he wouldn't take offence if I said that to his face – for Arthur age wasn't a barrier to new experiences and his positivity rubbed off on me. I wanted BoardFree to do more than just raise money for charity; the chance to inspire people to live life to the full was right here in my hands. And for someone who didn't have a job my hands were now getting quite full. It felt very good indeed.

*   *   *

'I'm a bit worried about you,' said Nick Bradley, friend and former work colleague. 'What are you going to do in the desert? I mean, how are you going to carry water and stuff?' He cocked his head a little, and stared at me. I was glad he had asked, not least because it was nice that people were thinking about my safety. But I'd spent a few weeks quietly considering the same questions myself and had come up with a few suggestions. I tried them out on Nick, just to see what he thought.

'Well, it's a fair point mate,' I said. 'There are a few possibilities. First, I could tow a kind of trailer behind me, some kind of carriage with space for my tent, water, that kind of thing . . .'

Nick looked at me without saying anything and I couldn't help noticing that one of his eyebrows was higher than the other. I remembered our first ever conversation. We were in the Students' Union media centre after a newspaper editorial meeting, and I'd been telling tales about my travels, which involved beasties and creepy crawlies. During one particular story involving waking up in Ecuador with a large, hairy spider on my face, Nick had let out a girly little scream and turned slightly away from me, almost as though the spider would leap at him at any point. 'I'm a bit scared of Dave,' Nick had told someone later, and although as time passed we became friends I did wonder whether Nick still thought I was, well . . . a little strange. And here I was, discussing the ins and outs of skateboarding across Australia, and I had a horrible feeling that Nick would soon be unable to repress another girly scream that so clearly was building up in his throat.

I continued. 'The trailer could be tricky to deal with, though, especially on steep uphills, so I was maybe thinking about having a support team, a couple of people on bikes, or even in a van.' This idea must have seemed more sensible because Nick nodded and said, 'That sounds like a good idea.'

Talking about Australia helped me get things in order, and the more I thought about it the more it made sense to take people with me. The advantages were endless: they could carry supplies – water, food, spare board parts – and would be able to help the fundraising drive at the end of each day, although in the middle of the desert there probably wouldn't be much to do. One thing became clear. If I were to make a proper go of this journey I'd need to get my priorities straight. Did I want company? This harebrained scheme had come about because I wanted a shot at freedom; did I need to be on my own to achieve that? Would I be able to carry everything on my own, if I was on my own? And if I was serious about doing my bit for the charities, would I really be able to make a good go of it after skating forty miles each day?

The thought that this adventure was still a year away started to nag, my feet were starting to itch and I wasn't sure if I could hang on for twelve months! To the best of my ability I tried to visualise what was approaching, and this meant preparing mentally, physically and logistically. Where do I start? I thought, staring at the map of Australia that hung on my study wall. And then it hit me. I wasn't going to learn about the ins and outs of a skateboarding journey by staring at a computer screen. I needed something tangible, something challenging and something that would teach me some good lessons. Kiwa strutted in, tail high, and stared at me unblinkingly, like only a cat can. 'You know what, Kiwa,' I said to her, 'I need a bloody warm-up.'

* * *

I loved my football as a kid. I fell in love with Manchester United when I was seven or eight and it was a passion that continued throughout my teens. When no one else was around I took three or four balls and walked miles to the nearest pitch to practise, commenting out loud at the things I, in mental costume as a professional, was performing. Even now, closer to thirty than twenty-five, I find few things more beautiful than the sight of a football goal with tightly strung white netting, bulging in glorious receipt of another goal. Football was my first passion, but by the time I was twenty I finally accepted that my dream of becoming a pro had fallen by the wayside. I was proficient but in no way excelled at other sports like tennis and athletics, but football had been my only hope. It is a sad realisation for a young man, completely dotty about sport, when he reaches the conclusion that he'll never make it, that his sporting life from thereon will be consigned to local leagues and evening telly. I thought I'd had my chips.

The papers were always full of individual pursuits; marathons, triathlons, the occasional round-the-world bike ride, but it never really took my fancy. Now and then my parents would invite friends to dinner and more often than not they were fitness freaks, joining my parents in an admirable chase to the sun by cycling and running long distances as the fifty and sixty-year marks passed them by. Some of them spoke about cycling the length of Britain from Land's End to John o'Groats and although I was trying my hardest not to break my moody teenager rules and make conversation with the elders, I couldn't help but wonder whether I'd ever complete that famous route someday. A seed had been planted; all I needed was some passion to push myself from one end of the land to the other.

And then all of a sudden I was 25, my passion leaning against the wall at the bottom of the stairs. A yellow deck, large green wheels, much more exciting to me than cycling or running had ever been. Upstairs, in a stand-off with Kiwa, this late summer's day was about to become a time for another spontaneous decision. 'If I was going to have a practise run where better than here, close to home,' I told my cat. 'Kiwa, I'm going to skate the length of Britain, from John o'Groats to Land's End, as a warm-up. I think it's just what I need.'

She purred, and wandered off.

*   *   *

I started spending some time with Becki McKinlay, a friend from my days in Swansea University and now the Students' Union President. We shared a regular morning session, chatting about BoardFree, coming up with new ideas, her with coffee, me with hot chocolate, marshmallows and whipped cream. She became bright-eyed as I revealed more about BoardFree and where it had all emerged from, and it wasn't long before she submitted an application form through the website to become a member of my support team. Strong, resourceful and passionate, it didn't take me long to decide that Becki would be the first aboard my currently non-existent support vehicle. While on campus I also paid occasional visits to Rae Howells, who was now warming my old chair as Editor of the university newspaper and had encouraged her fiancé Phil that being a part of the BoardFree support team would mean a memorable and quite unique honeymoon. Not including Rae and Phil, I'd received another seven application forms, and was seriously considering upping the size of the team from four to five, maybe even six. A team would widen the effect of the project on the ground in Australia, placing greater importance on supporting the charities. The prospect of having a support vehicle, especially during the Nullarbor Plain crossing, took a huge weight off my mind as well; BoardFree was becoming much bigger than the original one-man-and-his-board inspiration.

The make-up of the support team was foremost in my mind as an early-December selection get-together approached. I was confident in my instinct to pick a group of decent, hard-working people who could muck-in as a team, but was slightly concerned at the average age of applicants. Living in other people's pockets for months on end often results in cabin fever, which in itself becomes all-consuming, and avoiding the onset of this was going to be largely down to the experience and maturity of the individuals involved. At the same time, I was searching for people who could willingly take six months off to volunteer for the project, and realistically I was always going to be limited to applicants around student age. I'd received some promising and some not-so-impressive forms covering each position I'd advertised on the website. There were two or three places open for roadies, who would drive, cook, fundraise and do other odd-jobs, and I was also looking for two people to document the journey from within the team, a cameraperson and a photographer. I wanted to make sure it was all recorded, these memories would last a lifetime.

On Saturday 3 December, nine people gathered in my Swansea study. It was a relaxed affair, designed to give me a chance to make a judgment on who was support-team material. Friends who had applied – Becki, Owen, Rae and Phil – were joined by my housemates and two strangers; Simon Thorpe, a broadcasting student from Falmouth who had applied for the position of cameraman, and John Bolston, who targeted the position of photographer. Another photographer had applied two months earlier, a South African called Delia Farrer, but unfortunately she had decided to withdraw due to suffering from a dizzying condition called labrynthitis, an illness that severely affects balance and creates an almost chronic fatigue for the sufferer. Dee was on the mend from what she called 'The Labs,' but couldn't be sure how long it would take her to fully recover and didn't feel it was fair to leave her application open. I completely understood her reasons and appreciated her honesty, but was disappointed because it left the photographer's position wide open. John Bolston, the other photography applicant, had seemed enthusiastic, but it was instantly obvious on his arrival in Swansea that he wasn't right for the job. An awkward, high-pitched monosyllabic squeak followed most of his sentences, which, owing to an upbringing in Orkney, were embarrassingly difficult to decipher in themselves. He had even spent much of his application form criticising my methods of choosing a team, but despite this I felt he at least deserved a chance at interview, so I invited him to Swansea. Once here, though, he just didn't fit in, which was a shame.

One by one I took the applicants into a separate room, asking them to look into a portable video camera and spend ten minutes chatting about themselves and how they'd fit into BoardFree. I had already reached a decision about some of them, and at the end of their 'interviews' I officially invited Rae and Phil, and later Becki, onto the team. Becki especially was gobsmacked, sweetly accepting the offer by lifting her hands to her face and whispering 'Fuck you!' We hugged and she whispered in my ear, 'Thank you so much, I won't let you down.' There was bad news for Owen though, who didn't hold a driver's licence, a prerequisite for a roadie. I was dreading letting him down, but he took it well, saying he'd follow the journey all the way.

Simon had impressed us all with his laid-back, articulate attitude. He was good company and an outsider could have been forgiven for thinking he had been friends with us for years. My instinct kicked in the first time I spoke to Si, I knew he'd be a cracking addition to the team, and he proved himself so during the interview. He told me he was blown away by BoardFree and shared my confidence that the enormity of the Australian challenge didn't stand in the way of success. If I was looking for one thing from each team member, it was a complete passion for the project, a willingness to immerse themselves in the world of BoardFree just as I had. Simon fitted the bill, as did Becki. Rae and Phil had other commitments with their upcoming wedding, but I could make allowances for that as their maturity, I felt, would counterbalance the limited time they had to dedicate to BoardFree.

One person who was already an integral part of BoardFree but wasn't in a position to apply due to already-made plans to travel with his girlfriend, was Dan Loo, who as my housemate had been involved from almost day one. My delight at forming a solid base to the team was tempered slightly by a sadness that Danny wasn't going to be involved once the Australian project began. Even without the carrot of a possible support team position he had been my right-hand man throughout the summer, helping me form ideas about the project, skating with me and making little videos for the website. Danny would have made the ideal roadie.

Ten days later Becki, Rae, Phil and I sat round a ringing telephone, ready to welcome Simon onto the team. He had edited together a short movie from his time in Swansea, confirming that his suitability for the position wasn't tainted by a Stevie Wonder-like approach to filmmaking. Rae looked me in the eye, she knew I liked to play games. 'If you're nasty to him I'm never going to talk to you again,' she said, lip curling.

'Would I do anything like that?' I grinned. Her face fell. Then the phone stopped ringing . . .

'Hello?' said Simon's voice.

'Si mate, 'ello it's Dave, can you hear me?' I said.

'Hello Dave how you doing mate, all right!' he screeched, sounding half cut.

'Mate I got your video this morning . . .'

'Yeah, what did you reckon?' he asked, nervously.

'I've got good news and bad news,' I said, trying to keep myself together, 'what do you want first?'

'Ummm, bad news.' He sounded worried. Brilliant!

'The bad news is I didn't like it.' There was silence on the other end, and closer to home I could see Rae curling her hands into fists. Phil suppressed a snigger.

'Really?' said Si. 'What was wrong with it?'

I didn't have the heart to drag this on; the tension in the room was unbearable.

'Do you want the good news?'

'Yeah.'

'The good news is I'm lying, and I'd like you to come to Australia.'

'No fucking way!' he yelled.

'You're on speaker phone mate,' I said, 'and Rae, Phil and Becki are here too –'

'Hi Simon!' shouted Becs, who had been doing her best to empty the bar that afternoon. 'Congratulations!'

'You're fucking kiddin' me!' said Si, laughing.

'I can't believe he did that,' Rae piped up.

Becki spoke, 'The video camera's on as well mate so this is all being recorded!'

'You little shit!' Laughter all round.

'Welcome aboard man,' I said.

'Thanks very much,' said Si. 'That's the best Christmas present I'm ever going to get, and if I wasn't about to go and get drunk I'd pop in the car and come and hug you right now. Dave, I love you mate. I love all of you.'

'Si, good to talk to you man, I'll speak to you soon,' I said.

'Cheers, thanks very much,' he said.

And four became five.

10 Kate
December 2005

As a single man I constantly told myself I couldn't get attached to anyone and that while taking a girl to Australia was asking for trouble, leaving one behind was even more so. My heart was always stuck on one thing, BoardFree, and it was going to take an incredibly patient and accepting girl to demand a share of my attention. As the months wore on I did wonder whether or not someone would come along who would make me think twice about skating on alone, but always dismissed the thoughts as folly – the emotional concentration the long road was always going to require would be affected if my mind wasn't fully on the job, I told myself.

* * *

As 2005 drew to an end I took a train to London following an invite to the Link Community Development Christmas party. 'It'd be a good chance for you to meet everyone in the office and some other people who are doing good things for Link,' wrote Kate Brackenborough, from the charity.

I'd met Kate a couple of times before, hazily during a training session three years earlier when we were both university reps for Link's annual charity hitchhike to Morocco and, more recently, just a couple of months earlier during a hasty reintroduction when Kate, who had by then become Link's Events Officer, had just finished her first official Morocco Hitch training session with the event's new university reps. I sat beside her in a Golders Green pub having followed her legs down the road, and was feeling quite smug that as Events Officer she was to be dealing with me directly on BoardFree-related issues. Intelligent, lively and not a little flirtatious, Kate was enthusiastic about working with me and making BoardFree a success. I can safely say the feeling was more than mutual.

The Christmas party was expectedly eclectic; project leaders from Ghana and South Africa sat alongside admin assistants from the London office and middle-aged women about to head to Malawi, and after a drink or two we all swayed together on an underground train into the city, where a restaurant awaited for the evening meal. At the table, I perched myself next to Kate and as the meal went on we contributed greatly to the wine bill and rarely chatted to anyone but each other.

An hour later I was propped up against the bar, bottle of wine hanging loose in one hand, watching as the remnants of the party disported on the dance floor. I've never been a dancer; at best I have a stiffly wooden sense of rhythm, and over time have learnt to resist catcalls from rapidly twirling bodies that clearly just wanted to snigger at my incompetent footwork. In my late teens, while finding myself in Uganda, I'd fallen head over heels in love with a girl who was far too good looking for me. She was half Colombian and danced absolutely everywhere, skipping along potholed African streets, jigging through the jungle, gyrating on tabletops. I swear she tap-danced when she was on the toilet. I'd never seen anyone move like that and I couldn't have felt more out of my depth, but the whole experience did teach me one thing. In order to maintain my pride, I would have to resist joining her on the dance floor. She would reach out to me, brown eyes wide and eyelashes fluttering, beckoning me into her bosom. But I refused point blank, made an excuse about being comfortable where I was and drowned myself in a beer, quietly tapping a toe when no one was looking. Needless to say, the Colombian girl ditched me and left my heart screaming for mercy, but it had stood me in good stead. I was never going to be embarrassed on a dance floor.

'She likes you!' There was a shout in my ear. It scared the crap out of me. To my right was an assistant from Link, nodding over at Kate, who was involved in some kind of Cossack dance underneath the mirror ball. 'You should go and dance with her,' said the assistant, as if she knew everything. I thought on my feet and lied profusely.

'I'm not dancing, I've got some kind of trouble with my knee,' I yelled over the din, but my bottle of wine was already dragging me across the dance floor, defying all of my rules, leading me towards Kate who was by now bathed in a white glow, reaching out to me, blue eyes wide and eyelashes fluttering, drawing me in. And our lips met gently, then with a little more passion, and for the first time in my life I felt quite comfortable on a dance floor.

* * *

Oh boy. I'm in trouble now.

‖ Approaching Scotland
Jan – April 2006

A quiet Christmas drifted into New Year. I flitted between my home in Swansea and London, where Kate and I were spending more and more time together. She had knocked me off my feet and for once BoardFree wasn't all I was thinking about. I wrestled with myself, torn between a need to get to know this girl and a voice of conscience that argued quite strongly that I shouldn't be getting involved in anything romantic. I didn't have a choice. London developed a gravitational pull and weekend after weekend I found myself blissfully dragged into Kate's arms. The other Kate in my life, my cousin, had flown back from Australia for a family visit and we arranged to meet near Covent Garden in late December. En route I received a text from my housemate, Danny. 'Dave, is there any way I can be part of BoardFree Australia?' He'd split from his girlfriend. I typed back something along the lines of 'keep your chin up mate, we'll see what we can do', and continued to London, where Cousin Kate and I rambled excitedly about Australia and Sailability. She was to be my on-the-ground liaison with the charity and we mapped out a plan of action for the months leading up to the August send-off from Perth.

The early months of 2006 disappeared quickly. I stepped up my requests to sponsors with varying success. Christmas came early at least twice a week and piles of sponsored products ranging from MP3 players to water bottles began to stack up at the end of my study. There isn't a generic shopping list for people about to embark on a long-distance skateboarding journey so I went for the cluster bomb approach. The more people I wrote to, I figured, the more chance there would be of positive replies. Through Peter at rollsrolls I had all of the skate equipment I needed; a board, plus a spare, plenty of bearings and wheels, which the manufacturer in America was unwilling to supply. So Peter paid for them himself. Gavin Clarke from Surrey Skateboards, who are confusingly now based in Devon, had recently developed a groundbreaking longboarding truck called a Holey, and he kindly sponsored this side of things for me. Elsa and her bits were truly a multinational lot now, hailing from Germany, Poland, America and now the UK – it was great to have an English brand on board.

My biggest worry was finding a shoe sponsor. I'd written to all of the major brands without any response whatsoever. I understood mine was something of an unusual request and knew that I wasn't able to communicate my commitment to BoardFree through one hopeful email, but continued to hold out that my letters would catch the attention of someone. Anyone. All I had asked for was six pairs, but without so much as a whisper of reply I was starting to wonder whether it was possible to skate long distances in socks. Why are these companies being so rude? Is what I'm doing so worthless? Or do they get requests like this all the time from people who have no intention of doing anything? Well, I'll show them that I mean this, even without their bloody shoes I'm going to do it.

In mid-January the team and I invited Danny to join our ranks. There were six of us now, four guys and two girls, and I was humbled by the way I had found others to put so much into BoardFree. I had only been skating for ten months and the speed at which BoardFree had grown made me intensely proud. As the media coverage became more widespread I found myself doing two or three interviews a week. Messages of support came through to the website from around the world, giving the project a global feel and underlining the support base it had built even before the journeys had begun. Simple, heartfelt messages from friends and strangers:

> *I don't think even Paula Radcliffe calls 900 miles a 'warm up'. It's amazing to see so much ambition and determination. Good luck to Dave!*
>
> *– Victoria Brooks, via an article read in Metro*

My Oz housemate just found you in his paper, the Australian Times, you're on your way to becoming an international star!

– Amanda Shipp

This guy is a legend! I really appreciate things like this, especially when they are for a good cause. But he does have one heck of a challenge ahead, the Australian outback is a harsh environment, not the place for a fair skinned skater! He should get a sponsorship from a sunblock company. Only kidding! Full respect and best of luck to you Dave!

– David from California

I'm a longboarder too and I think what you're doing is awesome. I'd love to ride with you sometime!

– Sam in Perth

After a while, celebrities started to email:

What a brave man you are! Would be happy to help out in Oz next year. Keep me up to speed with your progress and congratulations on such an admirable effort. Cheers,

– Alan Fletcher, actor who plays Karl Kennedy in Neighbours

I'd consider doing this. If the skateboard had an engine. And a roof. And maybe sleeping quarters. Basically, if it was a camper van. But it's not. It's a skateboard. So I wouldn't touch it with a barge pole. So you – and some good charities – can be glad that another Dave is.

– Dave Gorman, Comedian

The world needs brilliant, imaginative and above all determined people like Dave – and never forget that each blister and fall is a step closer to your dream and to changing the lives of the children's charities you are raising funds for – good luck buddy!

– Bear Grylls, Adventurer

And then, towards late January, this arrived in my inbox:

Good luck Dave! Your journey is truly inspiring. I will never complain about my legs being too tired again.

— Tony Hawk, Professional Skateboarder

The support was all very nice, and it gave the team a lift as well, but I wanted to keep my mind on the job. We were still short of a photographer and I wanted to create a balance in the team, so hoped for a strong female applicant. In mid-February I was sat on a bag in Gatwick Airport, waiting to board a plane to Grenoble for a mirror image of the snowboarding holiday last year that had created the initial passion for BoardFree. My phone rang; it was Danny. 'Mate,' he said, 'you've just had an email from a girl called Holly Allen, she's nineteen and wants to be the BoardFree photographer.'

'Drop her a line,' I said. 'Tell her I'm away for a week and will be in touch as soon as I get back.'

The snowboarding holiday went well. In the back of my mind I knew that my length of Britain journey was only two months away so I put up a guard and didn't push myself. Saying that, ten months of longboarding had stood me in good stead. I'd improved an awful lot and although BoardFree had exaggerated my initial intentions for the sport it was a great feeling to clip my boots onto a snowboard and slide off down a mountain without needing to dust my rear on a regular basis. I also endeavoured to carry BoardFree leaflets with me on the slopes, leaving one on every chairlift and sparking up the occasional conversation with an amazed European. What a great feeling to have an ice-breaker like BoardFree! It often took a lot to get through to a stranger, especially when their face is covered by balaclava and goggles, yet here I was swinging in mid-air with an excited Dutchman who kept repeating 'Australia? Australia? You don't mean Austria?'

Back home at the end of the week I felt invigorated and ready for the two-month build up to BoardFree UK. I wrote to Holly and invited her to join myself and the team in London the following weekend, for when I had arranged a BoardFree awareness day in Hyde Park.

Five days later Becki, Dan, Simon and I were all descending on Kate's flat in north London, along with Peter Sanftenberg from rollsrolls, who had flown over from Germany to meet the crew. The next morning we headed for Serpentine Road in Hyde Park, which, weather permitting, was always going to draw crowds of walkers and skaters at a weekend. I'd discovered Serpentine Road by accident a month earlier, when Elsa and I scooted through Hyde Park to discover this thirty feet-wide, mile-long stretch of the smoothest tarmac imaginable. It was a skater's paradise and I was amazed by the contraptions on show: skis with wheels, slalom skateboarders weaving, inline skate schools showing beginners their first steps, other inliners gracefully dancing in between cones. This was a haven for people who had discovered the beauty of travel and movement, people who became happy when rolling around without a motor. It was the perfect place to promote BoardFree and the team poised, leaflets at the ready.

Kate, who of course wasn't an official member of the BoardFree team, had been accepted into the fold and mucked in immediately, donning a hired kangaroo costume and bouncing around with arms waving, teasing some poor sods who were being put through their paces by an army physical training instructor, and imitating a local performing tai chi in the distance. A big red kangaroo doing tai chi in Hyde Park, already BoardFree had created a first. Becki took charge of leafleting duty, stopping passers-by for a chat, her collection tin swinging. Danny skated around with me, Si filmed everything, getting strangers to contribute their opinions on BoardFree for a film he was due to edit for the website. Peter Sanftenberg had been the first person to see the potential of BoardFree from a sponsor's perspective and seemed impressed with the team's organisation. It was imperative for me that BoardFree gave off a professional air, however much we were winging it sometimes, but when push came to shove I knew that everybody was capable of seeing through the commitment they had promised when applying for a position on the support team. Pete saw this also, and told me so.

Holly joined us and I took her for a walk, getting to know her, delighting in her passion for BoardFree. Like Simon, she hadn't stopped thinking about the project since she heard about it and instinct told me this girl, despite still being in her teens, could offer us a lot. But could she take pictures?

'I want you to snap away,' I told her. 'On the journey I want every day captured on camera, the little things as well as the big. Just show me what you can do.'

Two days later Holly emailed through her pictures, a marvellous array of images, well-structured and high quality. During the day at Hyde Park I had worried that she wasn't taking many photos, but she sent through over one hundred, capturing the mood of the day perfectly and doing it without being intrusive. Holly offered more than just images, though. She already had her own camera and equipment, and another line in her application form had caught my eye: 'I have contact with a major skate shoe brand, what size feet do you have?' The brand turned out to be Vans and I wrote to Holly's contact asking for six pairs of shoes, and then waited. There was one more development involving Holly that would dramatically change the UK leg – she was ready to leave her job and dedicate herself to BoardFree: 'I'd be happy to drive alongside you between John o'Groats and Land's End,' she told me.

Even as February drew to a close I was preparing to carry out the UK warm-up alone, with just a rucksack on my back and board beneath my feet. I was looking forward to spending some time alone and constantly dreamed of collapsing exhausted on park benches, reading a good book for an hour before skating on. It was a romantic notion, but I knew it was logistically difficult, not least because of my biggest fear, traffic. More than 65 million people live in the United Kingdom and they drive over 32 million cars between them. Attitudes to non-motorists on the road in the UK are often impatient – my parents cycle regularly and I knew they shared my fears of crazed drivers – and I was terrified of sharing the roadways with speeding cars and trucks. Changing my thought process to accommodate a support vehicle was tough from a personal point of view, but for safety's sake it was a no-brainer. A support vehicle would drive behind me, providing shelter from traffic and carrying equipment and food. Its presence would make BFUK a very different journey, but it would heighten its chances of success. That was enough for me.

I met with the team in late February and we all decided Holly should fill the photography void. There was concern about her age and maturity: we all knew that while the BoardFree experience would create a more mature Holly, in the meantime we might have to deal with some growing pains. 'Despite all this she's a breath of fresh air,' I told everyone, and the decision was unanimous. A couple of days later I travelled to Portsmouth, where Holly lived with her boyfriend Nat, and delivered the news: 'I want you to come to Australia.'

She took a deep breath, little tears forming.

'I'm a little bit close to hitting you,' she said as Nat drummed the table excitedly, 'you have no idea.' She cupped her face in her hands. 'I don't know what to say. Thank you!'

Without giving her time to calm down I asked her to go outside and do a personal blog to camera, hoping it would make some great footage for the documentary. It did, as she started with the brilliant line, 'Hello, I'm Holly and I'm the photographer for BoardFree. OH MY GOD THAT FEELS SO GOOD TO SAY!'

*   *   *

We were now barely six weeks away from the beginning of BFUK. Holly had confirmed she was going to leave her job and drive with me, so I added vehicle companies to my list of potential sponsors to write to. I delegated little tasks to each of the other team members, who were all carrying on with their own jobs or studies but kept bugging me for things they could do to help. Becki was going through a hard time at work and was further out of the loop than she had been for a while, but BoardFree posters and leaflets adorned her office walls and door and she told me she was doing what she could. Si was busy with his degree in Falmouth, Dan with his in Swansea, and Holly did what she could from her home on the south coast, printing stickers up and having some vehicle graphics made, which she brought to Swansea to stick on Dan and Becki's cars, which were both a similar yellow to Elsa, my board.

Holls was sat in my study when a new email flashed up, it was from Vans. They had seemed pretty positive in the previous communication we had shared and I was sure they would come through for us, but it was bad news.

'We don't have the budget to give you six pairs of shoes,' they wrote.

'That's bullshit!' I shouted.

It was a real kick in the teeth. General support for the project was going strong, there had been plenty of media awareness and even celebrity support, but Vans couldn't supply six pairs of shoes. It took the piss. Holly was quiet in the corner, feeling responsible because she had put me in touch with them, but it wasn't her fault. I think the basic fact that a major skate-wear company wasn't willing to support BoardFree was the biggest blow; we still had a lot to prove. That same afternoon I shot off more emails, mainly to smaller, independent brands and shops, and was amazed to get an almost instant response from a shop called Vapourised, based in Leicester, who said they were willing to support us. The mood in the study changed. We were all jumping up and down cheering. My God we were on a rollercoaster, there was nothing like that afternoon to epitomise BoardFree, getting on with things after another letdown and turning it into a success. Vapourised were just a small company, but they were willing to support us although their budgets were a tiny fraction of a company like Vans.

Outside the study, the team kept BoardFree working. I'd spend most weekends with Kate in London, and she'd got used to storing BoardFree leaflets in her back pocket to hand to complete strangers who would glance inquisitively at my board. Meanwhile, the Dance and Drama Societies at Swansea University supported BoardFree by selling t-shirts, wristbands and the BoardFree Naked Calendars I'd produced earlier in the year, which involved individuals and teams from Swansea University posing scantily clad with appropriately placed longboards covering their white bits. More sponsored products kept landing on the doorstep: helmets from Bell, smoothies from Innocent Drinks, breakfast bars from Eat Natural. A running store in Peterborough called Advance Performance sent me a reflective jacket, vest and gloves. Clic Extreme agreed to become the team's sunglasses sponsor and provided a pair to each member of the team. Connecting above the bridge of the nose with magnets, the sunglasses were a quirky addition to the project and I was sure they could get some wide-scale coverage as the journeys went on.

March and April brought their own stresses. BoardFree had been growing slowly for a year now, and it was proving to be a difficult period for the team. The project was in a vacuum; media coverage and donations had tailed off, and although I knew it was fundamentally the calm before the storm, few of us were dealing with it well. My personal frustrations with a relatively low rate of donations and a couple of months of relative silence on the airwaves started to boil over. I often felt alone, fearing that the team had relaxed now they had won their places on the team and didn't need to prove themselves. Most of the team weren't going to have much involvement in BoardFree UK and it was going to be hard for them to get their heads around the concept of watching my progress knowing that Australia was still months away. I couldn't have expected them to be as committed as I was, after all, this was born of my dream and of course they had other commitments, but when reality set in I knew that I couldn't drag the project kicking and screaming towards success until I finally got on my board. The skate was where this had begun and ultimately it was going to be what BoardFree was judged on, and I made sure that I was in the right physical shape, skating between ten and twenty miles each day, using that time on the roads and paths to focus mentally. When it came down to it nobody else was going to be able to do the pushing, this was down to me.

Things were getting tense with Rae, who wasn't receiving much support from her family over her and Phil's involvement with BoardFree. Many of the concerns involved safety, especially across the Nullarbor, but I felt a strong negative spin was being self-generated by Rae, who hadn't travelled much before and was worried about so many aspects of the Australian journey that she'd worked herself into a hole of doubt. When this doubt became focused on my ability to manage BoardFree we had problems.

Rae questioned my commitment to the journeys, citing my snowboard holiday as proof that I wasn't doing all I could to protect myself from injury. It was all getting a bit silly, and while Phil was content to sit back passively it slowly became clear that Rae didn't want to be involved anymore. I couldn't dismiss their wedding either, which was set for July and still needed much work. It was a huge commitment in itself and BoardFree was becoming too much of a burden for them. Personally I had to put BoardFree first, and knew that if I gave Rae a way out she'd take it. So I sat down in her office and talked things through.

'If you have major doubts about this you have to do the right thing and nip them in the bud now. We can't afford for this to continue and flare up in the middle of the Australian desert. If you and Phil need to leave BoardFree I understand, Rae,' I told her, 'but we need to resolve this as soon as we can.' A couple of days later I got a call, she and Phil were off the team. The relief of settling the matter was tempered by disappointment. Si and Holly both expressed their upset at Rae and Phil's departure, but I knew it was for the best. They would be missed but there were more important things to focus on now.

I had a to-do list the length of my board. Because of this and heavy, consistent rain my training took a downturn, but I took heart from advice sent over from the USA by Jack Smith: 'You can't really train for something like this, it's mostly mental.' I kept myself sane with regular trips to London to see Kate, who was due to spend a fortnight in Florida and would be out of the country for the beginning of my UK journey. Her support had been invaluable to me since we met and we had fallen head over heels for each other, but deep down I was still trying in vain to keep her at arm's length, half-heartedly trying to protect both of us from the inevitable goodbye. This girl had not been in the plan, but here she was and like it or not, I was going to desperately miss her during the first two weeks of BFUK. The security blanket I had thrown far away when quitting my job and embarking on this project had been replaced in a different form by Kate's support for me, which was simply unbending. 'I love you,' she told me, 'you're an amazing person and you have so much to give. Whatever I can do to help, I will.' My original mindset of ensuring that nobody on the team should have a partner had been dented a little with Holly's addition to the team, and I couldn't help wondering whether I should stop being stubborn and create a place for Kate; she had contributed just as much to BoardFree as any of the team members. Meanwhile, an email from Ellen MacArthur, the inspirational sailor, provided some settling support:

Dear Dave, the team and I here wish you and Elsa every success on these epic journeys! I'm sure that just like the sea, the roads will bring their own set of challenges, but with lows come great highs and really I hope you realise your dreams. Good luck and stay strong. Just Go For It!

Ellen.

I pinched myself at recognition from people like Ellen, individuals who had achieved so much and continued to inspire millions around the world. How she had time to write to me I didn't know, but I soaked it up and returned my thanks and best wishes for her next journey.

I was starting to itch with anticipation. For twelve months I had been travelling down a new road, totally reinventing my life targets and working hard without an income just so I could make a difference. A great deal had happened and the team and I had received so much support, all I wanted was to justify the hard work. I longed for Land's End even before the drive up to John o'Groats had started.

Skating the length of Britain was no mean feat and had Australia never crossed my horizons everyone may have been similarly as awed had I approached them with just the one, nine hundred mile journey as my life-changing project. 'Wow, Dave,' they would have said, 'you want to skate the length of Britain? That's going to be tough man, but good luck, hey.' But that wasn't how it panned out. I'd gone and started off my dream with a task so unbelievably huge that John o'Groats to Land's End was a side salad. It was a means to an end, a not-so-basic learning curve and a pointer to everyone out there who was questioning my integrity, my ability, my determination. I knew that the time for talking was coming to an end. I was just days away from stepping onto Elsa and starting a journey fraught with obstacles. The comfort zone was about to be left far behind. I'm prepared for the nightmares; the misty images of a man with a swag bag stealing into the night with my board under one arm and our fundraising totals in his sack. But I'm also prepared for reality, that these journeys are happening and they're happening soon. It was time to put my longboard where my mouth was.

12 The Last Week
Late April 2006

Through Holly's boyfriend I made contact with Patrick Midland, a factual documentary director who had expressed an interest in filming the BoardFree journeys. With John o'Groats now just days away everything was falling into place and the opportunity to have the journeys professionally filmed was interesting. I was confident in Simon's ability to film and edit a good documentary of the Australian trip as team cameraman, but was conscious that with our lack of experience the production wasn't likely to get further than DVD. I met Patrick, who had recently started up his own production company, on a bench in Hyde Park and discussed the ins and outs of filming the journey, as well as the potential for getting the finished product on television. Of course, there were no promises that the documentary would air, but I was more concerned about the effect an outside influence would have on the team and needed to be satisfied that Pat recognised the importance of BoardFree to me.

'I know you have to see it as a business interest, but whether it's being filmed or not I don't want anything to compromise the original reasons for the project,' I told him. 'I'd want the documentary to be about the journey, not the journey to be about the documentary.'

'This is your baby,' he said, 'and if we filmed it I'd want you to be involved in decision-making all the way through. It's a really interesting story, you know, I'll have a chat to my business partner and get back to you.'

He called me a couple of days later with good news; they had decided to film the UK journey as a trial run. Pat's business partner, Dominic Beard, visited Swansea to film our preparations for the journey and spent three days stepping between boxes and skate parts, interviewing myself, Dan, Becki and Kate, who had taken time off work to offer another two hands before she flew to Florida. Two pairs of shoes arrived from Vapourised, and the irony couldn't have been more evident: one was a pair of Vans. Still, they were green and yellow, exactly the same colour as Elsa and her wheels, and I set about wearing them in as we all crowded around the computer and enjoyed the progress of an eBay auction, in which I was selling my calves as advertising space to raise more funds. It was a quirky publicity stunt: in anticipation of much growth my calves were already the subject of several Internet debates and I thought selling them would raise interest in the journey. We ran with the auction promoting 'unique advertising space in which the advert actually grows as time goes on'. Kate had called around searching for a company that specialised in creating temporary tattoos. One of them, The Magic Touch, agreed to help, and their managing director ended up buying my right calf, with the left one going to another sponsor, Dogcam Sport, who had earlier provided a three-inch bullet camera for some skater-eye-view shots. Dom joined me in a visit to The Footbed Clinic in Swansea, where chiropodist Chris Sharp, whose former clients included Colin Jackson, the Olympic hurdler, measured my gait – an embarrassing process involving me removing my jeans to reveal some horrendously creased yellow boxer shorts – and then moulded some custom insoles to slip inside my shoes. Afterwards, still wishing I'd worn different underwear, I thanked him and made haste out of the door.

Without doubt, the largest development in the run-up to BFUK was our acquisition of a support vehicle. One of my posts on a Volkswagen Internet forum had been seen by Dave Hulme, editor of an online publication for Volkswagen enthusiasts. His first email, offering use of his old, beige-coloured VW van, had me squealing in delight, but two days later he wrote with more good news, attaching images of a newer, not to mention larger, bright blue VW Campervan. 'The guy who owns this van runs a graphics business and will logo up the van for you, too,' chirped Dave, who was almost as excited as me.

'This makes a huge difference to the journey Dave, I can't thank you enough,' I told him. And it really did, having a big blue van as a support vehicle wouldn't have featured in my wildest dreams two months earlier, but now with Holly driving and Dom filming, BFUK was gaining momentum.

Back in my Swansea study, Kate was on the phone to companies who dealt with nutritional drinks, foods and powders. She hadn't so much slotted into the BoardFree system as taken it by one ear. As my partner she was determined to make sure I was going to be physically capable of completing this journey; looking after me was her priority and her passion on the phone was evident. Call after call, though, there was rejection on the other end and she was getting frustrated.

'I just want to make sure you're healthy and getting enough energy on the road,' she said, wide-eyed, 'but none of these buggers care.'

'Babes,' I said, giving her a squeeze, 'you're doing an awesome job. It's not your fault these people can't see past their noses.'

'But what are you going to eat?!' she asked, desperate.

'Bananas?' I shrugged.

* * *

On Thursday 27 April 2006, three days before I was due to push off and begin BoardFree UK, I hugged Kate and Kiwa goodbye and climbed into a heavily packed car with Dan and Becki, who would share the wheel on the three-day drive north. Dom filmed us go, and would meet us the next evening in Prestwick, where we'd pick up our support vehicle from Dave Hulme. With Swansea fading into the distance I knew that this was it. Thirteen months on from stepping onto my first longboard life had changed immeasurably; there was no more day job, no commitments except those I had set myself. As we crossed over the Welsh border I kept my eyes on the roads, knowing that I would be skating back along them in two weeks or so, the sense of achievement to even get this far swelling up inside me, the reality of distance and danger quickening my heart rate. I knew I was capable of becoming the first person to skate the length of the country, but as the hours drew on I knew that there would be many factors beyond my control that could snatch away this dream. All I could do was keep focused and treat BoardFree UK just as it was: a warm-up.

We spent the night at my brother Andy's house in Manchester, spread about on floors and mattresses. The next morning I hugged him goodbye, blinking away the tears, choking back the ache in my throat, my fears for the coming weeks rising to the surface. I was terrified of cars, of traffic, of sharing the road with drivers over whom I had no control. Saying goodbye to Andy, four years my younger, I dealt with the possibility that I might not see him again, all it would take was one swerve of a passing car, one bad fall, and that would be it.

'I'm so proud of you bro,' he said to me. 'Good luck and see you in a couple of weeks.' I nodded, turned, and climbed into the car.

Seven hours and several hundred miles further north, we pulled into a Leisure Centre on the outskirts of Prestwick to find a man in a luminous jacket poking around in our support vehicle's engine. Dave Hulme was there, arms wide, his face a picture of embarrassment. 'I'm not sure what's wrong,' he said pointing at the van, 'it was running fine until this afternoon.'

Personally, I couldn't have cared less about the technical hitch and trotted around the van, peering inside, staring at the logos that stated quite clearly what the van's role was. Tangibly, this vehicle was the largest product of the dream that began that morning a year earlier. Hundreds of phone calls, thousands of emails, tens of interviews, almost 200,000 visitors to the website's 54 pages, and this van, all blue and magnificent and clad in its fighting colours: JOHN O'GROATS TO LAND'S END, SKATING THE UK FOR CHARITY, WWW.BOARDFREE.CO.UK. Dom was already there having taken the train from London earlier, and pointed his camera at me. 'How does it feel to see the van for the first time, especially when a mechanic is working on it?' he asked.

'The van looks great, I'm so chuffed with it,' I said. 'As for the engine trouble, it doesn't really bother me. It's just a glitch. He'll fix it, we'll carry on, it's just one of those little obstacles we're going to have to overcome time and time again on this journey. Absolutely not a problem.'

Eventually the van started up to cheers all round. Picking up Holly from the station en route, Dave led us back to his charming little house on the edges of Prestwick Airport, where he made a full-time living as an air traffic controller. Dave lived with his wife Joyce and excitable dog Jacko, who instantly made us feel quite at home with several generous lashings of tongue. As dusk fell I sat in the conservatory writing a blog for those members of the public who were ready to follow this journey, some waiting to see the wheels fall off the attempt, others anticipating a month-long saga ending with a new world record. Messages of support streamed in and I felt strangely separate from everything, replying to each message but wishing I had done more to earn their backing. My time was coming, I knew: two more nights of sleep and then Elsa and I would be away. But there, airport lights blinking in the distance and the dark looming shape of the BFUK van right outside, I felt the real weight of responsibility on my shoulders. Despite the team's presence I suffered pangs of loneliness. I'd put myself in a position that invited effort, pain, fatigue and jubilation. Some very true rewards were waiting at the end of these journeys, but with some very real physical and mental suffering as a consequence. Nobody else, whether they were watching through the website or sitting in the van behind me, would be able to fully comprehend exactly what I was about to go through, and as the clock ticked past midnight I shuffled to bed feeling very alone indeed.

From Prestwick we drove towards Inverness, where Simon was waiting at the airport, having made a last-minute decision that he wasn't to be the only member of the team not present at the start of BoardFree's first journey. In Inverness we stopped for lunch, and leaving the rest of the team in the pub to watch a football match I ambled through new streets in search of knee supports. In a leisurewear shop a small girl tugged at my trousers, pointing at my board: 'What's that?' Her dad, a heavily bearded man named Ian, listened to my story and to my surprise pulled £20 out of his wallet.

'Thank you very much,' I said, sincerely, 'you're the first person to donate on this journey.'

'It's my pleasure,' he said, handing me his card. 'Good luck on the road.' I watched them go, the thrill of receiving a donation from a complete stranger steadying my feet, I was ready for this now.

The A9 north from Inverness was the road I'd be skating back along in the coming days and try as I might I couldn't take my eyes off it. The volume of traffic, decreasing as we approached the tip of the country; the quality of the road, so hard to judge when speeding across it in a vehicle; the topography of the land, fearfully hilly in places. Apart from the numerous bridges across inlets and waterways, there were few sections of road that could be called flat; the challenge ahead was growing with the mountains that surrounded us. We park up in a petrol station in Tain and three kids run out to see what's going on. One of the lads is called Josh, he's about six and wants a go on my board. I run alongside and catch him as he loses balance. 'I'm about to skate the length of the country on that board,' I tell him, 'would you like to do it too?'

He looks at me, face straight as an arrow.

'Yeah, I'd do it!'

In one year, he was the only other human being I'd spoken to who had given that answer. I patted his head and gave him some stickers.

Two hours later and fifteen miles south of John o'Groats is the small town of Wick. I'd been put in touch with Neil and Mary Thompson by a friend who worked in London. 'Welcome to Wick!' said Neil, as we wearily pulled into their driveway. Mary stood beside him in a quaint doorway, and immediately started offering food and making us welcome. The light was fading already and Dom interviewed me in the garden. Danny was there too, cradling the minicam. This was the last interview before it all began. I was aware throughout the interview that the next day was the start of a new chapter of my life, and found it quite ironic that this new chapter had been set up by a year of talk, and here I was, still talking. I rambled on about being prepared to fight the elements, my fears about the hills we had seen on the drive north. 'I'm not worried about pushing up them,' I said, 'it's coming down that poses problems, the potential injury not just from falling, but from the stresses of dragging my foot to brake.'

'Was it strange seeing the road you're about to skate?' Dom asked me.

'I think the very fact that each of us was feeling the strain just from driving here says a lot about the road. The conditions were good, obviously lots of hills and some tight corners too. But that accumulation of fatigue, I'm always conscious that I'm about to experience that in a whole different sense in the coming weeks. The scenery is superb and I can't wait to see it from a new perspective, the clean air is going to push me on several miles further each day, I am ready for this.'

Neil and Mary set out a glorious feast for dinner. Everything was being filmed so it didn't feel natural, but the camera was part of it and we accepted the stunted, directed conversation for sake of celluloid memory. Neil is asked to question me about BFUK, and for some unknown reason a laughing fit ensues. In seconds everyone is giggling. Each time Neil asks, 'Dave, is this your first trip to Scotland?' I fall about. Five or six times he tries with the same result. Holly is in stitches and is eventually sent from the room, Becki can't control her cackles and clamps a hand to her mouth. Neil asked me the question again and I manage an answer.

'Yes.' There's a pause, and in the midst of delight at finally speaking, I realise I've given the wrong answer. 'No,' I hiss, and we're all reduced to an exasperated, laughing mess. Eventually we calm down, but by then Neil is so determined to get his questions out and I'm so keen to answer them quickly that the conversation is so insanely robotic that it'll never be used in the documentary.

We all retired to bed after that. Exhausted from the drive, nervous about the coming day. I close my eyes and fall asleep with the excitement of adventure running through my veins, I'd been waiting so long for this, I thought, I wasn't sure if I'd ever wake up.

13 BFUK

30 April – 2 June 2006

I did wake, sick with nerves. Mary fluttered about downstairs, piling toast onto plates and making sure everyone was happy. There was a buzz in the air and it felt like the beginning of a relationship, the unquestionable electricity of something new and thrilling. Everyone was grinning; finally it was Sunday 30 April 2006. This day had been a long time coming.

Everything was packed into the van and I went into the front lounge to collect some Ordnance Survey maps. Then Danny came in with a grave look on his face. 'Dave,' he said, 'the van isn't starting.'

'You're kidding me,' I said. Outside, the ignition spluttered again and again.

'Sorry,' Holly said, each time. I called the AA out and forty minutes later a mechanic arrived, a real oiler who didn't want to be filmed. As he tinkered around in the engine text messages of support arrive to my phone, Neil brings out another mug of tea.

Simon, who was training his camera on the exhaust pipe, started to jump around like a mad man. 'My leg!' he shouted. 'Something's burning my leg!' He reached into his pocket and pulled out an AA battery, throwing it down as though it were a hot potato. Somehow, Si's positioning beside an outside fuse box had caused the battery in his pocket to heat up. Strangely, nobody else had seen this little episode, and for Si at least, it was an amusing, if not baffling story that only he would remember on this momentous morning.

With the mechanic still buried in the engine I had asked Becki and Si to drive to the start point to let people know that we would soon be on our way, but they'd driven back saying the only person at John o'Groats was a half-naked man in a campervan. I was split between disappointment and relief, disappointment that the media weren't interested, and relief that we'd kept nobody waiting.

I was tracing the day's route on a map when Becki came in. 'Can you hear the van purring outside?' she asked me. It was ready! It was time! Rushing outside, we all bundled in. Holly negotiated the tight driveway out of the Thompsons' house and began the drive to John o'Groats. I eagerly peered through the windscreen as the team nattered excitedly. It was a beautiful day and my heart started beating faster as the sea came into view and as we drew closer I felt serene and happy. Eight months of planning had come down to this moment, and in John o'Groats I slid open the side door and jumped out, ready to take on Britain.

'Can you do that again?' asked Dom, who wanted to film us clambering out of the van, so we got back in, waited for him to get into position, and did it again.

The place was silent, ever so peaceful. Wanting to register but finding no one in the John o'Groats Inn, which sat twenty metres from the start line looking for all the world like an 1800s country pub, we left a note on the bar explaining that we were about to start a journey to Land's End, on a skateboard.

As I warmed up I gave a little interview with Dom, explaining how I hadn't thought about what John o'Groats would look like, it was just a place where the journey was always going to start from. 'It feels amazing to be here,' I told him, looking around. 'This is the calm before the storm.' And then, with one last deep breath, I grinned like the Cheshire Cat. 'It's time,' I said. 'Let's do it.'

Everyone gathered around and we hugged as a team; spontaneously everyone kissed my cheek, everyone except Danny.

'Where's my kiss, Danny?' I said, and he puckered his lips and pushed a kiss into the air. It was so quiet, so sweet, that we all cracked up and the tension vanished.

'Good luck mate,' said Si.

'Good luck baby,' said Becki.

A small pause.

'Let's go guys, let's do it,' I said, breaking away and walking towards Elsa, who waited on the start line.

I was just about to push off without ceremony when Si piped up, 'Shall we have a countdown?'

'From five guys,' said Becki, and they began . . .

'Five, four, three, two, one . . .'

And I pushed off from John o'Groats with an awfully long way to go, the beginning of a journey I'd been planning for the best part of a year. The start of it all.

It was strangely quiet after the initial 'Wooo!' of celebration released by the team. The road immediately turned to ruts and potholes and I could hear little but the grinding of my wheels beneath the board. Dom had been filming everything as we prepared for the push-off, and it was only when I watched the footage of the start a month later that I realised just how quickly the presence of a camera had started to subconsciously control the actions of everyone involved. As I pushed on, becoming smaller and smaller in the distance, the team remained silent until Dom turned and pointed the camera at them. Only then did they react, and it was almost as though a drama teacher had said 'wait for my signal, and then act!'

'Yeaaaay! Go on Dave!' shouted Becki, before putting her hands to her mouth and staring stock-still into the distance after me.

'Oooh! Oooh! Oooh!' howled Holly, pumping her non-camera hand in the air.

Simon tilted his head back and cupped his hands to his mouth, 'Go on my son!'

'He is actually mental,' said Holly, finding some words.

And Danny clapped for a couple of seconds, then turned away towards the van saying, 'We need to catch up with him. No, seriously, he's off!' They jogged over to the van, jumped in and gave chase.

The first two miles were all uphill and the road surface was abominable. So much so that as the sun beat down I was out of breath not far out of John o'Groats and I laughed into my minicam that I was knackered and could still see the Scottish north coast. Beneath the humorous angle, though, I was concerned more about the roads than my fitness. I was barely managing walking pace on the old, badly maintained surface and to lessen the impact of the rough road I skated in between the lanes, trying to run my wheels over the white painted lines, which at least offered a relative smoothness in comparison with the road.

We stopped at a large John o'Groats sign to take some team photos and at the same time a maroon car pulled up. The driver handed us an End-to-End registration pack, clearly marked with the John o'Groats stamp.

'I don't open 'til half twelve,' he said in a thick Scottish accent. 'Didn't realise I'd left the door open until I found your note.'

'Thank you very much,' I said, shaking his hand. The owner of the local pub had absent-mindedly left his door open. John o'Groats certainly wasn't a hotbed of criminal activity, but I was still grateful for the man's commitment to his end of the Length of Britain bargain. It would have been quite disappointing being turned away from Land's End because the proper paperwork hadn't been made available several hundred miles earlier.

In the excitement of the start I had forgotten to put my helmet on, partly because the lack of vehicles in the John o'Groats area hadn't set any alarm bells off. Someone handed it to me and as I fiddled with the strap Dom asked me how I was feeling.

'Good,' I said. 'That was a long uphill from John o'Groats and the road wasn't good, and that always hurts for a little while. But it goes away, a bit like a bang on the shin; you just grin and bare it.'

The countryside rolled gently away to the south and west, short highland grasses lining the roads with green and yellow fields cross-hatched and spread across the hills all around. The sea, blue and inviting in the sunlight, still filled the horizon to our left, and as I skated on to reach the top of another hill, a new swathe of countryside opened up revealing a thin, silvery line of road heading down into the valley and then, painfully, up and up over the next ridge.

In the van, the team was showing some worry about my safety, and I suppose ability, to make it down some of the bigger hills.

'We're a little bit concerned about him taking a tumble,' said Holly to Dom, 'because down these hills it can be quite fatal.' She stared wistfully out of the open side door before adding, 'Hope not though, touch wood.' At which point she quite inexplicably reached up and tapped her own head. Despite her wooden-headed concern, Holls was glad of the opportunity to snap away freely with her camera, an opportunity she knew she wouldn't have once the rest of the team left later on, leaving her as the sole driver.

'Only nine hundred miles to go!' Danny yelled, and as I continued ahead of the van I was oblivious to what happened next.

'Oh fuck!' said Becki and Holly in unison. Dom, twisting himself around to get a shot of the team inside the van, had lost his balance and fallen out onto the grass verge.

'You berk,' said Simon laughing, after Dom had brushed himself off and climbed back in without injury. And that's what we all loved about Simon, he was the only one of us who would ever consider saying the word 'berk'. It summed up the moment perfectly!

'Calf massage?' offered Becki.

'Definitely, let me sit in the van,' I said, commenting about how hard the hills had been. Becki crouched down and grabbed my left leg and Holly knelt down to my right, exclaiming, 'Oh, why do I get the fat one?' She prodded my right calf as everyone laughed, and then Danny and Si took hold of a foot each and started to gently roll my ankles.

'That's good! Mmm, oooh yes!' I mumbled, my legs and feet in ecstasy.

'BoardFree porn!' said Holly, 'I feel like I'm grabbing a piece of meat! A big steak!'

'Let's see how far we've come,' I said, pulling my Garmin portable GPS out from beneath my hooded top. 'Five-point-four miles. Forty-four minutes, fifty-eight seconds. Moving average seven-point-two miles an hour, which is fair enough for those big hills.

'I think it's safe to say,' I looked straight at Dom and then down at Becs, Dan, Si and Holly, 'that at present we're travelling at precisely zero-miles-per hour. Shall we move on?'

An hour later and I was alone on the road, having said goodbye to Si, Becki and Dan. Holls had to drive them back to the car in Wick and with no other way to keep up with me Dom had go with them. I hugged each of them as they climbed into the van, staying positive despite knowing I wasn't going to see them for three weeks, but as soon as they had gone I felt empty and alone. Blinking away the tears I suddenly found myself longing for my cat, for a warm bath, for the security of the van and my friends, for Kate. The drive up to John o'Groats had been a real bonding experience for the team and I knew it must have been hard for them to leave so soon after the start. But it showed their commitment to BoardFree that they'd given up days just to be with me for the first twelve miles; I couldn't wait until I saw them again, not least because I knew I'd be very close to the end by then. I wanted to make them proud. Holly and Dom would be back soon, and although they had been the most recent additions to the team I was looking forward to getting to know them over the coming weeks. I continued, stepping onto the verge or pavement when cars drove by then getting back on the road when it was clear, and within half an hour I reached Wick. I gave Danny a call to see how he, Si and Becs were doing. As they drove south they were now aware, probably more than ever, of how road quality and hills were going to affect my progress. Tomorrow, he told me, was going to be a very hard day.

On the southern outskirts of Wick I skated past the journey's first major distance sign. Inverness 106. Jesus, I thought, One Hundred and Six Miles, that's a bloody long way. I pushed on, determined to cover the twenty remaining miles to Dunbeath, which I had scheduled as the end-of-day stop. This felt more like it, battling into a headwind and pushing up hills, I started to find a rhythm and felt much better than I had at the end of lunch. Pulling the van over for a drink at the top of a hill, I leant on Holly's door and gasped dramatically, 'Every road is uphill! I can't feel my left foot!'

With a sharp wind in my face, even relatively steep downhill runs were slow going, even to the degree that sometimes I was pushing downhill. When I was more fortunate to get a free run, I took the chance to practise foot dragging, my manual braking mechanism. Elsa's low deck was a huge help in this, making balancing on one foot simple as I scraped the sole of my right shoe along the road to slow down. Holly and I began to work out a system of communication, me using hand signals when I wanted a drink or needed to pull over, her yelling out of the window or beeping the horn when she needed to tell me something. Quaint cottages and farms littered the fields to both sides and livestock took a great interest in my passing. A farmer in blue overalls waved and I pulled over to explain what was happening, quickly getting the impression that he didn't find much in common with my desire to escape the rigours of a day job by skating across countries. 'Safe skateboarding,' he bid me with a toothy smile at the end of our conversation.

'Have a nice day,' I grinned back at him.

Dunbeath was a small hamlet situated on the northern edge of a daunting-looking valley, in skateboard terms at least. Again, as it had many times before, the road dipped down out of sight and re-emerged as it climbed a steep gradient on the other side. 'I'm not starting tomorrow knowing I've got that hill to climb,' I told Holly and Dom, and thus set a precedent for the long days to come. I remembered from the drive up that there was a bridge at the bottom of the valley with a relatively large grate, which had caused the van to jump quite considerably when we drove over it. I didn't fancy running Elsa over it at speed so set off tamely, rolling around the corner to huge cheers and wolf whistles from a bunch of people in a beer garden. Buoyed by their enthusiasm, I made it safely across the bridge and scaled the other side, the first half on my board and the second, for the first time that day, on foot with Elsa under my arm. The van was waiting in a lay-by at the top of the hill. 'I think we'll call it a day there,' I said as Holly came round for a hug.

* * *

Back in the lay-by the next morning, rain poured down. Nearby, a sign indicated 85 miles to Inverness. It was a daunting prospect. The drive up from Inverness had taken hours and I wanted to skate there in two days, but it was stupid to equate driving and skating, I needed to take the journey day by day and the previous day's success bred confidence, but I was cautious of the threat laid down by wet surfaces, one bad slip and it's all over.

I'd slept well despite suffering some unfortunate chafing from the first day on the road. Red raw, I'd explained the problem to Holly who took it upon herself to find a solution. 'I'm going to ask Mary,' she said.

'Try and be subtle,' I ventured, a little embarrassed at this latest medical issue. Blisters I could take, upper leg soreness hadn't been expected. Sure enough, Holls tried to explain the problem to Mary without actually explaining the problem. Hobbling downstairs, I was greeted with a tub of cream and a perceptive smile.

'Got some chafing, have we?' said Mary with a twinkle in her eye. 'This should sort it out.'

Reaching Tain sixty miles away seemed unlikely with vicious headwinds and a wet surface. My right knee was also giving me angst and occasionally Holly set about it with a vigorous rub and words of encouragement, 'You're doing well, babe,' and 'I'm proud of you,' but we both knew there was a big test on the way.

'Watch out for the Braes,' everyone we met had said yesterday.

'Sounds like the Scottish equivalent of the Minotaur,' I noted, shitting myself. The Berriedale Braes was indeed a beast of sorts, a cavernous hole in the earth, the decline on either side steep enough to make Land Rover drivers think twice. With the rain continuing to spit I decided to walk most of the way down, only cautiously skating the lowest section when I could see the road was due to rise up again on the other side. Heading towards the sky again. The van wasn't built to trawl behind me for an hour at such an incline, so I sent Dom and Holls to the top and walked along the verge. It took half an hour, and upon reaching the top the arch of my right foot jerked in spasm. I'd never felt anything like it and collapsed theatrically into the van. 'Could be a stress fracture,' I told the other two with a serious look on my face, 'hurts to buggery.' Holly turned on the van's heater, whipped out some cream and gave the foot a massage. It must have been the swiftest stress-fracture mend in history, and twenty minutes later I was timidly pushing myself towards another set of hills.

Despite grey skies and a feeling that Elsa was struggling to freewheel, I was making progress. Surrounded by pine trees and my face soaked with rain, I grappled with what was happening. A soundtrack Kate had made me played in one ear and I kept glancing around wide-eyed, mentally pinching myself that finally I was on the road. For little more than a year I'd been working towards this and here I was, skating south away from John o'Groats at the mercy of the elements. Despite a hazy presence of fatigue and the occasional ache of pain flashing up my legs I was happy. I caught up with the van to discover Holly trying to make a cuppa on a gas cooker that refused to work, and suggested we plough on to the next town and stop for a break there. Minutes later I was back on my board and had picked up a fair pace when indecision hit me. A car flew past my right shoulder on a blind corner, catching me in two minds whether to foot drag and slow myself down or stay steady on the board. I was travelling at over 20mph with just one foot on the board and all I wanted was to slow down, but the road was rough and Elsa began to wobble violently. I just managed to get my back foot on the board and rolled through Helmsdale with my heart in my mouth. My inexperience had shone through and I felt lucky to have avoided a bad fall, but I was spitting with rage over the stupidity of the driver who had overtaken on the blind bend. All it would have taken was a car coming in the opposite direction and there would have been a smash right beside the support vehicle and me.

Despite a plethora of supportive honks the British have an innate impatience when driving and I knew that we had to take responsibility for our presence on the road. My keenness to ensure this led to a bust-up with Holly towards the end of the second day. Sick of enduring angry beeps and middle fingers from passing motorists, I took to waving drivers through when I could see the road was clear. The A9 running through Golspie was narrow at the best of times and often traffic built up behind us. I hadn't talked to Holly about how to deal with this and in her protectiveness she yelled at me to stop beckoning drivers behind to overtake. It riled me and I pulled her over at the next opportunity, allowing the traffic behind to filter through but also for me to get my point across. 'Holls, I have to think about the other people on the road, we're doing a good thing here and I don't want them to get stuck behind us and start cursing BoardFree.'

'Well let me wave them past then, it freaks me out when you swerve into the middle of the road and do it,' Holly said.

'I'm only doing it when I know it's safe,' I told her. 'I'm just very aware that we're in the way and I don't want to cause any undue anxiety to people on the road. It's killing me when people who have been stuck behind us are swearing at me as they pass.' I stormed off, pissed off that she wasn't willing to look me in the eye as I explained myself. My close call earlier on had got to me, and getting sworn at wasn't doing my confidence any good, it made me more than aware of my vulnerability on the road and I just wanted to make things easier for everyone.

'I'm just concerned for your safety,' she told me, clearly angry at my stubbornness, but I was already on my board, skating on and letting the anger build up. With each push I remonstrated with myself, with Holly, not having any release except the road running beneath me. All too quickly I was getting beyond rationality, yet my angst had boiled up from a fair point. I knew we both thought we were right but Holly couldn't feel how I was feeling, she had a metal cage around her, I had nothing. Eventually I had to stop again, the issue was sapping my energy and I needed to try and resolve it by explaining my point again. Holls didn't seem to agree with me and offered a half-hearted 'sorry' when I was done. Burnt out, I didn't have the heart to continue and buried my head in my hands; my head was spinning. Dom moved in with the camera. 'I feel like crying,' I said. Holly sat in the front seat, saying nothing.

As the afternoon wore on the sun came out, a boost at the best of times. Scaling a slight hill with a beautiful lake glinting to my left, I made video messages for Kate and my parents as I skated along. 'I miss you guys,' I said, 'it's tough sometimes but this is worth it.' The issue with Holly over traffic had burnt itself out and all I wanted was to clear the air. I spoke into the camera and told it just how great she had been, her presence, after all, had made the support van possible. 'If she wasn't here I'd be skating alone with a rucksack on my back, probably twenty or thirty miles closer to John o'Groats than I am now.'

'You've done so well, I'm so proud of you,' said Holly, bear hugging me when I'd finally pulled up for the end of the day; the release of tension was palpable. Seventy-seven miles south of John o'Groats, we passed a country pub with a large car park. The landlord gave us permission to stay overnight and we set about putting up camp, erecting a tent and getting into dry clothes. It was another hour or so before we could fully relax, Dom wanting to interview both of us on the day's main talking point, the argument. We both came out of it smiling, had a hearty meal in the pub and stared bemused at the woman behind the bar as she bored us with all manner of strange facts, including her fiercely held belief that Australia had once been attached to Scotland.

'They both have exactly the same soil,' she said sternly, 'it's been proven.' I crossed my fingers that we'd all live through the night.

*   *   *

We woke just before eight and dressed quickly. My limbs hung loose, aching horribly and begging for more rest. Mentally though, I was ready to get moving. I spent twenty minutes on the phone, calling local newspapers and radio, and the BBC based in Inverness. A journalist from Dumfries and Galloway got in touch, saying he'd like to cover the story as we passed by. I had no idea where Dumfries and Galloway was, and instead of admitting my ignorance gave the old 'it's hard to say when we're going to be in your neck of the woods, but I'll stay in touch' line.

Having set down the night before several miles short of Tain, the scheduled stop for the end of day two, I was sure that I could make up the lost ground and reach Inverness before the day was out. Forty miles of road lay ahead, but spirits were high as I pushed off: we should go over one hundred miles today, it was a minor landmark and gave me something tangible to aim for.

All day the wind blistered into my face, gusting in from the east as I pushed over the Dornoch Firth, past Tain and onwards along the A9, which was becoming increasingly congested and ran through very Scottish-sounding places like Kilmuir and Ardullie. We pulled over into a lay-by to listen to the eleven o'clock news on Moray Firth radio, the bulletin ending with a lilting female voice: 'Heaven is a long gentle downhill slope for one skateboarder. Dave Cornthwaite is currently skating the length of Britain for children's charities and today will be attempting the stretch between Dornoch and Inverness.'

For hours I battled around the northern shore of the Cromarty Firth, pausing only for a roadside café lunch and an interview with the BBC's evening news crew, who followed for ten minutes to get some passing shots as the Firth loomed to my left, a swirling body of black water made all the more ominous by the obvious rise of ground beyond the road bridge crossing. With eighteen miles to go all I wanted was to get over the Firth, move inland and out of the headwind that had plagued me since morning. Bent almost double crossing the bridge, I waved the van on to the next lay-by, knowing that the wind was too strong and the traffic too heavy to justify my presence on the road. I walked much of the two-mile uphill drag, and by the time I reached the van it was past five. Legs heavy and body defeated, I sat half in and half out of the van, swallowed down two bananas and mulled over the ten miles I had left to skate to Inverness. Grumpy, I said little to the others, just staring back down the hill from where I had come, watching the sky darken; looking out to the west where snow-capped mountains lined the horizon. You're not beating me, I thought, and got back on the board.

By twenty past six I had crossed the suspension bridge over the Beauly Firth, skated around the eastern outskirts of Inverness and jumped into the van. Three days into the journey and almost one hundred and twenty miles skated. I collapsed onto a hostel bunk after a massage from Holly and stared at the ceiling. Only thirty miles tomorrow, I kept telling myself, Aviemore isn't far away.

* * *

As the crow flies thirty miles may not have seemed much of a challenge in relation to the average forty miles I'd skated each previous day, but with Inverness nearly at sea level and Aviemore nestling in the mountains I knew I had a task ahead of me when I pushed up the A9 out of Inverness. Holly drove behind taking up the inside of three lanes, the road surface was so poor I was often reduced to getting a good foot plant with my right and driving the board forward with my left. A four-mile uphill drag on a board, at walking pace, the headwind stifling, I couldn't help feeling like I was wading through mud. It took just over an hour to reach the top, a painfully slow process, which was only slightly rewarded by the views over Inverness and the bridge across the Firth. It looked like a toy town down below, ant-like vehicles slowly growing as they climbed towards us and roared by. The A9 was far too busy for my liking and we got off as soon as possible, heading down a winding country road through Craggie and Moy, by where I had skated twelve tough miles and eaten not nearly enough. We parked up in a caravan site and I crashed, Dom and Holly letting me sleep for an hour. When I woke they had bought everything containing sugar in the campsite shop, a wholly unhealthy lunch which sparked me into life.

I unfurled a tourist map to Scotland, which indicated that a cycle path ran alongside the A9, so when we reached it I waved the van ahead and followed the path. For two and a half hours I skated alone, the path becoming a country road, the map in my pocket not detailed enough to navigate properly. My water bottle emptied and I started to become delirious and desperate, I had no idea where the van was and tried to follow a mental compass, but it was all guesswork. I was pushing up a quiet country road and hadn't seen a vehicle in a while, so stopped for a toilet break. Exhausted and dizzy, I fiddled with my fly, humming to myself, swaying drunkenly. A minute later I came to my senses, realising I was still undoing my fly and had somehow turned anticlockwise so I was facing directly down the road. A car crawled past, the occupants staring at me in what can only be described as disgust. If it had been the police I would have been done for indecent exposure. I needed the van, badly.

Forty-five minutes later I skated beneath an aqueduct and the road started to decline. Although the surface was appalling I was rolling freely for the first time that day, wind whipping into my hair, waking me from my stupor. Dom had given me the minicam to record my little solo adventure, so I pulled it out and expressed a good deal of delight at finding a downhill section. Seconds later the van came into view. I started yelling into the camera, 'It's the van! The van! I fucking love these people!' rolling up to Holly who was almost in tears, standing there with arms open.

'I thought we'd lost you,' she whimpered, guiding me to the van and shutting the door just as it started to rain. We were still nine or ten miles away from Aviemore and reaching there looked like a ridiculous task today. I was resigned to falling behind schedule but was too exhausted to care. For half an hour I lay catatonic in the van, sipping water and scoffing down chocolate bars. Outside the rain stopped and a rainbow appeared. At half five I decided to give it one last push, food and drink blasting energy into my limbs. 'Let me know when it's half six and we'll call it a day,' I said to Holly, realising I'd left Elsa outside in the rain – a skate would do her bearings good. Almost immediately a car pulled over, the driver claiming he was a longboarder and had heard about us on the news earlier.

'I'm from Exeter,' he said. 'You're doing an awesome thing and I'll definitely join you when you get to Devon.' It was the beginning of a revival, passing cars started to respond to the radio coverage and honked and waved and threw raised thumbs at me. The roads turned smooth, aiming downhill, I was on top of the world! On the stroke of half past six I rolled into Aviemore's centre, arms aloft. I turned and grinned at the van, clenching my fist in delight. We're still on target, I can't believe it.

* * *

Since the first day I'd been suffering from stomach cramps and a loss of appetite and now I've got a headache and muscle strains to deal with, brilliant. The sun shines as I push out of Aviemore and along a country avenue bordered with thick pine forest. The trees block out the light and shadows fall upon the garden of a solitary house two miles south of Aviemore. Staring into the garden I feel like I've landed in a hybrid world, a spooky cross between a Tim Burton film and a good dose of LSD. Halloween decorations cover the white walls of the house, dummies riding bicycles with witch and monkey masks balance precariously on flowerpot legs, one of them holds a knife. The large plastic head of a polar bear rests disembodied on a fence and other random paraphernalia lies around, including, oddly, a typically Australian yellow diamond signpost with an image of a Kangaroo above the words 'Next 14km'. 'Go on,' says Dom, 'go and knock on the door!'

'You're having a laugh,' I say. 'The people who own this house are the types to walk around dark forests with spades, looking for rabbits to kill so they can skin them and make rugs.' It was safe to say that progress from that point on was relatively swift, and I pushed on fast, following a beautifully smooth cycle path, turning to see snow-capped mountains in the distance beyond Aviemore.

The end-of-day target was a tiny place called Dalwhinnie, a town that would have been largely insignificant were it not for its whisky distillery, the highest in Scotland. It didn't take a lot of investigation to decide that Dalwhinnie wasn't going to offer much in the way of accommodation, so I pushed on for a mile or so, only to find a rather daunting sign advertising that we were heading towards the Drumochter Summit. Cold, tired and hungry, I wasn't in the mood to head towards a pass in the mountains that belonged somewhere in the *Lord of the Rings* trilogy, and didn't take heart from the rest of the sign, which read: 'Weather conditions deteriorate without warning and are severe even during the summer. No food or shelter for 30km.' Beyond the signpost trailed a path that ran alongside the road and I made my way along it. A horrible surface, a foot wide, made from compacted mud and covered in stony grit. Skating on this was like riding a bicycle through water; Elsa's wheels sank into the mud, covered in grit. The next two miles were painstakingly slow, and the day wasn't about to get any better. The van was parked up on the opposite side of the road, Dom crossed over and walked towards me. 'Do you want the good news or the bad news?' he asked.

'The bad.'

'The bad news is the van has lost reverse and first gear.'

I stare at him, disbelieving.

'What's the good news?'

'There isn't any.'

Holly had her head in her hands. 'Sorry,' she said when I climbed in.

'It's not your fault Holls, it's this fucking van, it can't go a bleedin' day without spluttering to a halt.'

We still have all forward gears except first, so we drive twenty miles along the A9 to Pitlochry. An AA mechanic came out to us, instantly managing to pull the gear stick into reverse much to Holly's amazement, but a couple of tries later the original problem returned. He pottered around for a while and then agreed to do an interview for the camera. 'Do you think this van can make it to Land's End?' Dom asked.

'I doubt that very much,' said the mechanic, shaking his head with a wry smile.

We found a local traveller's hostel and called out a gearbox specialist, it was dark by the time they reached us. I was working through various options for the next day. It wasn't looking likely that the van would be in a fit state to accompany me, so either I take a day off or make my own way south, neither being an ideal solution. Shortly after midnight the mechanics headed back to Dundee, leaving the van in exactly the same condition as they found it. And they charged us £60 into the bargain. Perfect. Tired, aching and emotionally battered, I fell asleep with the feeling that someone up there was testing BoardFree UK.

* * *

Weary from the night before and still unsure about exactly how to progress, I found myself on the BBC Radio Scotland breakfast show chatting to a pair of jolly Scotsmen called Fred and John. They had a good laugh about my big right calf and couldn't get over the fact that I'd skated the uphill drag out of Inverness. I updated them on our current plight, putting out an appeal for locals to help us out until the van got fixed, feeling positive that someone would come through for us. By half past two it was clear that the appeal had fallen on deaf ears.

'Guys,' I said to Holly and Dom, 'we've got to make some progress today.' We pulled a map out and decided to go cross-country, avoiding the increasingly congested A9 and making a beeline for Abington, missing out Perth and Edinburgh, two cities which could pose big problems for a van without reverse. We were back at the point where I'd ended the day before by 3 p.m., feeling the combined effects of a stressful late night and one hundred and seventy five miles skated in five days. Without warning I fell out of the van and doubled over in pain, legs like jelly, stomach curdling. I looked up at Holly who didn't know what to do. 'I'll be lucky if I make five miles today,' I groaned. 'I'll be OK,' I told her, 'just give me a minute.' I was feeling the strain, still hadn't got my appetite back and the late start wasn't doing me any psychological favours. Slowly I pushed along the grit path that ran tantalisingly close to the glassy smooth northbound A9. The temptation to take advantage of a gap in traffic and make a quick dash up the road was thwarted only by paranoia of hidden CCTV cameras, so I stayed on the path and did all I could do, pushing at walking pace, music in my ears, keeping positive. I thought about Kate sunning herself in Florida and cursed her amiably, imagined I was chatting to her, played the songs she'd compiled for me. It kept me going and eventually I reached the Pass of Drumochter, hoping to goodness that it was all downhill from the Pass.

Sometimes it seemed as if there was no structure to the journey. I bumbled south, my legs moving despite my brain's pleas, and when the clouds drifted in over my eyes and I felt as though this was it and I'd have to stop for a while, something happened to keep me going. Suddenly the grit path became concrete and I turned a corner. Although the path led uphill I was rolling freely, arms outstretched embracing the moment. I could make out fingertips digging into my back, pushing me along. It must be the wind, I thought, but there was none. I turned around but was completely alone, yet continued to roll uphill. The phone in my pocket rang. A man named Martin. He had read an article about the journey on BBC Online and followed it through to the BoardFree website. He admired what I was doing, he told me, and offered us a place to stay if we passed near Edinburgh. 'My wife's a geography teacher and has access to every Ordnance Survey map you might need for the rest of the journey,' he said. 'We're ready to feed and water you early next week.' I can't thank him enough.

Minutes past 5 p.m. the path comes to an end. There's a junction with the main road, signposted to Trinafour, four miles away. Here my romance with the A9 comes to an end, I turn off, call the van and tell Holly and Dom I'm heading in-country, and push on leaving the roar of heavy traffic behind. This is more like it. I'm on a rural road, rolling fields layered in green tussocks of moss either side, a stream bubbling and bouncing down the hill, finding its way through a complication of rocks and grass. Three cars pass in half an hour and despite this I'm alone on the road, knowing that at some point the van will catch up. It drives me on, wanting to get as far as I can before they reach me. A hawk hovers above and a stag gallops across the road into a copse, and the road dips in and out of Trinafour. The road, still quiet, leads along the side of a valley. Up above me the gradient tapers towards a craggy edge and across the valley to my right hills line the horizon. Further in the distance snow caps some mountains, but they're to the west, I tell myself, they're not in my way.

The road descends and I freewheel for four miles, needing to carve the full width of the road to keep my speed down, leaning inwards with knees bent as Elsa approaches the gravelly, grassy kerbs, skidding slightly on the sharper turns but waking up with each one, an amazing hill, an incredible run, I scream with joy, exhausted but exhilarated. This is it, this is why I fell in love with this sport; I roll on and on, a new person. Tummel Bridge is two words on our map. In reality it is Tummel Bridge, Holiday Haven. The campsite owners give us a pitch for free. We order burgers and chips from the cafeteria, play arcades, laugh at the cheesy show they are advertising in the bar: Adam Quest, International TV Celebrity and Singer. We've never heard of him. Ian from Edinburgh, a VW expert, turns up and in exchange for a cheeseburger sorts out our gearbox problem. I kick myself for wasting £60 on the mechanics last night, but it's a problem solved nevertheless.

* * *

Our new, more southerly route had kept us relatively on track. Tummel Bridge was due west of Pitlochry, yesterday's original scheduled stop, and setting off from the Holiday Haven I had Crieff in my sights. In the early afternoon we stop for a cold drink at a pub in Weem. Heads turn as I roll up, eyes following the logos on the van, and we sit down beside a table of people who recognise us from a recent newspaper article. They all donate and we take photos together. One of them, a charming chap named Donald, tells me he's a caricaturist and will draw up a cartoon of Dom, Holly and I. The meeting leaves us all in good spirits and the southerly push continues. A car overtakes us and the occupants wave. Five minutes later they drive back with ten pounds hanging out of the window. 'Have a good journey,' they say smiling. We shake hands and they drive away.

We'd paused for snacks in a lay-by at Amulree when the air is filled with the roaring of engines. Seven Lotus sports cars speed past. 'That's William Shatner!' screams Holly, red faced and pointing wildly at the final car, certain she'd seen a celebrity. We spend the next five minutes wondering why William Shatner would be driving a Lotus in Scotland.

'Where is William Shatner from?' I ask, and we fall into giggles saying 'Hi, my name is William Shatner' in a variety of accents. He's definitely not Indian.

Thirty miles into the day a family peers at me from the side of a motor home. I scrape to a stop next to them and they thrust tea and sandwiches and cakes and a bottle of wine our way. They heard about BFUK on the radio show yesterday morning and couldn't be more complimentary, giving us a massive boost for the final stretch of the day. An hour later I roll into Crieff. I only know of this place because the actor Ewan McGregor grew up near here. We ask a couple for directions, they tell us where to find a Bed and Breakfast, then walk on. Seconds later the woman appears again, almost too fast for her high heels, and hands Dom a ten pound donation. 'Good luck!'

Another man turns up. 'Are you that dude?' he asks.

Word gets around.

'I guess I am!' I grin. 'Where did you hear about BoardFree?'

'You were on the radio yesterday. I think it's amazing. Good luck mate.'

I knock on some B&B doors, none answer. At the top of the hill a flurry of small bodies rush around a corner. I squint. They have skateboards! 'Get your cameras guys!' I yell to Holls and Dom. The kids skate down the road, they've been on the website already, heard about us on the radio. The smallest lad, Ryan, doesn't say anything and keeps staring at me.

'He's your biggest fan,' one of the boys tells me as Ryan nods. I don't know what to say, and sign his board awkwardly. They point us in the direction of a hotel and I invite them all to join me on the way out of town the next day, they say they'll be there. Later, Holly tells me that one of the lads said that BoardFree coming to town was the best thing that had ever happened to Crieff. Things like that make aching muscles seem ridiculous. We relax in the Tower Hotel, clinking glasses with locals and ending up with a small pile of cash on the table. The hotel's owner, Gilbert, lets us stay for free and gives us Internet access. Some days nothing goes wrong.

*   *   *

An alarm from a neighbouring hotel room wakes us. It rings on and on, slowly synchronising with the fall of raindrops outside. The boys from yesterday are out with their boards, braving the rain. We meet them in their 'skate park', two wooden crates in a supermarket car park, there is no official park here and they're involved in a fundraising initiative called Rampworks to have one built; they've raised £57,000 out of £80,000 needed. They join me for half a mile before we send them home with a BoardFree mug each, it's time to move on.

Despite the wet progress is fast and we reach Dunblane in less than two hours. Breaks are getting longer and longer now, my legs and mind struggling to get moving after a few minutes off the road. After a chocolate bar I read the map wrong and skate two miles up a hill. The road ends in a field and I take it out on Dom and Holly. I'm tired and pissed off, it was my mistake. The next two hours are hell on wheels. The rain falls as we edge around Stirling; a fat teenager peers out of a car window and yells obscenities at me, I stare at him as his vehicle passes and he stares back, his eyes wide and lifeless. Others are more helpful, beeping tunes with their car horns, giving thumbs up. As the afternoon draws into evening, rush hour forces me onto the verge. I wave the van on to the next lay-by and tread through the mud, only stepping back onto the board when a smaller, quieter road becomes an option. By 6 p.m. I've skated to the southern outskirts of Falkirk and called it a day. My friend Kerri offers us a place to stay so we drive east to Edinburgh in silence. I'm in a mood. Holly's in a mood. Dom's in a mood. I hope we all like each other at the end of this.

* * *

I haven't been online for four days and my inbox is overflowing with 'where are you?'s and 'are you ok?'s. Updating the route map and adding some videos and diaries takes a weight off my shoulders but I'm disappointed by the lack of donations. It's been a tough few days and the lack of height in our fundraising total doesn't reflect that. Another blow comes with reading the BBC Online article published a few days earlier. It's wonderful for the BBC website to cover BoardFree, but the article made out that I was doing this to alleviate boredom. I was furious and banged out a complaint.

> *Come on, the BBC of all media organisations throw in a bit of lightweight journalism and completely undermine the project. To whoever wrote it – I'm doing this to raise funds and awareness for three children's charities and promote sport to children of all ages. It's not something I'm doing because I was a bit bored. This has taken a year to organise, if I was bored I would have turned on my Playstation or had a game of chess. A bit of research and that article could have brought in a flurry of donations. Instead: bugger all.*

It hadn't been a good start to the day and it was about to get worse. My right shoe had worn through, just a thin layer of sole remaining, so I slipped on a new pair aware that barely a week into the journey I was onto my last set of shoes. My body is slowly wasting away – replacing all of the energy I use up each day is impossible – and although I feel fit BFUK is taking its toll mentally. Mood swings are coming thick and fast as I pound the road, I'm tired and I ache all over and I'm a grumpy bastard a lot of the time. At the beginning of each day I take ages to get ready and it must frustrate the hell out of Holly and Dom. I'm always losing things and it takes thirty seconds to pull my gloves on.

I'm slowing down, and it's awful to experience. 'Guys if we can avoid it let's not go on any busy roads today, I'm not feeling my best,' I tell them.

A few miles in we pass through a town called California, beyond which the land empties away. I raise my arms aloft in celebration as I head downhill, it feels like riding a giant wave with a strong sidewind and my knees soaking up the vibrations from the road. My GPS clocks nearly 28 miles an hour; this is the upper arc of the mood swing. Then the pendulum begins to fall. Despite running through the day's route before we began Holly misses three turns and I'm forced to skate along a busy A-Road as a result, a detour that added four miles to the day. We agree to take a side road half a mile in but when we reach the turn-off Holly stays in the left lane, waving me back in and shaking her head. There are no vehicles behind us and again she'd misread the map, I was furious! I skated on kicking at mid air until there was a chance to pull over. It's mentally exhausting skating on main roads; the surfaces are worse, the blowback from cars flying past at 60mph increases my awareness that on a board I'm without protection. It's not unsafe with the support vehicle right behind but the extra distance – added to the fact that now I felt I had to stop at every corner and do the map reading too – seemed so unnecessary. I walk to the van and ask Holly what she thinks we should do now. She doesn't answer. 'Don't I even get a sorry?' I ask her. Silence. I'm fuming but her unwillingness to accept responsibility makes me angrier. My way of dealing with that is to walk away, but without an apology from Holly my mood gets darker and darker with each push. The van drives on, leaving me to walk at the roadside for miles. Two lads walk towards me, teenagers, heads down. As they pass I feel Elsa lift up.

'Give us the board, give us a look,' they snarl.

I snap.

'Let it go,' I growl, bracing myself for a fight. They don't let go, pulling it harder, swearing at me. I look around for the van, for some help, but there's no one. One of the boys is tugging at the end of the board and I shove Elsa into his chest. He stumbles backwards and the other lad stiffens up, stares at his mate and begins to turn towards me, fists raised. Elsa falls to the ground and I push the second one full in the chest with two hands. He falls back over a two-foot high fence, bundling into the grass beyond. I pick up Elsa and run, adrenaline taking me beyond the shouted insults that chase me up the hill, my blood pumping, fury building. Half a mile later I see the van parked off the road, I walk straight past, not trusting my reaction. If they'd stayed with me this wouldn't have happened, I'd have been skating, not fighting. A mile later the van pulls in ahead of me, halfway up a hill. I'm exhausted and slump to the ground, burying my head in my hands. Holly gets out and leans against the van several metres away.

'Fucking kids. Fucking tried to take my board.' I took my helmet off and threw it away. 'Fucking hell!' Then silence.

Holly spoke.

'It was my fault and for that I apologise. But you know what, I don't apologise when provoked Dave . . .'

To me that was ridiculous. An apology in the first place would have diffused the situation.

'You know what,' I said, swinging my empty water bottle around, 'you need to have a good fucking think . . .'

'About what?' asked Holly,

'About whether you want to be a fucking part of this. I don't need you being in a mood. I'm just walking, and you're driving ahead and leaving me alone.'

'There was nowhere to pull over–'

'This isn't about you, it isn't about me, it's about fucking bigger things. So stop getting into fucking moods about your mistakes . . .'

I was furious, still slumped on the grass. Holly still leaning against the van, indignant.

'I'm not getting into moods–'

'Don't fucking refuse to talk to me about maps.'

'I didn't refuse to talk to you–'

'It's all about you isn't it,' I pointed at her. 'Don't fucking give me this. I need some support.'

'I'm trying my best–'

'You're not fucking trying, you're getting in a fucking mood every fucking corner.'

'I'm not at fault, you're having a go at me . . . I really don't know what to say. I'm asking you what I can do and–'

'Support, that's all I need. For five miles I've been alone. And two fucking kids, on the same pavement I'm walking on because I can't skate on the road, try to take my fucking board off me. I don't need to be fucking fighting because I'm left alone by the side of the road.'

'I'm not in a mard, I wasn't in a mard–'

'Yeah you are, and so am I funnily enough.' I banged my chest. 'JESUS CHRIST!'

'Why don't you just say what you're thinking?' Holly said, winding me up even further.

I got up, put my helmet on, picked up the board and walked on. I couldn't deal with this. If I had to do this alone I didn't need to deal with other people too. I was ready to put a rucksack on and skate the rest of Britain by myself. I was so close to telling Holly to take the van back to Prestwick and fuck off back home, this wasn't my idea of a fucking support team. I skated on and a few miles on the tension breaks. None of us want this hanging in the air; it's unbearable. Dave Hulme and Gordon, the owner of the van, appear. They've brought an orange flashing light and a bigger steering wheel for Holly. Holls hands me a piece of cake. We hug. She apologises. I apologise. Thank God.

Dave tells me thousands of VW drivers across the UK are looking out for the van and they're ready to help if we need them. It boosts my spirits. I was feeling alone and I couldn't expect anyone involved in this to fully comprehend how it's affecting me – even I didn't truly know – but the smallest things tilt me in either direction. Mary Thompson's cake, kindly donated on day one, plus Dave's enthusiasm for BoardFree – 'You've come two hundred and eighty-five miles on a skateboard, you're some man!' – made the day easier. Holly's conciliatory hugs soften everything.

Six miles on brief upset resurfaces after another bout of misdirection. This time Dom, who had hidden behind his camera during the earlier altercation, misread the map to add yet another three miles to my route. I don't have the energy left to be angry and Dom apologises, but what's done is done. Even crossing the three hundred mile mark at the end of day nine and rolling into Biggar under a setting sun doesn't completely soak up my frustration. We walk to a nearby pub and slump against the bar. A group of old men stand to our right and we explain that we're looking for a room. At first, nothing. Then a sparkle in the eye of one of the men, an old fellow named Jack, trimmed beard, old man's cap. He says we can park in his driveway. One of the other men asks Jack if he'll feed us, too. He says we can feed ourselves. Two minutes later he offers us a fish supper. Half an hour – and a drink – later we're following a taxi back to his place where he hands us fish and chips and shows us to the nice clean beds in which we'll be staying. Jack was sixty-one and a half, a gem of a man who loved his dog, Tallach. He uncorked the red wine and when that was finished another bottle was opened. I could see tomorrow becoming difficult, skating hungover is never recommended, but Jack was fine company, a self-confessed pedantic old bastard who said things like 'do you want a warm or cold bath' and then when a positive reply arrived looked over his shoulder with a shrug, saying, 'oh, so he assumes he's having a bath now . . .' His hospitality was an unexpected high at the end of a tortuous day, and two glasses of red sent me into a pleasant, much needed coma.

*   *   *

After a cooked breakfast and a tour of Jack's sports car hidden like treasure in his garage, the neighbours donate £35 and I get back on Elsa. The roads are tough and smooth, extreme contrasts every few miles. We finished twelve miles short of schedule yesterday and I was in bullish mood, ready to redress the balance and make Scotland work in our favour. Within an hour and a quarter we're having a break in Abington services, having averaged 11.7mph for the first twelve miles. The rest of the day is much the same, a hard slog, blisters starting to appear after two days in new shoes. The roads, even the cycle paths, are hard going, rough and potholed. Shortly before 6 p.m. I roll into Lockerbie having covered 42.5 miles. I'm elated at making up ground and getting back on schedule but it has come at a cost. The soles of my feet are covered in blisters, others wrap around my toes in white sacks, stinging when I walk, pulsing with pain. Holly finds a hotel called the Townshead where the landlady Caroline lets us stay for free. After a Chinese supper I check emails, disheartened to find a caustic message from a man in Bristol questioning my motives and the destination of the funds we raise. Why do people go to such lengths to knock others down? At some point we all fall asleep, knowing that this will be the last night we spend in Scotland this journey.

*   *   *

It's an altogether strange feeling waking up knowing you're about to make history. Breakfast is an afterthought, as is the photograph we take in front of the van with Caroline, who has been so kind to us since we arrived. We jump in the van and return to the spot I ended at yesterday. Holly helps me bandage my feet; it's a new addition to our regular day on the road but one that will become permanent as time goes on. 'It's time to do the old pierce and squeeze,' I tell the camera as Holly moves towards my blisters with a needle.

'I'm not used to this at all,' Holly says, accidentally gripping the bottom of my foot and compressing the blisters on the sole.

'That's really reassuring,' I say once I've finished screaming.

'No, no, no,' she says, 'I usually use pins rather than—'

'Pins?' I yell, wondering whether letting Holly loose on my toes is a good idea.

'Shush,' she tells me as I groan at her first incision, 'quite a lot of water comes out at one time . . .'

Water. She thinks it's water.

'I hope this doesn't go on the DVD,' Holly says, worried, 'because everyone will write going she doesn't actually know what she's doing . . . wouldn't it be wiser to attach it to the suction thing and suck it out?'

I stare at her, gobsmacked.

'What suction thing?' I ask, completely bewildered. Then the penny drops. 'God no, you're not syringing my toe.'

'Does it hurt?' Dom asks me.

'Like a bastard.'

'Do you feel like crying?'

'All the time.'

'I could really do with some tears, it would make good viewing.'

'You're not going to get any.'

'Bet I film you crying before the end of this.'

Bet he won't.

Holls finishes off the job with some fetching leopard print plasters, and we move on. A photographer from the *Dumfries and Galloway Standard* finds us on the road and takes a photo to complement an interview I did for the paper yesterday. An hour later I find myself pushing towards Gretna, the Solway Firth glistening down below to my right, the first open water since John o'Groats. Dom and I do a little Simpsons cameo as we pass through Springfield and then I'm skating with the minicam, the last mile running below Elsa's wheels. On the border I'm struck by temporary confusion. I turn to see the Scotland Welcomes You sign on the other side of the road, and my first thought is that somebody had stolen the England sign on the other side of it. But I'm in No Mans Land, and facing forwards again I see it. 'Twenty metres to go . . .' I say into the camera, my heart beginning to pump, a natural smile revealing my teeth, '. . . until I become the first man to skateboard the length of Scotland. How bizarre is that!' The sign, bordered in old brick and shaped with two turrets either side, reads Welcome to England, Cumbria. I laugh hysterically as I pass it, arms aloft, screaming with joy. I collapse on the grass verge a few metres along the road, instantly noticing that the first road England has to offer is an uphill climb.

We stay at the border for an hour, doing interviews and video blogs, enjoying the freshness of a new country, experiencing the moment. Dom looks at me and says, 'They put a man on the moon before anyone skated this country. Dude, out of six billion people on the planet you're the only one who has ever skated the length of Scotland. It's a real achievement.' He runs off, calling people on his mobile and running backwards and forwards across the border, taking his friends on a little journey between England and Scotland, Scotland and England. The enthusiasm the border crossing has injected into the team is wonderful. Scotland, the Highlands especially, was starting to take its toll, not just on my body but on our spirit and togetherness. But for all of the arguments we made it across Scotland as a team, we kept each other going. I returned to Elsa and pushed deeper into England, it's time for another country.

People have started to honk and wave again, probably in response to an earlier radio interview. It feels so good to get support from others on the road. A few miles later I reach Carlisle. A call to the city newspaper ends in disappointment, when they say our story 'isn't local enough'. Dom leaves us at Carlisle. He takes a train to London and will rejoin us in two days. I'll miss him, a stranger two weeks ago, he's been a big part of the most incredible few days of my life. Although he frequently drove Holly up the wall with his uncompromising command of the van's CD player his presence on the journey gave me a balance I wouldn't otherwise have had. It was good for me to have a bloke around and his sly humour added to the comedy of Holly's air-headedness. He was difficult to be around sometimes though, occasionally dropping into moods and contributing less money than Holly and I to everyday costs. At one point Holly was so angry with him for eating the snacks intended for me and slinking out of paying for petrol for the umpteenth time that she had to talk to me about it. I realised she'd kept it inside for so long, not wanting to cause upset and give me more to worry about. Both Holly and Dom provided support in very different, sometimes contradictory ways.

Holls and I decide to push on. My right foot is in agony but the adrenaline is still pumping and I'm keen to eat into tomorrow's mileage – it's a big slog to Kendal and I want to make it easier on myself. Four miles south of Carlisle I'm joined for a short while by a cyclist who is heading to a time trial in the countryside. This is the first time I've been joined by somebody on the road and it was as though an invisible rope appeared, the pull of mutual respect making my individual task seem easier. A car passes by and the elderly inhabitants look at me inquisitively. A few hundred yards on they've pulled in and are stood in a line, clapping. An old man steps out towards me with a pound coin in his palm. I like England.

My feelings for Scotland are tempered when I stop for the day, five and a half miles south of Carlisle. Holly and I drive to a nearby service station at

Southwaite, which I recognise as one of the stops I made with Dan and Becki as we made our way north towards Prestwick two weeks earlier, so much had happened since then. My right foot is burning and I'm torn between a need to remove my shoe and the looming dread at what lies beneath. I ease the shoe off, my sock drenched in blood. The bandage I'd put in place to protect a small blister on the back of my heel comes away easily, taking with it an inch and a half square layer of skin. The back of my heel is gone, worn down from two days of friction in new shoes; a second-degree burn is all that's left, angry red flesh. Other blisters on my toes and on the ball of my foot have grown too. I wash in the service station, it's the most painful shower I've ever taken but I feel better for being clean. I know that without a rest day scheduled my feet are going to be in pain for the remaining six hundred miles of this journey. BoardFree UK is about to become a test of mental strength.

*   *   *

At 9 a.m. I'm in the BBC Radio Cumbria studio, chatting away live on air. As we wrap up a television journalist pops her head through the door and asks if I'd be happy to do an interview for the lunchtime news. I oblige, for the first time realising just how understaffed and stretched the BBC's local budget is, as I have to show the reporter how to put a tape in her camera. She then holds the camera herself, struggling to find the record button, before conducting a brief and what must have been an extremely wobbly-looking interview. Our media duties are not over; ITV Borders meet us in town to film a piece for the six o'clock news. I'm very aware as I skate for the camera that the blisters on my feet don't need this extra pressure, but the more people that hear about BoardFree the more people donate, it's a no-brainer. We're not on the road until a quarter to two. As I wrap my feet up my mum calls, asking all sorts of cryptic questions, like what road I'm on, which direction I'm heading in, where I'm aiming for tonight. She swears blind that she's about to go to work in Oxford. When the call finishes I look at Holly. 'My mum is going to join us on the road today, expect a call for directions at some point.'

My right foot is in a state and I have no idea how to deal with it. Every push sends a spark of pain through my body and I try to work out how many more pushes it'll take to reach Land's End. I turn around and see Holly on the phone, shoulders shrugged in frustration. She's talking to my mother and has no idea where we are on the map. Her sense of direction has always been abysmal, but I'm in an odd position where I can only point and not talk. I don't want my mum to know her surprise has been foiled, and am quite aware that the first time

Above: Riding my first longboard, Uhuru the Tierney Rides T-Board, only two weeks into my boarding career.

Left: Heading downhill in northeastern Scotland on the first day of BoardFree UK.

Below: 365 miles into the journey, I'm elated to finally cross into England.

Left: Scotland and Cumbria took their toll on my right heel, despite makeshift work on the shoes.

Above: Fancy dress south of Worcester, an ideal way to celebrate crossing the 600 mile mark.

Right: The support didn't help the pain from my feet, though, and neither did the 'club foot' gaffer tape creation. I grimaced like this at every push through England.

Right: In addition to the heel injury, this blister on my right sole grew steadily and eventually became infected north of Bristol.

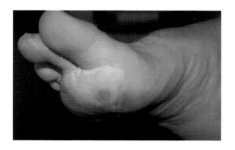

Below: The final push to Land's End. Having been skating for barely a year, I complete the 896 mile trek from John O'Groats and become the first person to skateboard the length of Britain.

Right: Several local skaters joined me for the early kilometers of BoardFree Australia.

Below: Two and a half months on from the end of BFUK we're Down Under. Becki prepares the fundraising push at the Royal Perth Yacht Club.

Left: Unfortunately the first day ended badly, our Jackaroo breaking down and forcing another three days in Perth.

Below: As Danny cycles behind me I reach the top of Greenmount Hill with the Perth skyline far in the distance. There's no turning back now.

Left: Remains at the roadside remind us that we're quickly heading into the desert.

Below Right: Once on the Eyre Highway, the three carriage road trains dwarf our support vehicles.

Below : As the Great Eastern Highway heads east, the roads stretch longer and straighter. Not always a pleasant sight for a skater!

Above Left: Finally emerging from 40km of roadworks near Balladonia.

Above Right: The sobering and all too frequent sight of dead kangaroos always put our time on the Plain in perspective.

Below Left: Elsa and I ponder the beginning of Australia's longest straight stretch of road.

Below Right: 130km from Caiguna, Danny and I shake on a good day's skating.

Above: I was so focused on rounding the first bend for three days that I didn't even see the enormous road train as it joined the highway. The jeeps behind me contained Doug Thorne and friends, who threw a BBQ for us in Mt Gambier six weeks later.

Above Left: The first of a few Dare Dave challenges, this one requiring me to bounce a Swansea University beach ball for a 1km section of the journey.

Above Right: The customary toilet paper line signals another milestone on BoardFree Australia. This time I prepare to go past the distance set on BFUK.

Below: As the winds whipped in unhindered across the Plain, I stretched my arms out wide to get a free ride as often as I could.

Above: Only from the air is the Nullarbor Plain's vastness this evident. I skate below with no trees in sight.

Below Left: The Bunda Cliffs stretch 200km from the WA/SA border all the way to the Head of the Bight, near the Nullarbor roadhouse.

Below Top: Holly and Dan enjoy a ride in Caroline Disney's Cessna aeroplane near the Head of the Bight.

Below Bottom: Simon took advantage whenever he could to open up the laptop and edit videos which gave the general public a fresh perspective of the journey.

she'll realise that I knew she was coming is when she reads this book. To make the plan fail-safe I skate with the minicam, screaming 'Mum! It's my mum!' as she appears on the road ahead, cycling towards me. Despite it being the worst surprise in the world, it is so good to see her. She hugs Holly and thanks her for being there, and we cycle on together, mother and son, side by side. We stop for lunch in a Penrith supermarket and my mum, a chiropodist, takes a look at my feet. After a local radio interview we push on, the Cumbrian hills taking hold and slowing my progress, my right foot crying out with each step.

At 6 p.m. we reach Shap and take up residence in the local pub. They change the channel and we all watch the news, the first television coverage BoardFree UK has received. When it ends everyone cheers and I continue for two more miles, emotional as I listen to Kate's soundtrack, missing her as I stare out over the Lake District National Park, wishing I could appreciate it more through the wall of pain, breaking my own rules and thinking beyond the end of the day, dreaming of crossing the finish line at Land's End. Tears stream down my face and I sit at the roadside with my back to the van, calling it a day at the top of a downhill run, knowing it will be a good way to start tomorrow morning. I'm twelve miles short of Kendal, my end-of-day target, and as we drive those twelve miles towards our accommodation for the night I witness the most terrifying twelve miles of my life. The hills were enormous and I stared blank faced as we twisted and turned, my foot in agony even as it lay still on the dashboard. Pulses of pain emanating from my fleshy heel, I have no idea how I'll cope with these roads tomorrow. There is nothing worse than seeing a road I have yet to skate, it's a revelation that will haunt me until the skating resumes. I'll have no choice but to carry on with my head down.

We spend the night in the most unlikely of places. A new friend, Piccia, who I met as she rolled past me on inline skates in Hyde Park weeks earlier, had pointed us in the direction of a friend who lived south of Kendal. Charlotte greeted us in jodhpurs as we navigated past another woman on horseback and down a steep drive, parking up outside an enormous country house. The day ends well, despite my dissatisfaction at a lack of miles covered and my diminishing pain threshold. Charlotte makes us a delicious meal and I have a bath in an oversize tub, the beds are scrumptious, soft and smelling of flowers.

*   *   *

I wake up terrified of the task ahead, a sick looming feeling kneading my stomach, like the feeling you have when a loved one has left you. My heel wound has seeped through its dressings overnight, leaving a horrible yellow stain on the sheets. I apologise to Charlotte who waves the damage away. I don't speak as we drive back to yesterday's end point. Fiddle with my knee strap, pull on layers, listen to music. I don't look at the road, geeing myself up for what I believe will be an enormous challenge. A general consensus of action results in a part of my shoe being cut out to relieve any undue pressure on my gaping heel. Blister plasters everywhere, padding and gauze.

A mental balancing act begins, the physical exertion of pushing up large hills versus the psychological lift of self-propulsion through astounding scenery. It is a true battle of worth, a determination not only to make it to the top of each hill, to keep pushing, just keep pushing, but to do all of this and not forsake the privilege I feel at being able to travel in this way. For all of the pain and the constant mental anguish at the onset of another steep incline, I vow never to lose sight of why I'm here, pushing my longboard south. I know I'm lucky and that I'm not going to stop for anything. In the recesses of my mind, I know that however much Cumbria heaves the length of Britain is barely a quarter of the width of Australia. I form a lock in my mind, filtering out despair and doubt, training myself to blend exhaustion and belief so that I can continue to push, whatever the pain, knowing the end of each day will come and with it a few hours' rest. This small journey, this End to End, is a mental workout. Physically, I know that forty or fifty miles each day in Australia is possible, but if anything will stop me in my tracks it's going to be my psyche. The sheer scale of Australia is critical; if I thought of it in terms of one big journey I'd never make it. Instead, I would take it day by day, never thinking too far ahead, focusing on the next bend in the road knowing that every mile I travel is one mile closer, one mile less. By training myself to think that way, and by concentrating on Australia, the UK journey became easier. I told myself that every agonising push took me four times as far in the UK as it would in Australia, and I kept pushing.

I ate into the miles, nudging Elsa forward over horribly jagged roads. We pull over and my mum trots off into the trees for a toilet break. Holly comes out, hands me a banana, gives me a hug. 'You're doing so well Dave, you can do this.' I show her my foot, it's bleeding again and the sock – and some of my shoe – is red.

'Don't tell Mum,' I ask Holly, easing foot back into shoe. She looks at me white faced. 'I'll be OK Holls, it's just blood.'

A long hill later we reach a peak, the ground all around is lower than we are. My mum, easily peddling alongside me, is a huge boost. She tells me how proud she is of me as sheep sprint awkwardly up ahead. The road falls away, a steep downhill for two miles with a vertical drop across to the right. It's too steep to freewheel and I drag my shoe, I feel every bump of the concrete and every stone jabbing at the blister that lies trapped between ball and sole.

At 1 p.m. I roll into Kendal and sit on bags of supermarket compost outside to give a recorded interview for local radio. They tell me it will be on at 6 p.m. My mum hugs me tight. Her clear plastic bag of plasters and orthopaedic felt stays with us, as does a bag full of homemade fruitcake, I'm so lucky to have her as my mother. 'Stay safe.' She smiles at me and climbs into her car. There are 23 miles to Lancaster, desperately far away. After ten miles the Friday rush hour kicks in and we pull over, planning to sleep until the traffic dies down. A car pulls up and a family gets out, a man, his wife and their son.

'We saw you outside Kendal earlier and had to see what you were all about,' says the man, handing me a ten-pound note. Holly and I listen to the 6 p.m. news, we're not on it. It's just local, but I'm so disappointed, longing for high points. Half an hour later, several miles up the road, we get our high point. Holly pulls me over,

'You were just on the radio!' she shouted. 'The family from earlier called in and said they'd met us!' From then on every other car that passed waved and honked. Some cheered. A family passed by and seconds later the three girls from the back seat were stood on a roundabout clapping and shouting 'Good Luck!' The father and son who stopped earlier and called the radio pulled up in their car again. They had two bottles of iced water and a marker pen. 'Go on, sign his t-shirt!' said the man, pointing at his son's clean white top. So I did, the boy quiet and shy but the dad jumping around in praise of BoardFree. Horns and beeps pushed me into Lancaster. I sped past a cyclist near the centre of the town who looked at me, confused. Dom joins us at the train station, he's with us for the week ahead, and then we drive around, finally settling down at a Holiday Inn. Nat, Holly's boyfriend, arrives for the weekend; his presence will be good for Holls. My foot is in shreds. I have no idea how I'm going to skate tomorrow.

*   *   *

It's doubly hard to prepare for another day on the road after a night in a comfortable bed. Outside Lancaster Nat joins me on the road, riding on Little Elsa, my back-up rollsrolls board. Rain falls gently and the country mildly undulates, Nat bends double and grips his ankles on downhills, it looks ridiculous and Holly laughs from the safety of the van. It's great having company on the road but Nat's not quite as traffic conscious as I am, swerving towards the middle of the road occasionally, without warning. I skate on, grimacing with each push, especially on uphill climbs when the back of my shoe digs in. The hole I cut out yesterday isn't doing much good and I need to find a new solution. I'm lifted when a white van pulls up in front of us. I see a hand hanging out of the window holding £10. 'We heard you on the radio yesterday,' the driver says, his passengers smiling, 'good luck mate.'

We reach Preston and the signposting is atrocious. We spend an hour and a half doing a figure of eight around the western edge of town, without a clue where we're going. Some kids run alongside us, excited at being part of this odd travelling troupe. I hand one of them my board and we take a photo in front of the van, then continue on with the pitter-pat of small feet still in hot pursuit. Nat hits a rock on a cycle path and I turn around to see him bouncing head over heels. He's a bit grazed on the side and arms, but keeps the rock as a souvenir. Nat and I skate alone for the last four miles of the day, meeting up with the van in Leyland.

A car honks and out of it steps my brother. He's here to lead us west to RAF Woodvale, where he is learning to fly. They've organised a Ladies Guest Night for us and I'm the guest speaker, so it's time to smarten up. Three-quarter-length trousers and t-shirt are swapped for tuxedo and shiny black shoes. I shave and am talked through the evening's protocol: the transition from the freedom of the open road to a regimented four-course silver-service dinner is striking. Holly hasn't been feeling well and is taking some well-earned quality time with Nat in a nearby town, so Dom and I represent BoardFree. Before dinner my brother shares a worry with me: 'I had a dream that you stood up to make your speech and rambled on and on. I looked like an idiot in front of everyone, they were laughing and pointing because I was your brother.'

'Well mate,' I said, 'I appreciate the confidence you have in me.'

'Are you sure you don't want to make some notes?' he asks, pressing the point.

'Nah it's OK, I'll wing it,' I tell him. It's not what he wants to hear and he slopes off tail between his legs, preparing for the worst. Andy and I are similar in many ways, but our differences are highlighted most by his connection to the Forces. We grew up as RAF brats and as my teenage years went on I gravitated away from the rules and uniform, repulsed by the idea of being judged on where my creases were. My attitude to public speaking was much the same; I'd rather not prepare and speak from the heart, so when I stood up after pudding I could see Andy out of the corner of my eye, already half covering his face with a protective hand. With the crowd mostly composed of my brother's friends I loosened the mood by bringing up the fact that Andy had been a fat baby, something that helped him immensely when faced with a four-course dinner.

I rode the resulting chuckles through to the end, which after a quick explanation of how BoardFree came about and a couple of stories about life on the road, came to something of an anti-climax. The BoardFree story was never meant to finish two weeks south of John o'Groats and I wished I had more to talk about, but I finished by thanking everyone involved in organising the night and gratefully accepted a £300 donation raised by all present. We were swept away by the after-show party – young company and free-flowing alcohol providing a much-needed release after two stressful weeks. Dom and I only found our way to bed when the sun was coming up, and I knew I'd pay the price a few hours later when it was time to board Elsa again.

*   *   *

Nat calls at 10 a.m. Holly is sick and the police have called after the mother of one of the children in Preston made a complaint about us taking photos of her boy. She's not pushing the charges any further but it's a dampener. The woman must have been on our website to find our number in the first place, surely from that she could tell there was no malice in our actions. Still, we have to be more careful in the future.

We're not back on the road until mid-afternoon. Nat drives back to Portsmouth, which isn't good for Holls. She's feeling unwell and the last two weeks have really caught up on her. I skate on autopilot for three hours, calling the day to a halt in heavy rain as we pass through Billinge. My clothes are drenched and I stumble into a local pub, the Stork Inn, rain dripping down my face, a small puddle forming beneath my shoes. I look like a drowned rat and a group of guys on the table by the door take one look at me and buy me a pint. Three minutes later, having dropped some kit in the van, I walk back in with Dom and Holls to find the men at the table have pooled some money to pay for one of our hotel rooms. After a shower we sit with them and Dom's eyes widen as the men tell him the Stork Inn is famous for being haunted by the ghost of an old Cavalier who died here hundreds of years ago.

'What room are you in?' asks one of the men,

'Room Six,' says Dom.

'That's the one,' the man says seriously. 'Good luck getting to sleep tonight!'

For the rest of the evening Dom talks about lights flickering and doorknobs shaking on the first floor, it's hilarious.

Kate has flown back from Florida and boarded the first train north. It's so good to see her walking down the station platform. Back at the Inn she tends to my right foot, which has swollen to double the size of my left since I finished skating. This new swelling phenomenon isn't welcome, and I put it down to a lack of sleep and the heavy rain. My heel injury is beginning to scab over, but a series of blisters below my big toe have joined together now, and are fit to burst. All I want to do is lie down with Kate and sleep, but we have to wait until half past midnight for BBC Radio Five Live to call. The phone rings at five to one, and it must have been the most incoherent interview I've ever given.

*   *   *

After a quick cooked breakfast we're off. Dom blamed the ghost of the Cavalier for a poor night's sleep, but Holly is quite unwell and I start wondering whether an unplanned rest day is needed. The swelling on my right foot hasn't gone down much overnight and I decide it's time to make a larger incision in the back of my skate shoe, still damp from the night before and laced with fluids from my foot injury. 'This shoe is like a Tarantino film,' I joke. 'God knows how the Club Foot is going to fit inside.' I cut the entire back off leaving a space like a keystone, and return to the road. Billinge is situated halfway between Liverpool and Manchester and the urban sprawl of St Helens, Widnes and Runcorn lies between us and the open countryside of Cheshire. My aim was to skate clear of what I called 'urbania'. It's horrible skating through cities and suburbia; there are more roads, the signposting is appalling, and the going is slow and mentally draining; the crow flies much further and faster in rural areas.

The rain falls again, drops hurtling off my helmet and streaming down my face. I squinted to see through it, wearing glasses was pointless. We struggle with directions, getting frustrated at each other but meandering slowly south as trucks thundered by, sending up drenching waves of water. The open gap at the back of my right shoe means the sock became sodden as soon as I started skating, loose wrinkles of damp skin compressing each time my foot went down. Not ideal conditions for healing. The agony of each push was now subliminally accepted as being an integral part of the journey. I take relief from brief stretches of freewheeling but even then I needed to use the soles of my feet to carve and my blisters are being pulled from side to side. I refuse painkillers; the only stuff strong enough to numb this pain would put me to sleep, and where would that get us?

After an eternity we find accommodation in Frodsham, a small town south of the Mersey River. Somehow I'd travelled past the endless urbania and reached our destination by half past three, an early finish by our usual standards. We fall into our bedrooms, Kate propping my foot up on pillows, laptops whipped out to update the website. I write a blog as Kate runs hot water into the Jacuzzi, telling me about the rollercoasters in Florida and how I'd love them. 'I missed you when I was away,' she smiles at me, and I can't bear the thought of her leaving again in two days' time. Her emotional support makes me stronger, helps me to keep going. She was in this with me and asked for nothing in return, I knew deep down I was going to struggle in Australia without her and the thought began to weigh on my mind as the Jacuzzi bubbles took me far away from the rain and roads outside.

*   *   *

BBC Radio Cumbria calls up in the morning. They introduce me as 'a friend of the show' and I chat to the presenter about the hills north of Kendal and the effect they have on one's feet. The poor weather continues and my right foot begins to slip out of its shoe as the gap I cut yesterday widens. Eventually there's no choice but to gaffer tape the shoe to my leg, but even then the rain loosens the tape and I skate along wearing what are tantamount to slippers. A team from BBC Wales turn up and films for the evening news and their presence gives me an incentive to block out the pain and make up some miles

With eight miles to go I'm struggling badly. I feel like I'm pushing and pushing and not getting anywhere. I blame my bearings, blame the hills, blame everything I can. I'm cursing under my breath when a red car pulls up and the three guys inside hand me all the change they have. Each rest turns into half an hour of gazing blankly at the sky. Kate hugs me like a bear and I'm ever so aware that she has to leave tomorrow. All afternoon she's been drawing up signs on pieces of A4 paper and sticking them on the windscreen. 'Keep Going!' 'You da Man!' 'Skaterboy Rocks!' 'You have one sexy ass!' These, along with a bangers-and-mash supper in a country pub gives me just enough fuel to reach Whitchurch, which all day has been a carrot bobbing at the end of an enormous, imaginary string.

We find accommodation at the wonderful Mile Bank Farm, the landlady Gill making us feel perfectly at home, even bringing over a foot spa from her home across the courtyard. Cutting off the back of my shoe has done the world of good for my heel, but with the blister on the ball of my right foot growing daily I'm daunted by the prospect of another twelve days of skating. The idea of resting for a day continuously crosses my mind but I'm caught up in the battle I set myself, determined to stay on schedule and reach Land's End on time.

* * *

Kate catches an early train. My heart sinks as we hold each other, privacy distinctly lacking as Dom films us. He's asked me to wear a mic but I turn it off for the whispered goodbyes. When the train pulls away Dom is straight in with the camera, asking me how I feel. I'm starting to be drained by not being able to deal with my emotions privately; I have to repeat them again and again for the camera and I'm very conscious that what is being filmed isn't going to appear very real, because it's not, really. I splutter out a couple of lines and withdraw, desperate for my own space. I'm keen for the journey to be filmed and be made available to the public and am trying to do as much as I can to make things easy for Dom, but the camera was becoming another exhausting factor for me to deal with. Kate's departure left me feeling incredibly low and, along with my injuries, the thought of two more weeks of pain and the combined effect of minor cabin fever and lack of privacy was taking hold. I felt hollow. Holly, too, had similar thoughts.

Gill bids us farewell and won't accept money for the room. She pushes a packed lunch into Holly's hands, we're incredibly grateful. I change bearings before getting back on the board. The pressures are piling on, I'm sick of the mess in the van, and all my socks are wet. The rain is falling again and on the southern outskirts of Whitchurch I pull the van over as my foot slips out of my shoe again. Laughing maniacally at the bizarreness of it all, I wrap layers of gaffer tape round and around until my shoe is a big black club inextricably attached to my leg. Twenty miles doesn't seem like twenty miles anymore, it seems like forty. A sweet old lady rushes out from her house with a bag of 5 pence coins for us

Outside Telford we fall asleep for an hour in the van, the rain drives down on the roof. It's all unbearably depressing, and when we wake I push less than two miles before calling it a day. We get a frosty reception at the Clairmont Guest House where the landlady, having previously agreed to give me a room, wasn't happy when three of us turned up. It was the last thing we needed. It feels as though a table tennis ball is wedged under the skin on my right foot. 'The only option is to not do anything for a day,' says Dom. And he's right.

'I'll make a decision in the morning,' I tell them.

* * *

Holly and Dom tap away on their laptops, searching for medical solutions to blisters. I sit on my bed my right leg raised, putting me in a permanently sloppy right angle. Emails arrive every minute in response to my decision to take a rest day. The self-imposed arrival date at Land's End, one month on from John o'Groats, is slipping away. I worry about finishing the journey without a crowd because I'm late, but friends and strangers tell me there's no reason to be ashamed of taking a day off. They send in blister and muscle treatments, some medically proven, some old wives' tales. Eileen, the Guest House landlady, had softened since our harsh welcome yesterday. She allows us another night in her beds and we're grateful for her change of tack. The rain bashes down outside and I'm dizzily happy to be doing nothing at all. Hopefully tomorrow will bring a new lease of life, and a smaller lump on my foot. My natural skating rhythm had changed since crossing the border, the ball of my foot now taking the brunt of each push, each swing of my leg now designed to alleviate the pressure on my heel injury. The skin on my heel is replenishing itself now, a yellow-red-brown-green web, still seeping with the lack of rest, but improving all the same. It is healing so quickly that walking to the toilet after an hour of non-movement means an excruciating stretching of new skin. I counterbalance by walking on tip toes, but of course this now has its own downfalls – the blister beneath my toes is spreading, a translucent, yellowy cover over red raw flesh. Without a crutch to balance on, I spend the rest of the day hopping to the bathroom. The ungraceful decline of a long-distance skateboarder thankfully hidden from view by four walls in Telford.

*   *   *

I need more rest but can't bear to be stuck in the same place on the map for another day. When the clock ticks on and the miles don't the urge to claim some of them back is stifling. Stagnant pause over, Elsa and I venture out into the rain. The blister on my sole has hardened and for a few blissful miles I skate almost pain free. By mid-morning though, the hotspots start to pinch at my feet, temporary relief over and a return to the minefield creating pressure points in an arc around from heel to the tops of my toes. Dom has returned to London for a day and Holly and I spend half an hour at a place called Ironbridge, which, funnily enough, is home to a large iron bridge. Yesterday's break has energised us, and Holly and I are getting on better than we have in a while. Our individual roles in this, while completely different, are exhausting. She has been wonderful, faithfully holding back her frustrations at not being able to photograph freely. Often I'd be overtaken by fatigue and slump into heavy moods, not talking for long periods and undoubtedly providing abysmal company, and I was aware that as the journey progressed I became less generous with my thanks. Despite this Holly was always there, but the journey was taking its toll on her energy levels at a rate I couldn't comprehend. Just as she could never quite understand what I was going through, I struggled to take her strains into account. Three weeks in, she was proving to be a remarkably strong character.

Approaching Bridgnorth Elsa and I break our personal speed record, but it wasn't through choice. When the road dips down into an unknown pit, vegetation rising up from both sides to obscure the road, I tend to lower my foot and drag it to create a natural brake. There's too much at stake to let go when you can't see where the road leads, a big fall with hundreds of miles left would be devastating. But this time, as I begin to foot drag, the friction on my blisters is too painful and causes me to jerk my foot up and back onto the board. By then I'm going too fast to brake again, because the process of lowering the right foot to the ground means for a split second I'm balancing on one leg. With Elsa rushing over treacherously rough and slick surfaces, the motion is too much for one foot to control. So, with the road below dipping and disappearing around a corner I have no choice now but to crouch down and go with it, my speed picking up as the metres fly by, wheels striking small potholes and Elsa jumping violently from side to side, my eyes watering as rain and insects buffet my face. I'm terrified, alone on the road save the van behind me but travelling faster than I ever have before, eying up nettle-clad verges for a spot where I can fling myself off the board and land in vague softness, rather than a nerve-shattering, skin-shredding slide along the road. I'm convinced this is it, that I can't hold this anymore, but the road bends round and turns uphill and Elsa eases into the gradient, slowing down as I hyperventilate, clutching my hands together and looking up at the sky, whispering 'thank you, thank you' to whoever, whatever, kept me standing. My GPS reads 29.6mph; that's too fast for my liking but I whoop with joy, not at the speed but the fact that I'm still in one piece.

* * *

With June approaching there was little sign of summer and the wet meant I used up more than my fair share of mental energy. With each, God-awful push, I needed to focus to avoid a slip. It was an extra caution that slowed the pace and drained my reserves. The first few miles were spent swerving around – and sometimes through – enormous puddles that had formed across the narrow, winding country roads that burrowed deeper into Worcestershire, the fifteenth county of the journey, but the poor conditions weren't a fair reflection on the day, which was about to get far brighter.

Three miles north of Worcester a car pulled up behind us, yellow and familiar, BoardFree website on the bonnet. It was Dan, Becki and Bev, a mate of Becki's from Swansea University. The moment they drove off ten miles south of John o'Groats seems unfathomable now in terms of distance and experience and there is nothing that warms the soul more than a reunion with old friends. I pushed on with a spring in my step, an odd convoy forming to typify the community this project had brought together. In Worcester the procession grew. Nat joined me on Little Elsa as Pat and his girlfriend drove behind, and then my parents appeared as if from nowhere, peddling towards me in luminous jackets, a complete surprise this time! I was bursting with emotion, only keeping myself together because I wanted to ensure the party remained safe on the road. Just south of Worcester I pushed over the six hundred mile mark and soon afterwards pulled into a pub car park in Callow End to celebrate the milestone, fifteen people or so bustling into the homely Blue Bell full of stories and smiles. I hobble around, the lady behind the bar looking down at my right shoe, which is swollen with layers of gaffer tape, raising an eyebrow when someone tells her I'm skating the length of Britain. The party has only just begun and when word gets around that Dom is outside. I stand by the door ready to greet him. A strange sound hums from beyond the door, it seems familiar but I don't know why. 'Dunnadunnadunna . . .' The door bursts open and a costumed man flies through it.

'Daaaaaave!' he shouts, pointing into the middle of the room. I have no idea what's going on and only twig when the man, dressed as Batman's sidekick Robin, finally rests his masked gaze on me and says, 'There he is!' Behind him is another stranger dressed as Little Red Riding Hood, then another in full Batman get-up.

'We've come to skate with you, geezer!' Batman tells me. An enormous wolf man struts through the door, followed by Dom's friend Eric, a Kenyan I had been expecting to turn up, but not dressed in full Masai warrior attire. Two girls, Dom and his mum complete the ensemble; I was blown away by the surprise and completely humbled that so many people would go to such efforts to join us on the road. A camera is pointed at me for a reaction:

'Well, I was expecting Dom and a couple of friends and family members to come through the door, and suddenly the whole cast of the cartoon world appears . . .' Everyone giggles and Pete, Dom's stepdad, masquerading as Robin, raised a glass:

'To you Dave, you've got the whole of Winchester behind you, we're all backing ya, we've been waiting all week for this and we're really up for it. Six hundred miles today isn't it? To Dave!' And everyone cheers, drinks in the air. Half an hour and a sandwich later we hit the road: my parents, Batman and Robin and Eric the Masai on bicycles, Wolf man on roller skates, Little Red

Riding Hood on a ridiculous mini-bike with legs spinning furiously. With even more cars in the convoy and a host of superheroes wheeling along behind me, morale is higher than it has been for weeks. 'Embrace the pain!' shouts Pete from a car window later on, turning my grimaces to grins.

Despite the occasion my foot continues to degrade and I'm forced to pull over at Upton upon Severn, startling a couple as they're passed by all kinds of characters in fancy dress. The crowd mulls about as my mum takes a look at my foot. The wear from the road has rubbed away the lower layer of gaffer tape and continues to eat into my right shoe, so I try to devise a plan to take the pressure off the ball of my foot. My dad, Nat and the superheroes walk to a skip at the end of the car park, Batman climbs up a ladder and rummages around for some rubber, then, *Reservoir Dogs*-like, the crew walk back shoulder to shoulder after a successful scrounge, a piece of old tyre swinging from Robin's hand. We cut slivers off it, gaffer taping them to the edges of my shoe in the hope that pressure will be taken off the centre of the sole, and therefore my blister. It's a sorry state of affairs and I'm sick of the pain, but the support is endless and I'm so grateful to everybody. My parents have to leave; my mum surreptitiously stuffs a bag of flapjacks into the van and winks at Holly.

* * *

John and Carole, our hosts for the night, sit in their car waiting to cheer me off, having donated some medical tape and carrot cake to the expedition. John has years of experience in the Forces and shared a few blister prevention techniques with me the previous evening, but I fear it's too late. The blister has grown to the size of a half tennis ball and is so much a part of this journey now that it almost has its own personality. Bloated and yellow, it has started to become septic. I'm regretting not searching harder for a sock sponsor.

The rain, yet again, is pelting down and I'm reluctant to climb out of the van, back out into the war zone. In a joint attempt to lift the mood and keep me dry, Pat decides to wrap a straw sombrero in gaffer tape, in turn sticking it to my helmet. 'That should keep the rain off,' he says, grinning. I start skating, waving goodbye to John and Carole but pull up two hundred metres later with the hat getting pulled around by the wind, the brim swiftly filling with water and sloshing all over the place. The driver of a passing car almost swerves into a ditch as he stares at me; a drenched and downtrodden man, clubfooted on a yellow skateboard, wrestling with an oversize hat which is somehow attached to his skate helmet. At least the helmet was dry. I rip the contraption apart, handing it back to an outstretched hand emanating from the van.

'It'd be great with a tailwind,' I say, but the words drift off in the rain. The bridge of my nose is a riverbed and a minute into the day my foot is damp, burning with every push. Sometimes I feel like the end of the day only comes because the pain is too great. Pushing on the next day seems impossible as I hobble around; I dread waking up now. I can smell my foot through my shoes and socks, even when I'm skating. I can't remember what it's like to walk without pain, to pull socks and shoes on without half an hour of preventative rigmarole beforehand. I don't know how I'm still pushing but I am, head down in a determined trance. I'm snapped out of it at the top of a hill in Maisemore. A view has appeared: Gloucester glistens in the rain, the cathedral towering above the city. It looks beautiful, just a couple of miles away, just a few more pushes. Come on, let's do it.

In Gloucester I fall into the van. I need to rest, I tell the others. Raindrops smack the roof of the van, rivulets and rapids on the windscreen. Becki and Bev play noughts and crosses in the sunroof condensation. Dom reads interesting snippets from the *Sun* out loud, he loves the *Sun*. Dan writes 'Poo' on the windshield, Pat and his girlfriend laugh at the madness. I can't bring myself to go out and skate. The rain. The pain.

The others understand but they're frustrated at the delay, I can't keep them waiting anymore. At 4 p.m. the sun blinks through the darkness and I get back on the road, the prevailing winds full in my face. Pat leaves to drive back to London, another sign that the weekend of company is coming to an end. 'Keep going mate,' he says, 'almost there.'

At Woodford Bev and Dan jump out and skate the last hundred metres with me, Dan on Little Elsa, Bev on her wooden board, I'm so grateful to them for being here. Bev and Becs buy me a meal in a nearby service station, then proceed to have a burger-eating contest. Bev wins. I can still smell my foot but nobody else notices, not with service station food on the table. Holly and Nat turn up; it seems to me like Holly needed a longer rest. Nat barely talks to me and I don't have the energy to ask what's wrong. There's a hotel across the car park and we check in, Dan, Holly, Dom, and I. The staff are rude and we stay in the room. I have a bath, soak in the nothingness of bubbles and throbbing feet. I miss Kate, she would have loved this weekend; the costumes, the camaraderie, the togetherness. Despite everyone and everything, she was my missing piece. I'm going to need her in Australia, I realise, I just need to convince Becki. Bev and Becs plan to drive back to Swansea, but first I chat with Becs in the corridor. We slump opposite each other, backs against the walls, and I tell Becki I want Kate in Australia, for me and for the team.

'Holly knows better than anyone what it's like dealing with me day in and day out on the road. Only Kate can truly do that,' I said. 'I need her there, for all our sakes.' Once Becki had been accepted onto the team our conversations over coffee and hot chocolate in late 2005 grew in intensity with the assumption that Becki would be the team member to take care of me when I was down, and I understood that Kate's introduction changed things. 'Becs, it'll give you more time to lead the fundraising team, and I've decided you could do with someone to help you with that, too.' She looked at me, confused, and I pulled a surprise out of my sleeve. 'Do you think Bev would consider joining us in Aus?'

Bev was a ball of energy, making up for her lack of stature with endless personality. I knew she and Becs got on well and over the weekend had seen them work brilliantly together. Instantly and out of the blue, I knew Bev would be a great addition to the team. 'Talk to her about it on the way home tonight,' I told Becs, who loved the idea. 'BoardFree has got to the stage where we can't have too many people.'

*   *   *

The mental battle the length of Britain has got going with me is tearing me apart as I lie awake, snores all around, my right foot hanging out of the sheets at an angle, exploding in pain, stinking like death. I know now that I need to let the blister heal. But I'm fifteen miles north of Bristol, a critical landmark for me; my path after the city will turn south-west towards Land's End, the home straight. Stopping now means that for the duration of my lay-off I'll be haunted by the fifteen miles between Woodford and Bristol. One more day, I tell myself, skate for one more day and get to Bristol, and then I can justify a rest.

I have to stop fooling myself. When the others are up I tell them it's time for a break. I tell them I need treatment. I tell them we're going to hospital.

I have a lump in my throat as I sit up front, the M5 flashing beneath us, my foot on the dashboard, smelling. Dan is driving and needs to open a window: 'Why don't you just cut it off, it's dead anyway,' he says. In Bristol I hobble into the Royal Infirmary and wait as Dom organises a consent form to film my treatment for the documentary. We're led to a cubicle and a kindly nurse asks how she can help. I explain the injury, how it came about, the urgency attributed to the rest of the journey. She doesn't flinch and laughs at Dan and Holly, who hold their noses.

'I can't smell anything,' says the nurse. I feel something like relief. She patches up my heel and prescribes antibiotics for the blister. She recommends full rest until it heals but accepts that the clock is ticking on this journey. The pills will kick in within the first three days, she tells me, so I agree to rest until Thursday. She's OK with that. I'm not, secretly. But there's a long-term aim to be preserved here, and I just hope that two days of rest can sort my foot out enough to send me to Land's End without further breaks needed. As we leave the hospital a fire alarm goes off and we're suddenly surrounded by people in white coats and gowns. Dom is asked to stop filming by an armed guard and starts to argue with the guy. My head is buzzing and I think Dom's aggression is unnecessary, I've never heard him admit he's wrong. At the same time I can't help feeling that there's something wrong with an armed guard patrolling around a hospital.

Holly and Nat had spent the previous day in Minehead with Nat's parents, and that's where we're going to rest up. We drive through Bristol and stop briefly at the headquarters of Lush Longboards. My first four-wheeled board was a Lush Bahari and in many ways the Lush website was my initiation into the sport. Rich Auden welcomes us into the lair, walls lined with brand new boards hanging from racks. 'I wish we'd got onboard with you guys sooner,' Rich tells me before we leave, 'you're doing an incredible job with publicity, I've been reading about you everywhere.' It meant a lot for him to admit that, and I feel sure that BoardFree and Lush will join forces at some point in the future.

We drop Dan off at the station and head to Minehead, where Nat's parents, Jo and Rick, await us at their holiday home, Primrose Hill Cottages. There's BoardFree stuff all over the place, the notice board in the games room covered in t-shirts and posters and a leaflet in every room's welcome pack. We settle into our cottage, pop an antibiotic and elevate the foot. Dom and I work on some videos – the website needs some updating. Even with two days of non-skating ahead the BoardFree project lives on.

* * *

For two, stale days my foot throbs. Throb. Throb. Throb. Towards the end of the second day of rest I experience the strange, draining feeling of the antibiotics getting to work, forcing the infection out. Holly and Dom inspect the blister and both agree that it looked like it had normal skin on it. You know things haven't been good when having normal skin on your foot is worth talking about. The smell still lingers, if I touch the blister the scent of infection stays on my hands. I hobble around, walking on the side of my foot. The new skin on my heel still hurts when it stretches, but not as much as it used to. I rest, my body recuperating, foot in the air, a painstaking game of patience. TV celebrity Jonathan Ross writes to me. I email him back. He replies. I get the feeling he thinks I'm mad, but it's nice of him to get in touch with a complete stranger. 'You'll be on his show one day,' says Dom.

'Not if my foot always smells like this,' I reply.

*   *   *

By Thursday morning I was raring to go. The mood in the van as we made our way north was very much 'let's get back to business'. The fifteen miles between Woodford and Bristol had haunted me for three days; the red line that had slowly snaked its way down my UK map had hovered teasingly north of the M4 for too long now. It was time to put things right. I felt better for a good rest and so did Holly, I thought. She had stayed relatively separate from Dom and I during the spell at Primrose Cottages but I put that down to a natural tendency to escape. For almost a month she'd been stuck with two boys, anyone would have wanted space after that.

It felt great to be back on the road. I was now wearing a new right shoe, one of my yellow trainers that had been brought from Swansea at the weekend, and although I had cut the back off it there was no need for gaffer tape just yet; it fitted snugly having been worn-in by my regular training sessions pre-BFUK. My blister had dried out after three days of pills and it was wonderful to be back on the road, skating with little pain. My first glimpse of the two bridges that cross the Severn just north of Bristol gave me something tangible to hold onto: for the first time on the journey, having skated six hundred and fifty miles, I was in familiar territory. My well-trodden route between Swansea and London intersected the BoardFree UK journey right here, and it was a mark of how far we'd come. Those journeys to London had in recent times been for one reason – Kate – and I was buoyed by the fact that she had taken a few days off work and was going to join us in Bristol. Since our goodbye ten days earlier in Whitchurch I'd found things increasingly tough and couldn't wait to see my little lady.

I revelled in skating without pain, the blister on my right foot itching a little but providing very little discomfort. I sped into Bristol, remembering what a slow process it was to skate through a heavily urbanised area but basking in the first sunshine we'd seen for weeks. I split from the van outside Bristol Zoo, Dom and Holly waiting for Kate to appear in a taxi. We arranged to stay in mobile contact and meet a few miles later. Beyond the Botanical Gardens was a view I had no idea existed. I reached a viewing platform and looked out across a narrow gorge, the Clifton Suspension Bridge gracefully spanning the space between, a backdrop of green hills with the River Avon carving its way into the distance. For all the pain, all the moodiness, the arguments, the headwinds, the uphills, it was moments like this that made travelling such a journey worthwhile. I took stock for a while, soaking it up, and skated across the bridge from Gloucestershire into Somerset.

* * *

For twenty miles I rounded the bend, my direction shifting towards the south west, squeezing along narrow country lanes and scraping down slimy hills north of Cheddar. It was a short day, the unforeseen rest periods delaying the journey by nearly a week and creating another mental challenge for me to deal with. I'd accepted that reaching Land's End late wasn't anything to be ashamed of. Nobody had ever attempted this journey before and whether or not I had been naive with my initial schedule my main battle was with myself, and I felt incredibly frustrated that I hadn't matched my initial expectations. The delay was also going to influence the next two days of the journey. Simon had arranged a celebration party in Falmouth for the journey's end but with the party just hours away I was still two hundred and fifty miles from Falmouth. Skating it, of course, was impossible, so in the early afternoon we were joined by Dan, Becki, Bev and a few other friends from Swansea and I jumped into the van, changed into dry clothes and motored to Cornwall.

Kate and I lay in the back trying not to look outside as the A30 unravelled, but I couldn't help taking a peek, knowing that early the next week it would lead me towards Land's End. I didn't like what I saw – a ten-mile tailback slowed us to walking pace and the poor condition of the undulating road becoming more than evident. 'Oh shit,' I whispered to Kate, 'it's horrible knowing what I have left to do.' I thought of the moods that overtook me as I dealt with the prospect of the section north of Kendal. The fact that this road to Falmouth was ten times as long and just as undulating terrified me. I slumped into Kate's arms, blocking out everything beyond her grasp, so grateful for the distraction.

The party was a storm, raising several hundred pounds and giving everyone a chance to celebrate, albeit prematurely. Si had managed to rake in a large pile of prizes from local sponsors and Dan had brought down a couple of custom boards from Swansea, which had been donated by various longboarding companies. I wilted halfway through the night as adrenaline was quickly filtered out by fatigue, and made my way outside to put my head down in the van, the vehicle's now legendarily dodgy alarm sometimes blaring for no good reason while Kate scrambled across bags and longboards to disable it. My dreams were haunted by endless roads and footsteps outside. Another restless night.

*   *   *

'I'm leaving,' Holly tells me in a supermarket cafeteria.

'When?' I ask, stunned.

'I'm driving back with Nat in two days. I have some worked lined up next week.'

'Why didn't you tell me earlier?'

'I thought you knew,' Holly said, knowing full well I didn't.

She explained that Becki was going to stay and drive for the final week, but I was furious that this had all been arranged behind my back and couldn't understand why Holly had been so deceptive. It was clear she had found the journey tough but I felt hurt she hadn't been honest with me. Others on the team had known she was going before I did, but Holly's reasons changed depending upon whom I spoke to. My anger grew as I pawed the road, confused at Holly's actions. If she had come to me a week earlier and explained her situation I wouldn't have had a problem with her going, but the late notice meant there was no time to organise a new camera, meaning several days at the end of the journey would remain undocumented.

A question mark hung over Holly's commitment to BoardFree now. Her ability to switch off from her responsibilities and abandon ship undermined the amazing contribution she'd made to the journey so far. Her boyfriend Nat was a factor, joining me for sections of the day but becoming more argumentative about the directions we were taking. His attempted dominance came out of the blue, was bang out of order and harder to deal with because of the situation. Tensions rose all over the place, Kate calmed me down as I simmered, Holly didn't look me in the eye all day. There was always going to be an element of personal conflict on a journey like this but bar the awful blow-out we'd had south of Falkirk Holly and I had got on well. Her lack of professionalism in this instance was simply unacceptable and it forced me to doubt her ability to see through the entire Australian journey. The possibility that she could fly Down Under and then decide to leave one day without explanation troubled me.

My mood lifted on a country road south of Bridgwater, where a now familiar yellow shape peddled towards me. Mum! We hugged, God I needed it, and she produced another load of homebaked snacks to keep us well fed. Pushing along with her beside me took away the short bursts of pain that had started to return in my feet, the knowing smiles and the determination in her face through the drizzle making me more aware than ever of how I was able to do what I was doing. We chatted about Kate, whom Mum adored, and I told her that once I'd reached Land's End I'd be asking Kate and Bev to apply for positions on the Australia team. Even though the girls had already showed their worth to BoardFree I still wanted them to apply officially, as the others had done. Mum, who perhaps more than anyone valued Holly's contribution to my welfare on BFUK despite her imminent departure, nodded cheerily when I told her about the high chance of Kate joining me in Australia. She gave me that knowing look that parents give their children when they've made the right decision.

Taunton was a hotbed of expletives, three separate vehicle drivers telling me exactly what they thought of BoardFree UK. 'Get off the road you fucking prick!' shouted a fat man in a 4x4. 'Twats like you should be arrested,' another man grunted as he sped past. I wasn't feeling the love, and my water bottle was constantly poised at chest height after that, ready to be used as a missile at the next expression of support. It was one of the things I'd become used to since the first mutterings of dissent that had been aimed my way on the busy roads north of Inverness, but the criticism, however inarticulate, was never easy to stomach. British roads are bursting with high pressure, blood vessels popping out of foreheads, clenched fists and teeth. For all the good we were doing and the support that was flooding in, I felt constantly drenched by passing venom. Even the kindest people turn into snakes when they climb into a vehicle and pull out onto Britain's roads.

In Rumwell I hugged my mum goodbye, sure that she was having me on when she repeated that she and Dad couldn't make it to Land's End. 'We'll be thinking of you darling, you've done amazingly. Just keep going, you're nearly there.' The rest of us found a country pub down a side road and gained permission to camp in the car park, the night ending amusingly when a group of six skinny lads, all brothers bar one, posed with me for a photo. All of us in shorts, twelve stick-like legs side by side and then my calves, bulging angrily.

*   *   *

Another day of company on the road. Becki takes over van-driving responsibility from Holly. Rae and Phil have driven down from Swansea, Bev's here as are Bec's parents and other friends. It's great to see Rae and Phil, both stressed from organising their wedding but glad to be here. The crowd drives along, stopping where they can to clap and whoop when I roll past. Spirits are high as we stop for lunch in Tiverton, Devon; BoardFree UK's penultimate county.

The Brennan family join us for lunch. Ann and Mark shake my hand, this is the first time I've met them. Their son, Connor, has Lowe Syndrome. At seventeen he's curled up in his wheelchair, exhausted from an epileptic attack that morning. He's small for his age and is completely blind due to the cataracts that form a symptom of Lowe from birth. His younger sisters run around mischievously, flashing cheeky smiles. I chat about Lowe Syndrome with Mark and Ann, a lump in my throat as I'm handed pictures of Connor abseiling. They've always had problems getting him into school, fighting for their son to be accepted. They're a normal family, upbeat and realistic, dealt a cruel blow with Connor's condition but dealing with it exceptionally, knowing that the discovery of a cure will come too late for their boy. Those who swear at us on the road and doubt the reasons behind BoardFree, they don't matter. Connor and his family matter. John o'Groats to Land's End is absolutely nothing compared to what they have been through. Ann and Mark thank me for raising awareness of Lowe Syndrome, but I wish I could do more.

I'm steely now, every push is for Connor. Kate jumps out of the van and runs alongside me as I force my way up a large hill. She's a star, holding my hand until she can't go any further. I skate beyond Crediton before calling it a day, finishing off with a long one-mile gradient. It feels as though the land is levelling out, the horizon widening. Five days to go.

* * *

We camp overnight, a BBQ dinner going straight to my head and feeding a deep, peaceful sleep. When morning comes everyone packs up and goes their separate ways. Only Kate, Becki and Dom remain. It's a rough, hilly skate to Okehampton, which sits on the north-western corner of Dartmoor, and I take a break just after 1 p.m., halfway up a hill. Dom eyes up Elsa. 'Dave,' he asks, 'do you think I could skate down the hill.'

'Course you could mate,' I say instantly, an evil plan hatching.

I turn my head away from him so he thinks I'm measuring up the hill, but in fact I've turned away so he doesn't see me laughing. Usually I wouldn't advise anyone to skate any kind of hill that was beyond their ability, but with Dom there was an instant difference. He's a cameraman. For four weeks he's been asking me to skate up big hills twice because he missed filming it the first time. Also, absolutely positive that he wasn't going to make the bottom of the hill, I knew that he'd appreciate the footage of his first big fall. He plucks Elsa from the verge and heads for the road, I spin and scrabble frantically around the van. 'I need the camera!' I hiss at Kate and Becs, 'Dom's about to stack big time!' I couldn't stop laughing and found the camera just in time, Kate and Becs hurrying around the van. Dom begins to roll faster and faster. Kate starts to worry. I'm cracking up trying to keep the camera steady. Dom is twenty metres down the road now, still gaining speed, wobbling madly.

'Be careful!' Kate yells, and the call triggers a reaction, one last wobble. Dom launched into the air then thumped to the ground with a thud. Elsa hit the side of the road just as Dom bounced. Yes, he bounced. I doubled over, my sides aching. I knew that even if he had badly hurt himself he would have been proud of me for filming it. He picked up Elsa and hobbled towards us, showing a couple of grazes like a boy in a playground. Dom had just had his first big stack and as I tell everyone I teach to longboard, once you fall like that you don't do it again. Dom fully agrees.

Dartmoor drifts by, the alternative routes to the busy new A30 are running out as Bodmin Moor approaches, and with the day drawing on and the light fading I hit the A30 for the last four miles to Launceston. The road quality is great, the traffic much lighter than expected, it's like skating on a motorway. One big downhill then two and half miles of up, but before the climb I zoom past a signpost. Welcome to Cornwall, it reads, our last county border. I raise my arms aloft, an unexpected bonus right at the end of the day. On the other side of the road, heading east, VW vans stroll by, returning from the Run to the Sun festival in Newquay. Another van had broken down on our side of the railings. The occupants, three guys, stand at the roadside as I sweat my way past them. We high five one by one and the buzz sends me on until the next junction. We're one day of skating from the last page of our dog-eared roadmap, a silent witness to our journey.

* * *

We spend the night in Exeter with an old friend of mine, Rich Taylor, and his girlfriend Maike. Maike and Kate, who spent a year studying in Berlin during university, exchange pleasantries in German as Becki dives onto a sofa, two days of driving already catching up with her. 'It's not easy following you around,' she says, sticking her tongue out, 'you're so frikkin' slow.'

Kate needs to go back to work and I walk her to the station before breakfast. This goodbye is easier, and she'll be back in two days for the final push. Land's End is so close now we've all relaxed, the need to chase down more miles isn't so urgent now, and I'm determined to maximise the fundraising potential of BFUK by organising more media coverage throughout the week.

Elsa and I resume our westerly route shortly after 2 p.m. We have no choice but to stick on the A30, bisecting Bodmin Moor, which dauntingly reaches out to the horizons north and south. The prevailing winds whip round and hit me side on from the left, disrupting balance as two lanes of heavy traffic create their own vicious whirlwind to my right. The bleak scenery not offering many inspiring views, I find there's not much to look at on the A30, except signposts. Bodmin 23. Bodmin 22. Bodmin 19. The constant countdown becomes an unwanted focus of my concentration, the miles passing slower as a consequence. It's a mind game, like watching a clock towards the end of a work day.

A police car pulls up, the dreaded flashing lights. 'Put that camera down, did I say you could film?' The officer gesticulates at Dom. The camera goes down but I suspect it is still recording. The officer is concerned that the support vehicle is going too slowly and that it's not visible enough to prevent a crash.

'But it's a huge van,' I say, pointing at it, 'there's a big flashing orange light on top of it.'

'These get hit all the time,' the policeman says, pointing at his patrol car, which is brighter than a fairground ride. I don't believe him but nod understandingly. I explain the situation, that I'd really rather not be on the A30, but there's no alternative route between here and Bodmin. Eventually the officer agrees, radios all the other patrols along the road to make them aware of our little chat, and drives off.

Half an hour later the three of us sup a hot chocolate in an old tavern called the Jamaica Inn, the setting for Daphne du Maurier's classic book of the same name. A former haunt for smugglers, villains and murderers, the Inn is the type of place where ghosts roam around. The walls are covered with foreign money. It is an odd place but not as blood-curdling as you'd expect from the scene of several violent murders. In fact, it's rather cosy. It is half past five, there are fifteen miles left to skate, it's windy out there and warm in here. Motivation lurks in the bottom of my mug.

The run-in to Bodmin is an easy one, the roads smooth and traffic easing off past 7 p.m. We don't go through the town, stopping just off the A30 where we are met by Jon Worsely, who got in touch through the website and offered to put us up for the night in St Austell. His house is full of boards and Jon, a member of the Middle Age Shred skate forum, is a great example of someone who rediscovers a hobby with utter passion. He, his partner Karen, rat Norbert and countless cats make as feel right at home, and promise they'll be there in Land's End.

* * *

I wind through the countryside, roads with high hedges either side capturing the sun and forming a sparkling golden pathway ahead of me, almost like the yellow brick road. The topography isn't easy, and neither are the occasions when we have to negotiate right of way with oncoming vehicles, but my foot is fine and the glorious weather makes skating a pleasure. I'm tired, four and a half weeks and more than eight hundred miles of skating catching up on me, chasing my rear wheels with gaping jaws. Recuperation is an added incentive driving me towards Land's End.

I brood for a while about negative comments posted online in response to an article recently printed in the London *Metro*, which detailed my upcoming challenge. The article was a piss-take, asking people to log-in to the *Metro* website and share their thoughts on whether there was a dumber way to cross Australia. There was no mention of the charities or the BoardFree website, which made it all the harder to stomach when a couple of posts claimed ego was the driving force behind the journey, and genuine charitability was dismissed. The fact that just two out of twenty posts were negative – all the others were incredibly supportive – should have told me something, but I was still coming to terms with the poison some people were willing to contribute in our direction. It riled me, just the reaction the posters were hoping for I suppose, and I skated along for part of the afternoon like a bear with a sore head.

I record a couple more interviews, one with Cornwall's Pirate FM and another with BBC Online. I ask their journalist to make sure they don't try to make out I'm doing this because I was bored. 'You should see the hole in my foot,' I laughed, 'this is no good cure for boredom!' The rest of the afternoon disappears in a flash, and Truro is behind me when I pick up Elsa and jump into the van. We're just a few miles north of Falmouth now and we drive south, settling in the student bar where the BoardFree party was held just five days ago, wondering exactly what I was worried about on the drive east following the event.

* * *

Kate, who arrived by train late last night, slips into the passenger seat beside Becki. My left foot slides into its green and yellow trainer, the right into a bright yellow one. Both shoes are battered and worn, dirty and misshapen. The weather is blissful, gradual hills shadow the main A-roads between Truro and Penzance as Elsa and I glide along them. I'm happier than I have been for a long time, the combined weight of the skating plus the additional responsibilities of running BoardFree are slowly lessening as the road ahead becomes shorter. I begin to huff and puff as I push uphill, wheezing like an asthmatic. This hasn't happened before and I don't associate the heavy breathing with anything but poor fitness. I'm tired and thoughts run away with me, but the disconcertion of skating almost nine hundred miles and still being unfit, however ridiculous the notion was, just makes me puff even more.

We spend two hours in a beer garden, playing music and soaking up the imminent completion of the journey until we feel obliged to leave. The landlord, incredibly friendly until we had paid for lunch, starting to glare at us, huffing and puffing almost as much as I'd been doing earlier. Penzance is on the cards, let's go. We take small, quiet country lanes through Porkellis and Nancegollan and Godolphin Cross, smooth and mainly downhill as the coast beckons.

Penzance comes quickly – almost too quickly – and I trace the cycle path around the bay. It's been 33 days since I last saw the sea. Then it was in April, on the northern shores of Scotland. Now, here I am having pushed the length of two countries on a longboard. Penzance and its ocean remind me of Swansea, nostalgia bubbling not necessarily for South Wales but for those twelve-mile training runs I took around the Bay, one easy smooth direct path backwards and forwards. And now I see signposts directing me, Land's End 12 miles. The length of just one training run. I'll save it for tomorrow.

*   *   *

Lands End is so close, just hours away. I'm shaking with anticipation, the nearness of it all hard to grasp, as though this journey had been talked about so much it couldn't possibly be anything other than a myth. And I suppose, at that point, it was a myth. It still hadn't been completed, not by anyone. Had I been asked at 23 years old what I'd be doing two years later, I guarantee I wouldn't have said skateboarding long distances. I wouldn't have said skateboarding at all. This was brand new, all of it, thirteen and a half months on from stepping onto my first board I was about to break, no, *create*, a new record. A brief moment in history, scratched from nothing with the help of a cat named Kiwa and a determination not to paint by numbers anymore. I bind my feet for one last time, cutting a hole in a square of orthopaedic felt and placing it over my heel injury, taping it in place, plasters on my toe blisters, socks, another pair, shoes. Ready.

I call two news agencies from a horizontal position as the van heads to Penzance. We have five or six recorded interviews going out around the country today: several Cornwall stations, BBC Radio Cumbria, and some online stuff including the BBC site. BBC Radio Four wanted to speak that evening, but no national news. It wasn't worth being disappointed, this was a warm-up and bigger things would come later.

Nat skates with me, three other cars in convoy with the van. Holly is in one of them, snapping away. Gael, a friend from Swansea, towers through the van's sunroof taking more pictures from another angle. The van struggles on a steep hill as we climb out of Penzance, the smell of burning rubber and fuel drawing out worried faces. Becs apologises but it's not her fault, and we manage to push-start the vehicle, getting it to the top of the hill where it needs to remain static for a while. The van's mechanical issues had dominated the first day of the journey and were taking centre-stage again, the toxicity in the air a crucial factor omitted as I gave an on-the-spot interview to Dom to sum up the situation. It was a blip, the engine starting after half an hour, the procession continuing along smaller country roads as we missed the main turning which would take us onto the A30. We pass through St Buryan and Trethewey, locals waving as I wonder which uphill will be my last.

For the first time directly ahead of me on this journey, I see the sea on both sides, the blue expanse converging at one spot, the end of the land. I'm handed a video camera and speak as I roll past a sign telling me that Land's End is just two miles away. It's time for a final speech.

'This is for every child out there who has Lowe Syndrome. This is for every African child and teacher whose lives are made better by Link Community Development. This is for every disabled child in Australia who benefits from Sailability's work. The lives that are going to be benefited by the funds and awareness raised by BoardFree, both this UK trip and the Australian one, those lives are full of pain and hardship . . .' I look around, then down at Elsa, '. . . and let me tell you, this isn't pain and hardship, it's a little bit of a struggle. Nine hundred miles on a skateboard is nothing at all.'

I thank my sponsors for believing in a complete stranger who wanted to embark on a mad escapade, for sticking their necks out when they didn't have to and making a journey like this possible. I tell anyone who is planning a journey from John o'Groats to Land's End not to listen to people who say that it's downhill, because it's not. John o'Groats is right at sea-level, Land's End sits at the top of a hundred foot cliff, so actually it's uphill! I thank the team, their families and all of our friends who had shown so much support, then wind up with a sign-off: 'Less than a mile to go now. John o'Groats to Land's End, April thirtieth to June second two thousand and six, this has been BoardFree UK, signing out for the final time.' Behind me there are cheers from the van, they sail and echo on the wind and I realise they'd been listening to it all via the microphone on my shirt.

I handed the camera back and skated along by myself, taking a solitary few moments to reminisce and look back on what had been an incredible journey. The sea drew nearer and I remembered setting off from John o'Groats with a band of five screaming into the emptiness. I thought about Holly and how she'd been there for me, the times we were angry and upset and the times when we'd hugged and everything felt OK. I turned around and saw Becs in the front of the van. She'd given up a lot to drive for the last week and had done a wonderful job. Sat beside her was Kate, smiling widely. She'd played such a huge part during the journey, travelling back and forth from London to various places on the route, knowing that I needed the emotional support and doing everything she could to give it. I longed to take her to Australia, knowing now that having a girlfriend on the road with me wasn't such a bad thing after all.

A T-junction approached and right ahead I saw a sign. Land's End ½. I had skated 895½ miles from northern Scotland, and only had half a mile to go! Cheers went up from the van as I carved down the final hill into the Land's End complex, having one last panic attack and waving my arms furiously in search of direction as a fork in the road approached, but it was a one-way system and I was wasting my energy.

'You're not there yet, keep pushing!' shouted Becki, cackling loudly as the gates approached. I could see Land's End ahead, just a hundred metres or so, a finishing line pulled across the road in front of the building surrounded by a large crowd. I walked back to the van and quickly changed into a new t-shirt.

'Good luck mate,' said Gael and Dan in unison, both of their heads poked out the sunroof, they were ready to photograph and film the finale. I winked at Becki who was ready to drive the final stretch.

'Are we ready?' I grinned rhetorically, walking back to Elsa. The barrier opened and I pushed forward, realising that I had no idea what I was going to do when I crossed the line. It came up all of a sudden, champagne spraying into the air, people clapping, the van's horn honking behind me, my arms raised aloft. 'Yeeeeeeahhh!' I scraped to a halt, running off my board, turning in a crouch, grabbing Elsa in complete elation, 'You beauty!'

Everything else is a blur. I kiss the line. I kiss Kate, our noses touching and eyes closed tight. I hug everyone else. Dom has a tear in his eye and I can't help thinking that's a bit ironic. I walk into Land's End with the team, register my journey and make it official. Dom buys me my first beer and we sit around a wooden bench, the sea down below, endless beneath a clear sky, silver horses twinkling on the surface, the same way that they had done at John o'Groats.

14 In Between The Journeys

June – August 2006

The train rumbles west towards Swansea, through fields and past lakes, my head up against the window as the countryside north of Bristol passes by, road after road running by the tracks. I wonder which one it was that took me south, the reality of the past month's journey slowly sinking in after a long weekend in London with Kate. I pull my laptop out and start to type as small memories flash back from the last day at Land's End:

I reached Land's End five days ago: the whole team was there, official and unofficial, the loo-roll finish line held up by Bev and Nat, the glorious arc of champagne. Small things come back to me: I can't remember if my momentum broke the toilet roll or if it was let go at one end. I remember hearing a voice saying 'well done Dave'. It sounded like my Dad but he and my Mum couldn't be there. I've watched the video back ten times, it still sounds like my Dad.

A swig of champagne sends me dizzy. We all walk to the famous signpost, New York 3147. John o'Groats 874. That signpost is a family business and we're told we have to pay to have a photo with it. You travel the length of Britain and have to pay to have a picture taken with a piece of wood. I'm not here for the photos. I sign a few BoardFree leaflets for interested tourists and wonder if the people who own the signpost have ever travelled from John o'Groats to Land's End.

Done it. Deep breath. The realisation won't set in for a few days but less than fourteen months after stepping onto my first longboard I've become the first person to skate the length of Britain. The BoardFree team celebrate with pasties, beer, ice cream and a brilliantly steep inflatable slide. Some things I couldn't have imagined as I pushed off from John o'Groats thirty-four days earlier . . .

Several national tabloid newspapers ran stories on the culmination of BoardFree UK over the weekend. The *Sun* gave me a nickname, 'Superfit Dave Cornthwaite'. The *South Wales Evening Post* fill page 3 with the story, I'm introduced as the 'Chairman of the Board'. It's all so laughable, the way the journey is pulled to and fro in a search for different angles; *it's a new record, but just a warm-up. How can a 900-mile journey be a warm-up? Australia is coming, watch this space.* This was the aim, to make sure as many people hear about BoardFree as possible. Now and then someone writes after chewing on the wrong end of the stick, claiming I'm doing this to become famous, that my motives are all wrong. They rarely sign their name and clearly don't know me, but it's an unwanted form of criticism and I can't fathom the vitriol. The direct correlation between the amount of people who hear about BoardFree and the amount of people who will then donate places an emphasis on BoardFree having good PR; I'd be a fool not to have capitalised on this. I'm a little frustrated that we've only raised £3,500 and despite some decent press coverage I honestly thought the efforts from the journey warranted more, but I want to learn from the experience rather than blame the traditionally stuffy British media for not wanting to cover a long-distance skateboard journey.

I'd been running media relations at the same time as completing the journey and it hadn't been ideal office conditions. Only help from freelance journalists like Dave Roberts, who I met shortly before BFUK, meant the story hit the national papers. I knew I needed to rethink our media strategy and as had happened with almost every other element of BoardFree to date, a new piece of the jigsaw was being shaped to fill the gap.

With little more than two months to go between my crossing the line at Land's End and boarding an aeroplane bound for Perth, Australia, I was keen to get on with things and ensure that logistics were arranged with time to spare. The most critical decision was also the easiest: Kate and Bev had proved to the rest of the team that they were dedicated to BoardFree and were ready to eat, sleep and breathe the project. In mid-June I got them both in the same room and welcomed them aboard, Bev to help Becki with fundraising, Kate in charge of BoardFree PR.

I had a team, but I needed to get them to Australia. British Airways declared that they weren't willing to help with BoardFree, not even by alleviating the costs of excess baggage, so Air France, Singapore Airways and Qantas were recipients of new emails. A stipulation of each team member's part of the project was a £3,000 contribution to the costs of the Australian expedition, and I had budgeted to allow this figure to cover flights should we not be fortunate enough to find sponsorship. One by one the airlines replied with shaking heads, except Singapore Airways, who were kind enough to offer us an additional 10kg of baggage per person. This was a big relief, as paying for the excess baggage we'd undoubtedly be lugging Down Under would have run into silly money. After that, I felt a strange moment of calm when finalising the flight bookings, the confirmation of our passage to Perth via Singapore stamping an air of decision on BoardFree Australia. We had managed to achieve so much from one room in Swansea that the prospect of flying to Australia and finalising our preparations there didn't seem as daunting as maybe it should have done.

The combined benefits of my completing the UK journey and receiving a fair bit of media coverage at the same time was having the knock-on effect I hoped it would. Before John o'Groats to Land's End there was always an element of doubt about BoardFree when I approached sponsors, who potentially had a lot more to lose by supporting me than a newspaper journalist did by simply printing an article. There was positive anticipation about the Australian journey now and although the United Kingdom was a mouse beside Australia's elephant, enough determination had been exhibited during BFUK to make people look twice as I filed off sponsorship requests.

One of the companies who had no hesitation in supporting BoardFree was Kangaroo Poo, a leisurewear clothing brand that seemed to thrive in the shadow of the big brands that herded around the same arena. Quiksilver, Billabong and Ripcurl were world famous, but for those that had heard about the brand Kangaroo Poo was popular because its roots seemed deeply embedded in the brand's lifestyle philosophy. More importantly, there was a clear Australian link that Kangaroo Poo wanted to forge with BoardFree, and I could barely believe my eyes when I read their initial courtship email, which came at a time when I was wandering around wearing none other than a Kangaroo Poo t-shirt. Always happy to venture from Swansea to London and tie-up some BoardFree business with some downtime with Kate, I skated from Paddington to Gloucester Place, where Roo Poo's brand manager, Rebecca Richardson, was waiting for me. She immediately impressed, the pair of us connecting instantly and reeling off several hundred ideas in the first ten minutes. I felt like the brand was going somewhere and that it shared a similar philosophy to BoardFree in that there were roots being built on with enthusiasm and belief. A mutual respect formed between Rebecca and I. She said Kangaroo Poo had been watching my progress since reading about BFUK in the *Metro* and that they wanted to be a part of the Australian journey. 'My team and I need a clothes sponsor,' I prompted.

'You've found one,' said Rebecca, piling t-shirts and hoodies into a bag for me. 'Here's something to keep you going.'

We had good luck with other sponsors, too. The IT side of BoardFree was critical, with the website our main tool of information, and five months of video footage, images and other files required some serious hardware to store and back it all up. Iomega came through for us with a varying collection of hard drives. Meanwhile I'd struck up conversation with Juergen Hagedorn, director of The Magic Touch, who had supplied the temporary tattoos that adorned my calves as I pushed the length of Britain. Juergen offered further support to the Australian leg, instantly taking advantage of The Magic Touch's prided printing systems and arranging for a supply of customised reflective jackets to keep the team and I safe on the road. 'Our company in Australia will help you out too,' he told me on the phone from his office in Amsterdam, 'we support you all the way.'

In addition to logistics and training, I had two major issues to deal with: Becki and Holly. The manner of Holly's departure from BFUK had been amplified by her behaviour on the day I reached Land's End. I had hoped that her week away would give her fresh perspective, as well as a chance to relax, but it seemed she had found neither. I sat down with her on the one occasion everyone else was absent, and asked her what was wrong. She told me it was Bev and Kate, the fact that they were being invited onto the team purely for emotional support, Kate for me and Bev for her best friend Becki. 'If you and Becki can have that, why can't I? It doesn't seem fair,' Holly said, before the others came back.

It was out of the blue and highlighted Holly's problems with communication. I'd thought four hard weeks on the road and the hangover of pinched nerves from unresolved arguments had been the issue, and now she was bringing her boyfriend into the equation. He hadn't excelled himself earlier that day, forcing Becki to tears with an unnecessary phone call, and there had never been talk or consideration of him joining the team. He couldn't offer what Kate and Bev could, not in terms of teamwork or relevant skill, and Holly's insinuation that BoardFree was becoming a love-in showed me her personal needs had quickly overtaken her professional understanding of how she sat in the BoardFree tree. If she had struggled with BFUK she was certainly going to struggle with Australia, and if she couldn't be open and honest about her feelings there wasn't a place for her on a journey five times as long and just as stressful as the one she'd just experienced. Her photography, on the other hand, was second to none, but that wasn't enough. Two weeks after Land's End it became apparent Holly wasn't going to be able to meet me in person, so I emailed her, laying the situation on a plate:

Holls, I want you to know that I haven't forgotten what you gave up to be a part of BoardFree UK and had you not offered to come along it would have been a very different journey with a very different impact. You mustn't think I'm not grateful because I am, more than you know. But before we can move on there are some creases which need ironing out. I was willing to forget the moods, you leaving the journey without explanation, everything, had you gone away for a week and come back bright, refreshed, happy and excited. You weren't, you hid away in your tent on a night of celebration. You felt you could leave without giving me any reasons, any notice, and no explanation. And I'm not even sure that you know what you did was wrong. If this happens in Australia I'm left without a photographer and now, with you having proved you can walk away without any word of explanation, I need reassurance that you're not going to be committed to a small section of Australia and then leave the team in the lurch. That's a risk to me. I want you to be there Holls, the team wants you to be there, I need you to be happy with the idea of months without Nat and reassure me that it's not going to affect your moods or your performance. It might be hard for you being without your partner for so long, but you said in your application you could deal with that. I'm yet to see solid proof of this. This isn't all bad chick, I have to cover all bases because this is getting bigger. We can't head out to Oz with any cracks in the armour. Let me know your thoughts . . .

Her reply was enough for me. She categorically wrote that she'd learned from her mistakes, she was going to be fine for months without her boyfriend and she categorically wasn't going to walk away from the team. Satisfied with Holly, I was still weighed down with another team issue, which had been boiling under for a while.

Becki had exploded at me halfway through a day-long training session with the Expedition Care Program, which was putting us through our paces during a crash medical course. Bewildered, I listened as Becki brought up how badly I'd been treating her, how I didn't appreciate the work she'd done, how I'd been bullying her. I was stunned, none of it adding up. I'd been focused wholly on the job in hand, ensuring BoardFree Australia was ready to fly, literally, and undoubtedly I'd been grumpy and blunt after long hours, but I'd assumed everyone had realised the pressure I was under. Becki had been treated no differently but she made out as though all I did was bring her down, which simply wasn't true. She'd become irritable herself, snappy too, and my way of dealing with it was often to ignore it for the irrationality it was, we all suffered from it now and then. That had been the wrong way for me to deal with Becki, who had actually been doing a bloody good job for BoardFree in between her actual working hours.

The blow-up at the Expedition Care Program bisected classes on dealing with major wounds and acting quickly in case of snake bite, and I zoned out for the majority of the latter session because of the Becki situation. She was a high octane character, with all that entails. I knew it was potentially a recipe for disaster in a closed environment, I just hoped having Bev aboard would take some of the pressure off me. All said and done, I had often thought about taking Becki off the team for just these reasons, but never rested on those thoughts because I knew her positives by far outweighed the negatives. She brought things to the package that nobody else could and she was invaluable in that respect. Just as I had done during our tiffs before BFUK, I dampened down the flame as best I could and reassured myself that when it got down to the nitty-gritty, Becs would come through for BoardFree when the chips were down.

There was no denying the potential of this project now. With the UK warm-up a success, thousands of pounds were already in the bank for Link, Lowe and

Sailability, new sponsors were poking their heads above the wall of cautiousness and more media coverage came through as the clock ticked down to our departure. BoardFree became ingrained into the vocabulary of tens of thousands worldwide. As the project grows everyone realises that there is far more ground to cover than the four thousand miles separating Perth from Brisbane, and that this journey isn't just about one man and his board. I'm aware that I'm the figurehead of this but am determined for the team to get their dues. I worried about some of them, how they will react to their own personal journeys in Australia and how, in turn, they will react to mine, the only one in the public eye.

*   *   *

Dom joined Kate and me in a visit to my parents' house near Oxford, as he wanted to interview them before we flew off to Australia. I had been impressed with his professionalism from the beginning: an ability to be blunt and request a repeat of an answer or an action if it had been missed reassured me that the final documentary would be an accurate portrayal of the project. Dom had been editing footage from the UK journey and continually updated me on his progress. Initial plans to get the UK journey on DVD by August were looking unlikely but the edited segments he sent through to me were excellent, although the argument between Holly and I south of Falkirk was painful to watch. His contribution towards costs on the UK journey was still outstanding, but with a promise to pay by the beginning of the Australian journey there was no issue between us. Indeed, he and Pat had decided that they would like to go ahead and film the Australian journey and I set about working out a way to accommodate them.

After discussion with Simon and the others it was agreed that it would be best if Dom became an official member of the BoardFree team. He would still be responsible for the documentary, with Simon's help, but he was there on the proviso that his priority was to the BoardFree cause, as was the rest of the team. He and Pat agreed this was the best path to take and Dom signed the team contract, thus ensuring there was no grey ground between BoardFree and the production company. A separate, rather basic contract was also signed between the production company and me, agreeing joint rights of all footage and that the company would provide all cameras and tapes needed. This was a big help to me, as financially that would have placed an extra stress on the expedition budget. Money aside, I was happy with the part Dom played on BFUK and trusted both he and Pat where BoardFree was concerned, so much so I told them both that a handshake would have sufficed, rather than a contract.

Although Dom and I got along well I was aware we were different in many ways. I was an organiser, and there was no doubt Pat filled that particular role in the production company; Dom and I had different temperaments, especially when it came to confrontation. Dom had flared up on BFUK occasionally, usually when criticism had been made about BoardFree, but whichever way it was directed his passionate personality had an aggressive, angry streak that I found unsettling at times. How would he cope in the pressure-cooker environment Australia was undoubtedly going to throw at us?

During my early training runs around Swansea Bay in 2005 I had been fortunate enough to meet Jason and Sue East. They ran a small kiosk beside the arcade as the Bay cycle path rounded its final corner and led towards Mumbles Pier. Jason and I got talking, his enthusiasm with Elsa and my plans for her becoming contagious. He and Sue ran their own business, had four great kids and were wonderfully genuine and kind. From that first day Jason made an offer: 'Every time you come round here mate, you make sure you have something to eat and drink, on the house. You're doing something inspirational, you should be proud of that and we'll do anything we can to help.' The offers of support continued, and in the heat of summer the entire BoardFree family gathered outside the kiosk armed with a barbecue and a marquee full of t-shirts, naked calendars, wristbands and leaflets. The burgers and sausages, all bought by Jason, went down a treat with Dan and Pat at the helm, the scent drawing hundreds of people to the stall all day long. As the queue grew Becki, Bev and Kate pounced, drawing out donations and getting people to sponsor a section of the journey, £5 for a five-kilometre section of the road. Not one person passed without walking away with a leaflet or a wristband, or both. It was a tremendous day, we raised over £200 thanks to the Easts' generosity, and the team had bonded just as I hoped they would.

'This kind of spirit will take you a long way in Australia,' I'm told by a passing couple who just happen to be from Brisbane, Queensland.

'I'm hoping it'll take us all the way to your hometown,' I said to them, laughing.

*   *   *

In both London and Swansea I was getting used to being recognised, or more accurately, Elsa was getting used to it. As I rolled through Hampstead a man pointed at Elsa and said, 'A bloke is going to skate around Australia on a board like that.' I grinned, handed him a BoardFree leaflet, and skated off with a wave. On the Underground an Australian man asks to look at my well-formed right calf and when I roll up my leg he exclaims, 'Jeez mate, it looks like a chicken fillet!' Whenever I'm in London for a weekend I make my way down to Hyde Park to say hello to the inliners and slalom skateboarders, Elsa enjoying her celebrity among boards. Mike Stride from Octane Sport gets the slalom lads together and brings some prizes along to raffle for BoardFree. Between them they throw another £75 into the pot. As if to balance out the support, my inbox receives regular letters of criticism and warning. 'You don't know what you're letting yourself in for, mate.' Another: 'If you attempt this you're not going to survive.' And another: 'Who do you think you are, saying you'll raise that much money for charity without knowing whether you can complete your journey?' And then *that* message from the Australian, Steve Furness: 'My mates and I are taking bets on what day you will end up in hospital from dehydration, sunstroke or third-degree sunburn. I am finding it hard to get someone to take anything beyond day 4 in the pool.'

It's too late guys, I think; you're not stopping me now. With each spurt of venom I grew a slightly thicker skin, but it'll never be quite thick enough. All I could do is what I set out to; no matter what is said and what is done, I can only be judged on how it all ends up. Theodore Roosevelt's wise words are never truer when you read them as a person who has a self-made struggle on his hands:

> It is not the critic who counts; not the man who points out how the strong man stumbles, or where the doer of deeds could have done them better. The credit belongs to the man who is actually in the arena . . . who does actually strive to do the deed; who knows the great enthusiasm, the great devotion, who spends himself in a worthy cause, who at the best knows in the end the triumph of high achievement and who at the worst, if he fails, at least he fails while daring greatly. So that his place shall never be with those cold and timid souls who know neither victory nor defeat.

I took heart from these words, told myself that those cold and timid souls who persisted in writing had never – could never have – achieved anything of note, and then I focused on the good words which came through, which were far more regular.

*   *   *

The postman knocks regularly in the final two weeks. Bearings from Swiss Bones, a medical Pack from the Lifesigns Group, satellite phone from Applied Satellite Technology and cooling neck wraps called Cobbers from Bodycool UK. Without doubt the quirkiest product we had sponsored was called a Shewee. A bag of these conical devices arrived, giving the BoardFree girls the gift of urinating standing up, ideal for the desert! However, two critical items hadn't arrived yet. First, I was still waiting on shoes. After the damage sustained to my feet on BFUK I was suffering from a very literal Achilles heel. The skin that had worn away as I crossed the Scotland–England border had grown back, but it was weaker than before and sub-standard shoes were asking for trouble. For two months I had been chasing my sponsors, asking for shoes that were all the same brand and same size to arrive in good time so I could wear them in, but they only arrived three days before I was due to leave Swansea. Relieved and frustrated all at once, I pulled on a new pair and skated into town to post a couple of letters. They weren't skate shoes, per se, and boasted an angled sole, like you'd see on a running trainer. At a set of traffic lights I put my foot down to brake, and it went. I looked down and could see the sole of the shoe, which was still fully on my foot. I start the Australian skate in twelve days, I thought as a sharp pain shot up my leg and I fell like a sack of potatoes, fearing the worst. Somehow it was just a slight sprain, but it could have been so much worse. I called Kate, who was back at the house. 'Babe, can you call Vapourised for me, and tell them we can't use these shoes. I almost broke my ankle a minute ago. We need a new shoe sponsor.'

By the time I got home she was already on it, laptop at the ready and phone to her ear, the BoardFree spiel flowing freely. 'Hi, my name's Kate and I'm calling on behalf of a guy called Dave Cornthwaite . . .' She finished the call. 'Looks like we've got some interest,' she told me. 'They're a company in Bristol who are agents for Circa shoes, they've heard of you and are going to call back later.' Hours later, miraculously, Kate spoke to them again, and secured BoardFree a bona fide skate shoe sponsor in Circa. 'We'll pick them up on the way,' Kate said, 'and we've got the contact details for the Australian branch.'

There was one more critical item missing. I'd sent Elsa to get a new yellow coat at the rollsrolls European base and she'd been posted three weeks earlier, but hadn't arrived. The only board to have travelled the length of Britain, the only board I'd considered using for Australia. I woke up on the Thursday morning knowing that Kate and I were only three hours away from leaving Swansea. Elsa still wasn't there. And then, with barely an hour to go, a smiling postman, well up-to-date on the BoardFree saga thanks to the local papers, handed over the box as another neighbour walked past saying, 'I thought you'd gone, well . . . good luck!'

'We're flying on Sunday,' I tell the postie. 'You might not be,' he said, 'you should go and switch on the news.'

So we did. Kate and I side by side, Elsa downstairs safe in her box. And thousands of people across the UK stranded in airports as security shutdowns follow a foiled terrorism plot to blow up nine aeroplanes over the Atlantic. We hoped for the best, stuffed the kitchen sink on top of everything else and drove east with Kate's brother, Simon, who had kindly come to pick us up.

* * *

Kate's parents, Margaret and John, had the patience of saints. Their front room spent the weekend strewn with kit. Bit by bit, Kate and I packed it away into holdalls, inching through the mess. By Sunday morning flights out of Heathrow were still being cancelled. All hand luggage had been banned, a 22-hour long-haul flight without entertainment loomed. The news looked grim; thousands of people were still queuing at Heathrow. One last meal; I couldn't help feeling guilty that I was taking Kate away from her mum and dad, but I was so glad she was coming with me. Our bags were packed, waiting at the door. I slipped my feet into some new Circa shoes, that had a little slogan written on the side below the ankle. They read, simply, 'It's Time'.

15 Here We Go

August 2006

Rain had played a major part in the first instalment of the BoardFree story and none of us were too surprised that the weather was abysmal as we convened in the corner of a Heathrow Airport car park. Dan set to work repacking bags and sealing boxes, his blue and white rollsrolls board slotting in on top of Elsa and Little Elsa, all three decks disappearing beneath a padding of BoardFree t-shirts and wristbands. Enormous puddles formed across the driveway leading to Terminal 4 and the team stared down into them from the third level of the car park, stood in a line with elbows on bars. We were one body short, an hour and a half after our agreed meeting time Simon still hadn't arrived, but no one was surprised, this was Simon, after all. Eventually a phone rang, 'He's here!' someone said. All peering down again, there was Si leaning out of a car window with one arm aloft, wearing the same wooly beanie hat he'd worn during his first visit to Swansea nine months earlier.

We filed into the terminal, funnelling like cattle through maze-like queuing systems, fingers firmly crossed that our bags weren't going to be overweight. Armed guards with guns patrolled around and there was a strange hush in the place. Airport terminals are usually abuzz with the excitement of journeys ending and beginning for thousands all under the same roof, but the presence of guns and stringent security puts a dampner on things. You want to lighten the mood and say, 'Hey, at least we don't have to be worried about getting blown up today,' but you don't because even hinting at it could get you bundled to the floor and handcuffed.

Eventually we reached the end of the line – thanks to Simon, we were the end of the line! – and loaded our bags onto the belts. A couple were over the limit but a quick reshuffle of heavy items to other bags and we were through, walking down sterile corridors, turning into the departure lounge, down the gangway, finding our seats, which is a much easier process without hand luggage to worry about. We were half an hour late taking off, and I suspected our bags had something to do with it. I wouldn't have wished them on any luggage-handler, not for the world. The rain continued to fall, pattering against the wings. We backed away from the terminal, taxiing into position behind four other jumbos, following them round as one by one they blasted off. And then it was our turn. I peeked out of the window as a dull, grey England shrunk before my very eyes, Kate squeezing my hand as we climbed – she hates take-offs and landings. I glance over, her eyes are squeezed shut. We're all facing our fears here, I have no idea how it's going to be in Australia. Two months of groundwork, sending blurb-sheets to the Australian media, posting on Internet forums, liaising with Sailability, trying and failing to find a vehicle sponsor. How far would it get us, this long-distance work? I wondered how Australia was going to receive us. Will they care, will they be intrigued, will they say 'you're mad' and turn their backs? I don't know. There are no guides to road conditions; nobody has skated across Australia before so there's nobody to ask. In the UK we seem to live in a culture where everyone gets their heads down just to get through the day: you don't talk to strangers on buses, in England. My life is my life and yours is yours, and that's the way it is. I'm hoping Australia will be different. I need them to sit up and take notice. There is an awful lot of the unknown ahead.

We had been given just fifty minutes transit in Singapore but the delays at Heathrow meant we missed our outgoing flight. The next plane to Perth was seven hours later but there are worse airports to be stuck in than Changi. On the roof there's a small botanical garden, a dense humidity instantly closing in as I stepped through the sliding door, droplets of water from the garden's sprinklers adding to the growing moisture on my forehead. Later, I found the team enjoying themselves in a sports bar and was struck by worry that they hadn't taken advantage of the surrounding crowds to raise awareness of BoardFree. I played pool with an Irish guy who was flying in the opposite direction as us, and he nodded at the team: 'If they were my lot I'd have them all over this airport handing leaflets out. You're not going to raise any money with them sat there, drinking.' After that I had a word with the team and then wandered off, bothered by everything. It was the middle of the night and we were all tired, it was wrong of me to expect the team to be on their game. Kate calmed me down by a pool full of giant goldfish and I ranted, releasing the tensions and doubts built up over two months of non-stop preparation, feelings that had nowhere to go now we were on our way.

*   *   *

On the small digital screen embedded into the seat in front, our plane is shown slowly edging its way down the screen, Australia looms into view, its northern edges appearing like mountainous horizons with sheer bulk beneath them. I have to laugh at the absurdity of the task ahead. I was an ant about to run a marathon, a full-blow human marathon; all the other ants would be running around carrying scraps of food, looking at me sideways and trying not to catch my eye because they know something doesn't quite add up. I wonder briefly whether I'm out of my depth. I'm not, I know I'm not. Far below the land seemed endless. I'd peer through the window, shake my head at the expanse of it all, return to my book, read seven chapters and then glance out again. It still looks the same.

It was raining in Perth, the skies tormented with greys and blacks prominent in the early light. Australia is so far away from home it had often seemed mythical, but the common persuasion that it was a hot, dry, red country instantly came crashing down around our ears. The weather was worse here than it had been in Heathrow. We were tossed around on the approach, horizontal streaks of wet marking the windows like new cracks in glass, a hard and turbulent touchdown and the team glance at each other grinning. We're here. It's five in the morning.

All our bags made it. They were thrown into the back of a maxicab, a spacious twelve-seater driven by John, who has lived Down Under for thirty years but still has a Scottish accent. 'There's a storm front coming,' he says as I stare at the torrents of water rushing along the roadside, 'it should be here by ten . . .'

Welcome to Australia.

*   *   *

A couple of weeks earlier Bev had emailed countless hotels and hostels in Perth, seeking support for our arrival. Lewis Stannard, manager of the Emperor's

Crown in Northbridge, a conveniently central district, had responded positively: 'I think it's great what you guys are doing and it would be an absolute pleasure to help you out.' Our maxicab pulled up outside the hotel, I spun around in my seat and beamed at the team, 'We're here peeps, let's get inside.' The delay in Singapore meant we had to get someone out of bed to book us in. The day was just beginning but we all decided to battle on to get our body clocks in sync with the seven hours we'd accumulated in mid-air. Half an hour of spaced-out staring in our rooms was followed with a short team meeting, and breakfast in the café next door, enormous rashers of Australian bacon raking us out of our stupor, dropping energy into our legs and thrusting us out the door and through nearby neighbourhoods in search of vans for sale.

The wide streets were lined with confusingly inconsistent architecture, western without pattern, making it increasingly difficult for us to come to terms with the fact that we were, indeed, in Australia. We filed in and out of travellers' hostels, emerging each time armed with several pieces of paper torn from notice boards, each showing a picture of a second-hand camper with its relevant details. Our priority was to find support vehicles and with six days until the launch of the journey there wasn't much time. By noon we were sodden, but the predicted storm hadn't arrived so laden with second-hand car adverts we walked the path alongside the Swan River to the Royal Perth Yacht Club, from where I was due to set off on Elsa in just a few days time. Rachael Cox, Sailability's chief in Western Australia – which we're to refer to from then on in the local abbreviation of, quite simply, WA – greeted us warmly and showed us around. She bears bad news, revealing that the weather isn't looking good for the launch, but she's buoyant at the fact that it's looking bright for tomorrow, a chance for the team to join Sailability's regular sailors on the river. Rachael had also taken receipt of a box of BoardFree leaflets, printed up by Clic Australia, our sunglass sponsor who had kindly offered to cover printing costs for us too. These leaflets were our weapons to inform.

The next morning we gathered in the hostel's television room for a team meeting. I outlined everything we needed to achieve by Sunday, now five days away, and assigned individuals with tasks. 'Kate, you get on with letting the media know about BoardFree. Becs and Bev, start sourcing some fundraising potential in Perth for the rest of this week. Danny, you help me find vehicles. Si and Dom, film everything.' I brought up the Singapore airport situation, stressing that from now on everyone needed to be on their game. 'Whatever our individual roles in this,' I said, 'our priority is BoardFree as a whole. Get a leaflet in the hands of everyone we meet, don't stop thinking about BoardFree, how we can promote it, how our actions affect its reputation, we have a long few months ahead of us but we've known that for a while, let's make the most of this guys.' Other jobs were dealt out; we needed cooking equipment, medical supplies, a bicycle so the team could take it in turns to ride with me, emergency flares, sleeping bags . . . the list went on.

Everyone quickly mucked in, some heading straight into town, others perching at computer terminals in the lobby. I emailed various contacts built up over the past few months, one of them *TNT* magazine who had suggested a potential vehicle sponsor. They got back to me quickly with details of the company and later a few of us went to their garage to look at campervans. Sponsorship hadn't been confirmed yet, but viewing vehicles started to give me an idea of what we were looking for and what budgets we were talking about should the sponsorship not come through. I was hoping to buy two vans out of my own pocket, and was crossing my fingers for some corporate support to lend a hand. It's Tuesday now; we leave on Sunday. Dom asks me when I'd start to panic about support vehicles. 'Thursday,' I told him and his new camera, 'I'll panic on Thursday if we don't have vehicles.'

We rushed around town, arranging mobile phone contracts and vehicle viewings, paying a cursory visit to the army surplus stores just across the railway track. Dom and I walked to King's Park and did an interview for the documentary, a sweeping vista behind me with the Swan River snaking gloriously east, the high rises in the central business district glistening in the sun, people milling around us in the Park, including a ranger who questioned what we were doing but let us be when we explained ourselves. 'You should really get permission to film here,' he said, 'but good luck anyway.' Dom asked me the predictable questions: What does it feel like to be in Australia? How are the Australians accepting BoardFree? In truth, two days into our stay in Perth it was too early to answer with any great substance, Perth was much like any western city and I didn't really feel like I was in Australia yet. The Australia the team and I were experiencing wasn't the country European backpackers experienced, nor the everyday bubble that Perth's residents lived in. We'd landed at a sprint and hadn't stopped running, certainly hadn't had the time to take in the city. It was, however, a comfortable place to exist. It's easy to understand why Perth defies its 'most isolated city in the world' label and attracts visitors from all over with its easy-going, lifestyle-driven atmosphere. We were all tired but running on adrenaline, and it was unfortunate that we weren't going to have much quality time in Perth before the push off on Sunday.

Our roles were made all the harder because until we had our own van we were forced to rely on public transport. The irony of being restricted in our viewings of vehicles because we didn't have a car to drive across town was thick in the air, but we had to be mindful of time and budgets, and vehicles that were twenty miles north up the coast were too far away. We didn't have half a day to waste. An English couple responded to an online advert Becki had placed, and kindly drove their Mazda campervan to our hotel. It was a beauty. Clean, spacious inside, well maintained. It even had a name, Bruce. I felt the excitement of knowing that finally just what we were looking for had driven right up to our front door and explained BoardFree to the couple. I told them that we were looking for two vehicles and were interested in Bruce, then asked if we could get back to them by Friday with an answer. They were enthusiastic, liking the idea that they could follow their old vehicle around on our website. At $A7,800 the price was a little heavy, but I chatted to the guy and made a deal: 'Obviously we need a couple of vehicles and we are still holding out for sponsors, but I'd really like to know if someone else makes an offer on Bruce,' I said, 'will you do that for me?'

'Of course mate, absolutely,' he said. We shook hands and Bruce drove away. I felt sure I'd see that van again; it settled my stomach instantly.

Kate was working wonders with the media, and as the week drew on the phone began to ring. On only our second morning a few of us wandered down to the river for a chat with Fleur Bainger from the ABC. She set the tone for the coverage ahead, starting my first Australian interview with the words, 'Dave I can't believe you're even considering this, why are you going to go across the Nullarbor . . . and further, on a skateboard?' Fleur was genuine and down to earth, even asking me to give her some tips on how to ride Elsa, but she was obviously intrigued not only by the basic logistics of a long-distance skateboard journey but also by the idea of a guy from Britain who had only just taken up skating, and was about to push into the outback with no prior experience of road trains or kangaroos.

The incredulity factor was always going to be a great way to encourage media coverage, but I was determined that BoardFree wasn't going to become a running joke in Australia. It was an easy target for a two-line factoid at the bottom of a newspaper page, but I knew deep down that the only way I could really alter the general perception of the journey was to get out there and actually do what I'd said I'd do. A day after the ABC report, which went all over Australia, more interest was coming in. 'You have to head down to the river again,' Kate told me, 'a photographer from the *West Australian* is going to meet you.' I duly did what I was told, skating up and down as the man snapped away. 'You really are going to try this, aren't you?' said the photographer rhetorically. 'Mate, I take my hat off, the Nullarbor's a big place.' On the way back to the hotel even the taxi driver had heard about the journey. He warned me about the road trains and advised that we get some sun cream. I was starting to get the gist, and was beginning to yearn for the days to go by so I could justify all of this media coverage. I hadn't done anything yet and everybody was talking about it. I felt almost guilty. Sunday couldn't come soon enough.

Well, Sunday couldn't arrive soon enough for me, but by Thursday I was beginning to think it was coming a little too quickly for the team to get everything sorted in time. A swell of panic was starting to rise; we still didn't have a van, let alone two. The auto company who had expressed an interest in sponsoring us had ignored my pleas for a quick resolution and after three days of waiting still hadn't been in touch. Pissed off and desperate I called the office in Sydney, where I finally reached the Marketing Manager. After a yo-yo session of calls the final answer was 'No, sorry we can't help you, good luck and goodbye.' I couldn't believe it: just up the road that same company had a vehicle hire office with five un-hired vans which would have been perfect. Determined not to wallow in disappointment I decided to call the owners of Bruce the Mazda. They hadn't been in touch so I assumed the van was there for the taking, even with the asking price being a bit above my budget. Time was short now, and we needed to get some wheels. With this is mind, and without a call from Bruce's owner to confirm he had found any other interest, I was ready to make him an offer. So I called the guy, and he told me they'd already received an offer and accepted it.

'But mate, you promised you'd let me know if that happened so I could make a counter-offer,' I said, trying to keep calm but failing miserably.

'Sorry mate,' he replied, 'I'd feel like I was going back on my word if I told this other bloke the deal was off.'

'All due respect, you went back on your word to me, why not do it again?'

'I'm sorry mate, I really am, but that's that.'

I hung up, unleashed a barrage of expletives into Dom's camera and then slumped backwards, sliding down the wall into a tuck position, exhausted from a long day and furious at being let down by someone I thought I could trust. If there's anything that gets my goat, it's being let down. It's the lack of honesty on their part, and the bad judge of character on mine. With less than two days until I was due to push off we still had no vans, a delay began to seem inevitable.

It wasn't all doom and gloom, though. Holly flew in from a holiday in New Zealand, all smiles, nice and tanned, camera in a hard case. The team was complete for the first time. Becs and Bev managed to piggyback a pool tournament in a local hostel and came back with a box of cash donations and countless stories about well-wishing Aussies. Simon had even managed to win the tournament with a sequence of ridiculously lucky shots. He threw his $A100 prize into the charity kitty and quite bizarrely won a bogey prize: an old racing bike. Bev was always in high spirits, putting her musical talents to good use and making us all laugh with her hand-didge – it's amazing what noises that girl can produce. Dan had come up trumps, successfully lining up mechanics to service our vehicles – for when we found them. Si had earlier started work on the first web video, a series of which I had asked him to edit to give the outside world a soap-opera style view into the world of BoardFree Australia. I sent out a charity appeal via my blog:

> *We all know the real hard work hasn't quite begun, but to date we've raised thousands, please help us go over the £5,000 mark by Sunday morning, it'll boost everyone here. We're a small bunch of people in a big city at one end of one gigantic country. In a few days we'll be a dot travelling east, keep watching that dot, people. Your support will get us through this, and will show that with a bit of effort dreams can come true.*

The growing interest in BoardFree was remarkable. Newspaper articles were being printed not just in Australia but in Turkey, Romania, Germany, the UK, South Africa, even Dubai! Tens of thousands of people were logging onto the website, which I kept updated as often as I could with diaries, photos and progress reports. Kate had ensured that media coverage was maximised and that a spontaneous idea cooked up in a Swansea bed sixteen months earlier had turned into a project that millions were hearing about. The seven of us were exhausted, halfway around the world from our homes, using very meagre resources to pull together a project that from the outside may have seemed lunacy, but to us was our lifeblood. The team was putting everything into BoardFree and I couldn't have been more proud of them, they're as much a part of this as I am. If they were feeling the pressure they hid it from me well.

* * *

Kate and I have commandeered Danny's mobile for the length of the project, and given it the predictable title of Media Phone. Its *Knight Rider* theme tune ringtone has become the soundtrack to BoardFree Australia, and it's ringing again. My eyes snap open and I roll over onto my side. The bedside clock says 04:11. Give me a break.

This is the third time we've been woken by a *very* early morning call, and as usual it's unexpected. I sit up, try to dig up some composure from somewhere, rub my eyes, and press the button. As I do all this, Kate is scrabbling around on her side of the bed, still looking for the phone. 'Hello?' I say blurrily. Kate stops wriggling when I talk.

'GOOD MORNING DAVE, MY NAME'S BRUCE!' boomed a horribly chirpy Australian voice. 'I'M CALLING FROM ABC RADIO QUEENSLAND AND WE'D LOVE TO GET YOU ON THE BREAKFAST SHOW IN A BIT MATE, WOULD THAT BE OK?'

I paused, trying to get my head around why anyone would be this happy at this time of the morning, and then I realised it's a few hours ahead on the other side of Australia. 'Erm, yeah mate, of course it's OK!' I said. Bruce must have noticed a bit of bewilderment in my voice as he followed up by asking where I was.

'I'm in Perth, mate,' I said gently, not wanting to sound too bitter.

'OH SHIT! I'm really sorry mate, we read about you in the *Sydney Daily Telegraph* and just assumed you were in Sydney. Man it must be really early in Perth!'

I glanced at the clock, 'Yeah mate, it's about quarter past four.'

'Jeez I'm really sorry again Dave, I'll let you get back to sleep. Would you mind if I called you up in an hour to get you on the show?'

'Not at all Bruce, speak to you then.'

'Good on you Dave, in an hour . . .'

I didn't get a chance to ask him why he was calling. Clearly it wasn't about my imminent Perth to Brisbane skateboard journey, otherwise he would have known I was in Perth, surely? By 9 a.m. I had done four live radio interviews, two in Queensland, one in Western Australia and one in the Northern Territory. Just as the last one, a ten-minute cross with ABC Darwin came to an end Paul Kane from the Getty Images Picture Agency turned up and drove Kate, Dom and I around Perth for a shoot. After skating through Kings Park and posing in central Perth beside some enormous bronze kangaroo statues, we finished up east of the river in a nature enclosure inhabited by a mob of real kangaroos, which we discovered sleeping in long grass. Paul squeezed some bread out of his pocket and handed it to me, 'Probably shouldn't be doing this,' he said, 'but it'll make a great shot.' Paul was a good guy, friendly and über-efficient, and I was impressed that we weren't driving aimlessly for inspiration. Everything was planned out; he knew where he wanted to go and what shots he wanted from each location. Shortly before the kangaroo finale he had got me hanging upside down on a playground monkey bar. 'This'll make a great Down Under shot,' he grinned as my head turned purple from strain and gravity.

The positive media attention was lifting moods all round. Iain 'Hopper' McTavish, the owner of the Emperor's Crown, had been openly unsure about my sanity upon hearing about BoardFree, telling us he had driven across the Nullarbor many times and wouldn't wish an endurance journey 'across there' on anyone. He was, however, keen to help out wherever he could, giving me the number of a friend of his who ran a second-hand vehicle business. 'George is a good guy,' said Hopper, 'he'll probably have something for you.' One phone call later and George was on his way, pulling up outside in a Toyota Hiace camper. The van was bare but spacious, and George was like an uncle you could trust, his complete unwillingness to sell it to us until he'd serviced the brakes was reassuring. He said he could build and fit a bunk bed in the back for barely more than the $A3,000 asking price, and by the time he had driven away I was convinced we had finally found a van. Two hours later, having discussed it with the team, I called George and left a message to confirm that we'd like to buy the Hiace, lightening the weight on one of my shoulders but knowing we still needed at least one more vehicle to house everyone. Simon had found out about a second-hand car market in Fremantle the next morning, and having exhausted every other apparent option in Perth, our laurels were firmly dependent on this sale turning up the right van.

Saturday morning. No *Knight Rider* theme tune to raise us, but the alarm is still set for fifteen minutes to seven. I switch it off quickly and pull myself out of bed. Kate stays under the covers and will be the only member of the team not to board a train to Fremantle this morning. She's shattered from five days of phone calls, emails and early morning interviews, which she doesn't conduct but still has to endure. Just one of the prices she has to pay for being my partner. I kiss her forehead, then her lips, and tell her to sleep well. She groans like a zombie and turns over. I love her blonde mop. I skate tomorrow and with the clock ticking and a large pile of dissatisfaction lying in a bin somewhere in the form of discarded campervan adverts, we're all excited and positive that the car market is going to find us our van. We scoff down a breakfast roll, wander to the station and read a copy of the *West Australian* on the platform. There I am with a big smile on page 42, pushing along beneath the headline DAVID AND ELSA TAKE TO THE ROAD FOR CHARITY. The article is well written but the journalist has referred to me as Welsh, which wins me much jibing from the team, and there's another slight error. I set off yesterday, apparently.

By the time we pull into Fremantle the skies have opened. This feels like our final option, a last chance for the god of campervans to redeem himself and help us out. We walk a kilometre to the car market, soaked to the skin but brimming with hope at what is around the corner. Which is, quite simply, a car park sat beyond a closed café named Captain Munchies. Old cars littered the tarmac, just one lone campervan in the middle of them, which unfortunately turns out to be the market's mobile office. Simon shrugs his sodden shoulders, and then points. There is another camper here, but it's a Shetland pony-like

Toyota, so small we couldn't see it past a normal car. I approach the office-van and the lady tells me they have a pop-top Toyota on the books, and that they'll call the vendor and get him to bring it down. Ten minutes later it appears and the owner, Tim, shows us around.

It's clean, seems to be in good condition. Well laid out interior, poky but big enough. Wardrobes, storage space, a sink and a canvas annexe attached to the upper outside of the van, which creates a good spaced awning for shade or sleeping purposes. My mind was working overtime: is this van big enough to be our second vehicle? Is this our last chance to get something half decent? We all squeezed into the van and I was vaguely concerned about the puddles pooling on the cushions when a white 4x4 pulled into the car park. I shake Tim's hand, thank him for showing us the van and promise to call him by 2 p.m. with a yes or a no. Then I lead the team over to the white jeep, a Holden Jackeroo. The owner, a round chap with a lot of facial hair, tapped me on the shoulder. 'It's two thousand five hundred and seventy dollars, priced to sell.' The Jackeroo ran on LPG, a much cheaper and more economical gas alternative than diesel or petrol, and it suddenly dawned on me that it would be perfect to drive along behind me on the road. Keeping myself to myself, I walked with the team to shelter from the pouring rain and revealed a cunning plan.

'Guys, why don't we buy three support vehicles? The Jackaroo, the campervan we've just seen this morning and the Toyota George brought round to the hotel last night?' My reasoning was that two small campervans weren't really big enough for eight people, their belongings and our kit. Plus, the uneconomical fuel usage of a campervan cranking along at 15kmph behind me didn't make much sense now that we'd seen an alternative option. So, with time knocking on the BoardFree door I put cash down for the Jackaroo. Devoid of a driver's licence, I had just bought my first car and then, not satisfied with that, I made two calls, one to George and another to Tim, and became the proud owner of a fleet of three vehicles in what must have been one of the most decisive two hours of my life. The disappointment of losing out on the Mazda a day earlier still plagued me a little, though, and I was very aware that although Tim and I made a verbal contract and that I would trust George enough to let him take Kate out for dinner, the two Toyota campers weren't settled until I'd handed over the cash in exchange for the keys.

The rest of the day was spent making final preparations. Kate was much better off for her lie-in and handed me the phone to talk to a man from SNTV, responsible for Australian contributions to the international sports show *Transworld Sport*. I had grown up with this programme, waking early on Saturday mornings to hear familiar male and female voices describe well-known and then quite unique sporting achievements. As my teens went on I realised that, much like my childhood dream of having a career in football, I was just as unlikely to have much success in any sporting arena, meaning *Transworld Sports* was always going to be a programme that I'd watch and enjoy, but never feature in. Now, all change. They wanted to join the journey near Melbourne for an interview to air on *Transworld*. I thanked him a little too eagerly and hung up, jubilant and not quite believing what was happening. That evening, stickering up Elsa and my helmet with Danny, I left him to it to complete my final interview of the day, an 11 p.m. round-the-world chat with BBC Radio Five Live. 'In twelve hours,' I told the journalist, 'I'm going to step onto a skateboard and head east into the desert.'

'Do you think you can make it?' asked the man.

'I wouldn't be here if I didn't,' I replied.

* * *

Bloody hell, it's time. I woke up on Sunday feeling completely exhausted, not the best condition to be in with a 6,000km journey ahead. We were due to return to the hotel following the first day's skate so didn't have to worry about clearing our rooms. Instead, I gave a couple of interviews, one of which was with national youth station Triple J, which I was reliably informed was to be 'cool'. I realised later Triple J was the Australian equivalent of the UK's BBC Radio One, quite a coup.

Board, helmet and other essentials gathered, we drove in the Jackaroo to the Royal Perth Yacht Club. Bev, Becs and Kate had been there for an hour or so already, preparing the send off and inflating balloons that filled the air already swirling with the delightful aroma of our first Aussie barbecue. *Knight Rider* blared again and I made my excuses and wandered over to the shores of the yacht club, chatting to Liza Kapelle from the Australian Associated Press, who would send this interview through the wires and all over the world. Liza asked me how I felt about the prospect of skating across the Nullarbor Plain and I gazed out over the Swan River, staring at the hazy Perth skyline across the water, and answered, 'I have a great team behind me and we're all raring to go. Besides, if I squint hard enough I can almost see Brisbane from here, Australia's not that big!' Shortly after the call ended, a dolphin broke water halfway down the marina, smoothly arching and diving three or four times before heading out into the wide reaches of the Swan, its dorsal fin waggling in a humorous goodbye.

Almost thirty people turn up for breakfast and I address them on invitation from Mark Fitzhardinge, the Yacht Club's Vice-Commodore. I commend the team individually and collectively, seven people who have put a hold on their lives to travel halfway across the world to follow a guy on a yellow skateboard. 'It's almost cult-like, isn't it,' I said, drawing laughs from the crowd, 'but in truth what is happening here is the honest pursuit of a dream. Initially it was mine, now it belongs to many others. I can't promise we'll make it, but we'll give it everything we've got, however big this country is.' After a plethora of typically sarcastic Australian heckles, which covered everything from road trains to my pale skin's obvious need for sun cream, I thanked Rachael Cox, who coordinated the launch, and then handed the microphone back to the Vice-Commodore, who kindly bid us good luck with 'fair and strong winds on your inspirational journey'. After the customary applause I hugged and thanked Rachael. She was in a wheelchair when we arrived here last Tuesday but today was walking stiffly with a leg brace and no crutches, lifting equipment and cooking food to raise more funds. Everything was carried out with a smile and a wonderful dry wit. There are people here who are blind, without limbs, sometimes both. Yet they are active and happy and capable of great achievement, and in many respects this is down to Sailability's work. Here, on the back of a bizarre pursuit of an unpredictable dream, myself and my team are in the presence of some remarkable people. I haven't spent much time at the Royal Perth Yacht Club, but the time I have spent here has left me humbled. I'm not sure that 6,000km is enough. But for now it's all we have, and we're going to give it our all.

A group of skaters, fifteen or so, arrive with bright eyes and a handshake each to offer me a tailwind of company for the first stretch. One of them, a young lad named Sam, tells me he sent me an email months ago and I twigged, remembering him telling me he wanted to skate with me. The skaters are joined by television cameras from ABC, Channel 7 and Channel 9, for whom I give interviews as more people spill out of a Vietnam Vets function next door. The team pose for the cameras and I break away, high fiving Danny and walking towards Kate. We share one final kiss before the off, nobody else mattering for an instant. I walk up the pontoon, posing for the last press shots in the calm before the storm, colourful pink and yellow sails behind me as the Access Dinghies used by Sailability bob in salute.

A song bubbles up from a section of the crowd as I put Elsa down, I can't make out the tune but I see people swaying from side to side and the atmosphere swells with anticipation. I am holding Dan's minicam, the one that joined me between John o'Groats and Land's End, and speak into it, noticing at the same time that Elsa is the wrong way round. Turning her with my feet I begin the launch speech, a stream of unconnected sentences: 'I'm about to skateboard to Brisbane. Here's everybody who's with us. The weather's lovely. I'm going to try my best not to fall off in the first ten metres. I'm quite tired already.' Then I pause, taking five seconds to stop and think. Breathe heavily. My own time, the last seconds I have before this journey begins. Before it all changes again, even more so than since last March when I stepped onto Uhuru, my first longboard. Fifteen months of skating is all I have under my belt, and now this. Well, there's no time like the present, let's do it.

'Let's go to Brisbane.' I push off, negotiating the downhill run from the pontoon, carving around the wall at the bottom and setting off up the drive as the scrape of fifteen sets of wheels begins behind me, a feast of reflective jackets in hot pursuit. The cheers fade as I roll away, joining the cycle path that will take me along the banks of the Swan River and around the central business district, telling a group of passing men that I'm heading to Brisbane and receiving the instant response, 'Good on ya mate!' Danny joins me on the bicycle Simon won the other night; honks from passing cars confirm that the day's media attention has done its job. The TV cameras are positioned along the pathway, grabbing some final shots before the rush to edit in time for the evening news, but I'm already focused on the task in hand, getting to the end of the day. Before handing the minicam back to one of the support vehicles I have one more thing to say, 'I'm about to skate across Australia, why didn't anyone tell me how big this place is?!'

The skaters tail off after a couple of kilometres, finally leaving just Dan and I to head east, where we were met by Paul from Getty Images. He had been present at the launch but wanted to get a different shoot with the looming backdrop of the Swan Bell Tower. The yacht club was only three kilometres or so downriver; it was time to make some ground. I had earlier signed paperwork for the Toyota pop-top we found in Fremantle and Becki had happily taken control of the wheel, immediately naming the van Kylie. The Jackaroo, which Dom had inexplicably named Cheech due to the number plate starting with 1CHH, was also around, both vehicles driving ahead and parking up where suitable until I passed. Beyond the WACA, Perth's famous cricket ground, the riverside cycle path began to meander, crossing the river on a causeway and then only occasionally hugging the southern bank. Dan and I remained on the path, at one point not having a clue where we were going but finally meeting up with the vehicles as the early stages of the Great Eastern Highway trickled through suburbia. Dom took over on the bike, to be replaced by Kate for the final stages of the day as I skated past industrial stores with wide front yards stocked full of brand new tractors, lawn mowers and golf buggies. Finally, four staggered hours after I pushed off from the Royal Perth

Yacht Club to begin BoardFree Australia, the first day was over. Thirty kilometres on Elsa's new wheels had taken me to the Perth suburb of Midland where the team, left alone now by all outside parties, hugged as a group in recognition of a very good day. Becs and Bev had managed to raise several hundred dollars at the launch party and three cash donations on the road had been gratefully received. 'Let's head home,' I said cheerily, jumping into the passenger seat of Cheech the Jackaroo. We got going and had been on the move for barely a minute when Danny pulled into a shopping centre car park,

'We've got a problem, looks like it's overheating,' he said, the engine squealing like a stuck pig. The temperature gauge had hit the ceiling and smoke was rising from the bonnet outside. Fluid leaked onto the concrete below. I was flummoxed; yet again the first day of a BoardFree journey had been struck by bad mechanical luck. Dom couldn't believe his good fortune, eagerly filming every bit of the drama. He stayed behind with Dan as the rest of us returned to Perth in Kylie, flustered by the turn of events, red dollar signs in our eyes.

We had found an angel in George, the mechanic who was selling us our second Toyota. He took the news of the breakdown in his stride and quickly peeked around Kylie. 'You've got a good van here,' he said, nodding, 'a good buy.' Becki took control, sending me back to the hotel to rest as she and George drove back to Midland to tow the Jackaroo. If anyone could fix it, George could. Three excellent evening news reports on the launch of BoardFree Australia eradicated our disappointment in the breakdown, the ABC piece going out all over Australia. It'll be several months until we actually get there, but knowing that people on the east coast were already aware of the journey was an enormous boost to the team's spirits. Far away from home, we certainly didn't feel alone. Later, Becki, Dom and Dan returned having left the Jackaroo with George. They had bought a cheesecake to soften the blow of the breakdown, and we gobbled it down for pudding.

Because of the breakdown, the lateness of our acquisition of vehicles and the subsequent need for more preparation time, I decided we needed three days more in Perth before moving on. It was frustrating staying put having had such a good start but it wasn't wise to continue without being ready. Australia isn't a country that takes pity on foolhardiness. We were all very aware that after two weeks of skating we would be heading into the outback, the dry and empty Nullarbor Plain taking on an added significance in radio interviews, as did another challenge which had to be overcome first. During an early morning show with Perth's 6PR radio station, the presenters brought up a subject that had been raised by a few Perthites the previous week. After a quick chat about the launch they said, 'So the first thing you encounter in the next hour or two is the Greenmount Hill, good luck Dave!'

'Ha!' I replied, 'I've been told about that one.'

'You haven't actually surveyed the route you'll be going on?' the second presenter asked, incredulous.

'Not so much actually,' I said, which drew a little snigger from the studio. I ignored that and continued with the explanation. 'It's a bit of a tricky thing you know, once your body is used to these endurance events then it becomes a mental battle, and if you know too much about your route then it makes it a little bit harder.'

'So you've given up work until 2010 to do this?' These guys weren't having any of it.

'I'm aiming to get in by New Year actually guys, so just four and a half months.'

'No way, that'd be an almighty effort. How strong is your groin?'

'It's pretty strong!' I said, trying not to let the conversation drop into crudeness. 'I'm feeling fit, and warmed up for this with a little one and a half thousand kilometre trip from the north of Britain to the south of Britain so I'm still feeling good from that one. I'm ready to go.'

'Good on ya mate,' they said, winding up the interview. 'Good luck, keep skating. Dave Cornthwaite, I don't like his chances of doing that . . .'

The Australian leaning towards over-exaggeration was magnified by the fact that everyone commenting on the journey, especially where topography was concerned, hadn't actually travelled anywhere on a skateboard and therefore didn't know how easy – or hard – it really was. Psychologically though, the constant jibes about Greenmount Hill were shoving questions into my mind and I couldn't help wondering what these people knew that I didn't.

However uncertain people were about my chances of success, word was getting around about the 'pommie who wants to skate across the Nullarbor'. On a shopping trip into town I crossed a road without waiting for the green man, only to be stopped by two policemen. 'Come here, Dave,' one of them beckoned to me, much to my astonishment. He was a right jobsworth, threatening me with a $A200 fine if he caught me doing the same again. As he spoke, several other people were doing just as I had done right behind his back, but I wasn't getting anywhere with this guy. 'You can go now,' he told me, his partner chuckling next to him, 'and don't think you'll be making much ground on a skateboard, either,' he finished, nodding at Elsa. There had been plenty of piss-taking since we landed in Australia, sure, but this guy was plain rude. His uniform didn't put me at ease either. I'd done all I could do to gain permission to skate on the road from the State police forces but had received no reply to my attempts at contact. On my list of things to do that day was 'Visit Police Station', but after that meeting at the corner of Barrack and Wellington I decided against it, hoping that any trouble with the authorities would just be extra drama for the documentary rather than the end of the journey. After all, it was just as likely that no reply meant that they had no problem with the venture, rather than the fact that they hadn't got around to telling me it wasn't possible.

Some of the team took their mind off the stresses of preparation with an afternoon off at the kangaroo sanctuary where I had posed for Paul Kane the previous week. Then, gravity starting to tug at our stomachs, we received an invite from some of Simon's relatives who ran an award-winning Thai restaurant in northern Perth, Saowanee's Place. Robert and Saowanee herself put on a marvellous dinner, the other diners looking over now and then as word got around what we were doing.

The last minute jobs were pulled together on Tuesday and Wednesday. Danny and I went hardware shopping, piling storage boxes and tools into the third van, which we'd named George after the mechanic who had sold it to us and was overhauling the other two vehicles. Becki was overseeing the final vehicle checks at George's yard, relaying to me the final costs and confirming that Cheech's problems on launch day had been resolved. A crate of beer found its way into Lewis Stannard's arms, who as the Emperor's Crown's manager had done all he could to make our stay in Perth as easy as possible. The to-do list was diminishing at last, and I placed a call to my cousin Kate in Sydney to let her know we were just a few hours away from departure. She told me she had been listening to the radio coverage. 'It's everywhere Dave, what an amazing job! A Sydney show even called *me* up earlier and I told them that it would take a lot for you not to make it, but that Granddad thinks you're barmy!' She also told me how a Sydney-based Sailability meeting had gone, relaying disappointing news that while most of the city's representatives were keen to support us one man, who was in charge of one of the city's northern clubs, had openly said that he didn't know why the journey was being discussed. 'He just stood there and said there was no point in it because there was no chance that anyone could skateboard across Australia,' Kate fumed. 'I was fucking mad, Dave, I put him in his place by saying that when you did finally reach Sydney then BoardFree would have nothing to do whatsoever with his club. I'm ashamed that some people in this organisation think like that, it's unbelievable!' I chuckled, knowing that my cousin was capable of giving someone a good telling-off.

'I guess he can just add himself to the list,' I told her, 'I've got quite a few people to prove wrong at the moment. Thanks so much for your support Cuz, I'll see you in a few months.'

The next morning final items were packed into the vehicles, now newly liveried with BoardFree graphics. I was dismayed to hear some bitching in the air; my room was directly above the car park to the rear of the building. Two mornings prior I had called a team meeting and asked whether everyone was satisfied with the way things were progressing. 'We've got two days left, if we need to buy anything else then this is the time to suggest it,' I had said. Everybody was fine, there were no suggestions. And yet on the final morning I heard Becki down below cursing me, telling everyone how stupid I was not to have bought more storage boxes, that I never listened, that I'd really fucked up. My blood boiling, I stayed in my room until I'd calmed down, and then went down to the cars and called everyone around. They stood in a semi-circle, waiting.

'Listen,' I said. 'I've got the misfortune of having a hotel room right up there,' I pointed skywards. 'This morning I've heard some things I really didn't need to hear. I've tried not to be too strict so far but I'm going to make a rule now. From this minute on there will be no more bitching, no more backstabbing, no more slagging anyone off behind their backs. It's poison and we have enough to worry about without dealing with issues in the wrong way. In future, if there is a problem, deal with it openly. Come to me if something needs to be done. We've had long enough to sort out everything we need to leave Perth comfortably, there is absolutely no excuse for anyone to be complaining now.' The rhythm of my message was broken halfway through by the *Knight Rider* ringtone. Kate answered the phone and started to hop up and down in excitement. 'What? What is it?' I whispered as everyone looked on, intrigued. I held out my hand, wanting to speak to whoever was on the other end, but didn't get a chance. Kate put the phone back in her bag.

'That was the British High Commission in Canberra,' she said. 'They want to sponsor our media calls.' It was good news that provided some relief from the disharmony earlier, but I wondered if Becki would have the heart to come up to me afterwards and apologise. She didn't.

Shortly after noon, I finished my third radio interview of the day to find that we were ready to go. One by one Cheech, Kylie and George, looking the part as a convoy of support vehicles, squeezed through the tunnel beside the hotel, pulled out onto Stirling Street, then turned right and made their way back to Midland.

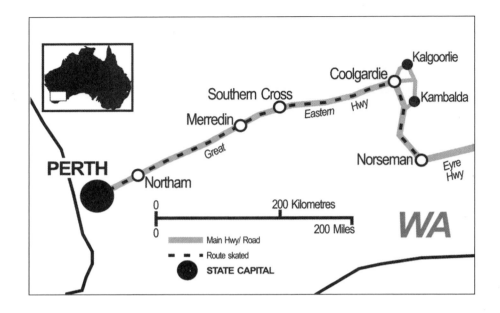

16 The Great Eastern Highway

24 August – 9 September 2006

Western Australia is enormous. Covering an area of 2.5 million square kilometres, the equivalent of continental Europe, it sits proud as the largest of Australia's eight states and territories. If you could turn Britain on its side and lay it down over Western Australia, Land's End to John o'Groats would barely take you three-quarters of the way from the west coast to the state's eastern border. It would have been folly of me to think in those terms when I placed Elsa on the ground with her nose to the east in Midland. As the team came together in a circle at the side of the road we formed a chain of arms and shoulders, a brace of comfort that we were facing the task ahead together. When I broke our circle with the words 'Let's go to Brisbane' I actually meant 'Let's go to The Lakes', because The Lakes, 47km further on along the Great Eastern Highway from Midland, was my end-of-day target. For the remainder of the journey I would wake up each morning with only one major milestone on my mind, my destination for that day. Of course, the journey would be dominated by talk of the larger goals; of the next state border, of the next city, of the east coast and, of course, of Brisbane. But had I pushed off from the Royal Perth Yacht Club on 20 August 2006 and thought hard about skating the full six thousand kilometres I wouldn't have made it to the end of the club's drive. This journey was going to be a mental battle and I was prepared to fight Australia with my mind as well as with my feet and my board. As I pushed through the final layers of suburbia workers rushed out from fast food restaurants and other stores to wave me on; theirs was another small contribution to the BoardFree Australia jigsaw that now had nothing to do but start assembling itself bit by bit.

After all of the talk Greenmount Hill wasn't much of a problem at all. The steep gradient and the passing of dauntingly large trucks were superseded by a smooth road surface and a good dose of natural adrenaline. I was on my way and so was Danny, who had opted to ride up the hill on the bike. Each time a police car overtook us or I saw luminous jackets up ahead my heart started beating ten to the dozen, paranoid about being called to the side of the road and having the journey stopped in its tracks. Each time though, the occupants of the police cars waved in appreciation, and the luminous jackets belonged to workmen who had their cameras ready to snap pictures of the guy who was going to skate across the Nullarbor. It struck me, as I waved in delight at the lenses of the workmen and of other passing motorists, that BoardFree Australia was becoming a national event of sorts. Halfway up Greenmount we pulled over for an interview and my feelings were corroborated by Lucy Carne from Queensland's *Sunday Mail*. 'So Dave, how does it feel to be Australia's man of the moment?' she asked, and I replied, quite honestly, that I didn't know I was, but it felt good to hear it all the same! I chatted to Lucy for ten minutes, told her I'd see her in Brisbane, and took another call from Triple J radio.

'Davey, how's it going?' asked Robbie Buck, the presenter of the Top Shelf afternoon show. 'You're on the way now man! Hold on, we're on in ten . . .'

I wondered whether the noise of the traffic outside would hinder the conversation or add some character, I was always conscious that interviews should be as professional as possible and the team were still learning to ensure quiet when I was live on air. Kate opened my door and I frantically gestured that the interview was about to start. The door slammed, and Robbie went into radio mode: 'Well, regular listeners will know by now that there's a pommie guy out there who has taken on one hell of a challenge. Dave Cornthwaite is in Perth, in fact, he's just outside of Perth, and he's slowly making his way towards the east coast . . . you're not going to believe this . . . on a skateboard.'

Ten minutes later I was back on the road, polishing off Greenmount Hill and finding my rhythm, each push taking me two or three metres on the glassy surface. Elsa was running well as intermittent honks of support from passing motorists added to my energy, although the horn of one passing truck was so loud it scared the shit out of me and caused me to stumble! As the hill levelled out I looked back to see the Perth skyline far behind through a gap in the trees. I bade it a silent farewell, and turned towards the job in hand.

By mid-afternoon the traffic had calmed and the verges had turned to red dust; finally after ten days holed up in the concrete jungle I felt like I was in Australia. It was a hot day, the sun bouncing off the bitumen causing me to sweat more fluids than I could take onboard. At Mundaring we pulled over for a cold drink, instantly provoking interest from passers-by. A family offered their congratulations despite the fact I was only 50km from central Perth. I chatted to an old lady as a man from a nearby shop donated a crate of Coca-Cola to the expedition, and before we moved on a moustached man appeared as if from nowhere and right there and then on the pavement proceeded to erect a pop-up tent, of which he was the inventor, he told us. Deconstructing it almost as quickly as it had formed, he said it was ours and handed the bag to Danny before hurrying off down the road.

Mundaring is the birthplace of the Golden Pipeline, which carries water from the outskirts of Perth 530km into the desert, supplying the goldfields around Kalgoorlie. The Goldfields Water Supply Scheme was the brainchild of Charles Yelverton O'Connor, an Irish engineer who was subjected to much derision and criticism by the Western Australia Parliament and press who thought the pipeline was beyond completion, not to mention a large waste of money. As a direct result the beleaguered O'Connor committed suicide in March 1902, just ten months before the first water successfully pumped through the pipe. Still thought to be the world's longest water main, the Golden Pipeline was to become a regular feature of my first ten days on the road, running alongside the Great Eastern Highway like a giant peaceful snake.

In the early evening I rolled across the Highway and into The Lakes Roadhouse, the first outback petrol station we'd encounter on the journey. The manager of the roadhouse came out to welcome us, filled our gas canisters and refused to accept payment. We made camp behind the petrol pumps, tried Kylie's awning out for size and showered in some ramshackle units, which were filled with bugs and other creepy crawlies. I had to scrub my face doubly hard, having been layered in yellow and green zinc stick by Bev before setting off from Midland. By the time I emerged from the shower it was dark, and I joined the rest of the team in the Roadhouse café, my eyes fixed on a BP map of Australia stuck on the wall. We were barely a finger's width away from Perth, the map was over a metre wide.

* * *

The next morning most of the team stayed behind to clean up. I used this as an incentive to push on, trying to get as far as I could before they caught up. I'd skated over 15km by the time Kylie and George passed, horns honking and white arms waving out of windows. I was filled with an enormous sense of pride seeing the vans drive past, yellow and black logos spread over white paintwork, the vehicles as much a part of the team now as the humans within them. An elderly couple asked Elsa and me to pose for a picture behind their caravan, which was crawling with bumper stickers. The couple told me they were on their way home to Melbourne, I suggested they might just beat me there.

The surface changed from rough to smooth but progress was steady. Beyond the six-foot-wide red dust verges trees formed a permanent avenue for the highway, coloured in the dull greens that typify a hot, dry environment. Overhead the sky was grey, reminding me that we were still in the Australian winter and that rain wasn't out of the question despite the mid-twenties temperature. Paul Kane drove out from Perth for one last photo shoot before we moved out of his range. 'I can't believe how much you fly on that thing,' he said, 'I didn't think you'd be this far along by now, I'm starting to see how this journey might be possible.'

I reached the end-of-day target by 2 p.m. Northam, 100km along the Great Eastern Highway from the Perth outskirts, is the largest town in the Avon valley region and would be the biggest settlement we'd see for over a week. Becki and Bev had driven ahead and had done a fantastic job, organising free accommodation at the Avon Bridge Hotel and inviting children from the local school to join me in a skate through town. Several skateboard signings and a local radio interview later I was using the hotel manager's laptop to update the website, when a newspaper article published in Wales hit a nerve: Running under the headline, *Are Silly Stunts Pointless?* the article began with this paragraph:

Dave Cornthwaite, from Swansea, has begun a 4,000-mile journey across Australia on a skateboard. Success would beat the skateboard distance record by over 1,000 miles. But does anyone really care about that record attempt or any of the other endurance and daredevil feats that are guaranteed to hit the headlines? Have we reached the point where silly stunts have become pointless? YES – says Guy Pargeter, journalist, Taliesin Communications, Ceredigion.

Pargeter went on to write that I was 'yet another sad, self-publicising egotist – drawing attention to himself with an endurance-style stunt which the media has fallen for.' He mentioned journeys by Hillary, Scott, Drake and MacArthur, suggesting that while they may have loved the limelight at least they made their names doing something worthwhile. 'Skateboarding across Australia?' wrote Pargeter, 'Do we care? . . . What we need are people with real talent and ability to get us off our bums and realise that we can each be a hero in our own way. Live our own lives, instead of living them through someone else's.'

Another journalist had been allowed the opportunity to counter Mr Pargeter's claims but hadn't once mentioned BoardFree. There was a great difference between an individual posting a personal opinion on the BoardFree website and a national newspaper actually printing such an article. Deeply hurt by the insinuations and frustrated at the potential damage the journalist's article could have on BoardFree, I rattled off a furious email to the editorial board:

Dear Western Mail,

I'm the chap who is currently skateboarding across Australia and have just come across Guy Pargeter's journalism in the article 'Are Silly Stunts Pointless?' Guy, who I have never met and who has never in any way attempted to contact me with regards to this project, seems very derogatory about a project he clearly knows very little about.

I appreciate that there are a feast of 'pointless' world record attempts occurring every day, but for Mr Pargeter to suggest that skating 6,000 kilometres across one of the largest islands in the world is an endurance-STYLE event is grossly misinformed. I am crossing the country in this way to raise money for three children's charities and not to create a flood of self-indulgent media attention. Your printing of Mr Pargeter's unbalanced views (and they were unbalanced, the counter-argument didn't even touch the subject of this journey while Mr Pargeter had plenty of personal remarks printed) is a shame, and I would appreciate the chance to respond to the article in print in the Western Mail.

Many newspapers, radio stations and television networks including Sky, CNN, ABC, BBC Television and Radio 4 and Five Live have covered this story because of the true nature of this expedition. It is an endurance event – and a bloody tough one at that – designed to create attention for charities that really need some support. I echo Mr Pargeter's viewpoint that the general public should stop watching other people and start living their own lives, because it is exactly how I felt last year when I decided to carry out this journey. To date several hundred people have started skating or longboarding because of my journeys and their lives are better for it, or so they tell me. Several groups of people have even decided that the BoardFree cause is so worthwhile that they themselves are now preparing for long skate journeys.

I suggest Mr Pargeter follows his own advice and travels out to Australia to witness at first hand exactly how silly this 'stunt' is, I am quite sure that he would offer an apology when he sees a combination of blisters, several thousand pounds raised for three worthwhile charities and the culmination of 16 months of planning which has resulted in a nation of 20 million people get behind this journey so much that the major newspapers radio and TV stations are calling us every day to follow our progress.

A quirky and unique idea skateboarding across Australia may be, but let me tell you it is not easy, and reading Mr Pargeter's comments after skating 100km in the last two days is actually quite laughable.

I look forward to your response,
Dave Cornthwaite

The article had been in a position to be read by tens of thousands of people, many of whom would have had their first taste of BoardFree through those very words. What was the likelihood that any of them would donate after that bitter mouthful? I felt it was a slur on myself and most importantly on my team, who had chosen to give up life as they knew it to make BoardFree a success. It was yet another case of the people we couldn't win over not being able to appreciate the sheer effort that was going into the project. I heard later that the *Western Mail* had printed letters of complaint about the article as well as several supportive articles about the journey.

*   *   *

I was warned about a few things by knowing locals in Perth. 'Don't end up on a Road Train bull bar,' they told me, and straightaway I decided to heed the advice. The road trains joined the highway not far beyond Northam, the Road Train Assembly Point ominously signposted as we approached. The trucks so far had been huge, some carrying enormous loads such as yachts and construction machinery. The prospect of vehicles over twice the size of these was terrifying but by the time we passed the Assembly Point we had adopted a sure fire solution to dealing with them. Whether Becki or Bev were behind us and communicated via the radio, or the looming bulk of a Road Train began to fill Cheech's rear-view mirror, a single honk of the horn would alert me to the danger. Fluidly, then, I'd pull off the road, as would Cheech, and we'd wave as the juggernaut flew by. These trucks are enormous, sometimes reaching 45 metres in length and stopping for no one, their sheer size creates a draft that sucks me along the hard shoulder – it's like being blasted in a wind tunnel for five seconds. Reassuringly though, almost all of them raise a thumb as they pass, pull down on their horn or show a palm of appreciation – making friends with the largest beasts around is the first rule of survival. Their impact on the highway is clear to a skateboarder who yearns for a smooth surface. The vehicle tracks became darker and more trodden, the weight of the vehicles combines with the heat and the older the road the smoother the tyre tracks were.

My pace quickened. It's only Day 4 and the team is developing a pattern. Dan and Kate and a cameraman join me on the road early as the rest of the team up-camp, shop for food if possible, edit videos and organise images before jumping in the vans to give chase. When they reach us someone grabs the bicycle and joins me on the road, the difference company makes to me is invaluable. I can't thank Si enough for winning the bike in Perth! It's Danny's birthday today. Becki presented him with presents and a chocolate muffin bearing a single candle as we gathered at the side of the road. Twenty-four today – probably one of the most bizarre birthdays Dan will experience – he unwrapped water pistols and a bendy straw that played Happy Birthday when he sucked through it. Then, satisfied at his birthday in the Bush, he jumped on the bike and joined me on the road for 40km. For most of the way he had his iPod in, listening to Ricky Gervais podcasts and giggling to himself. He's a good mate, Dan is, he keeps me going.

The people in Perth had more warnings. 'Boredom,' they said, 'it's very boring out there.' But actually, it isn't that tedious. Even as the roads became longer and straighter and there becomes less to focus on, the only monotony is the swinging of my right leg. Every little change in the road surface is an event. Each time the Golden Pipeline gets a little larger or smaller or splits into two. Perspectives change when a bright green parrot flies across the road or we pass a field containing hundreds of stock-still, staring sheep, their wide eyes seemingly addicted to movement or my luminous jacket. Something happens every minute and the little things keep us going, I think it's probably harder for drivers to keep their concentration. By lunchtime on the fourth day we are more than 150km east of Perth. A small blister sits atop of a toe, but it's the only sign of damage so far. Even this far out people have read about the journey or seen us on television: a couple of families donate and ask for autographs as we munch peanut butter sandwiches outside Meckering Roadhouse. I never call for a lunch stop before I've skated at least half of the day's projected distance. Stopping for a prolonged length of time leaves me no option but to think about how much road remains that day and no matter what the gradient, it always feels easier during the second half, as though it is virtually downhill. Across the road from our lunch table there is a building that excites Holly, a photography museum shaped like a giant camera. It's the first of Australia's Big Things we've seen. The country is famous for the oversize statues and items, which form part of its road-trip folklore; enormous bananas, crayfish and galahs are just a few of the giants to come.

I pushed into Cunderdin before 4 p.m., completing the longest day yet. Becs, Bev and Si had travelled ahead and had a fine reward for the 62km skated: we had been granted permission to spend the night in a vehicle museum. The curator, a sprightly sixty-something named Chum, showed us around, explaining snapshots of local history and inviting us to sit in the Earthquake House. It was there, shaking around and gripping tightly to my bench, that I realised we'd stopped for lunch earlier directly above the epicentre of Western Australia's most devastating quake. The Meckering earthquake of 1968 was also the world's second biggest quake to occur away from a plate boundary, but the low population numbers meant that amazingly only twenty people were injured, with no deaths recorded.

Danny's birthday meal was a delicious sweet and sour rice dish concocted by Bev and Becs on our neat expedition gas stove. We washed it down with a celebratory drink across the road and railway track in a typical pub-cum-betting shop, the girls doing their thing with collection buckets dangling and leaflets finding their way onto each table. Proud of everyone and delighted at the 179km skated so far, I wandered back to the vehicle museum and snuggled up with Kate in between old train carriages and antique cars, listening for a while to the bumps and creaks up in the museum's corrugated iron roof, wondering what surprises the next day had in store for us.

'You know what I find most bizarre?' Kate had said, staring around the museum foyer before lights out. 'It's that this doesn't strike me as bizarre. It's something I've come to realise is synonymous with BoardFree. Randomness, complete and utter randomness!'

* * *

The land levelled out, the countryside visibly changing with tree-cover receding and green fields starting to dot with red spreads of sand. The first 8km out of Cunderdin were flat and straight and after eagerly pushing towards what was apparently a sizeable hill for ten minutes I realised the heat haze was playing tricks with me and although it was indeed a hill, it wasn't big enough to warrant a mention on any other day. The team enjoyed a long brunch on green lawns in a small homestead called Tammin, population 450, area 1,800km². The day's final 25km were slowed by an ever-increasing headwind – cause for concern as this wind has been growing in the last two days and we don't plan on changing direction any time soon – but flocks of galahs and enormous kilometre-long trains following the India-Pacific track a kilometre north of the highway provided enough motivation to see us roll into Kellerberrin by the middle of the afternoon.

Holly had been a revelation. Arriving into Perth later than the rest of us she had slotted straight in, helping to prepare meals and making curtains for the vans in addition to her photography role. Once on the road she was all smiles, cheering me on as I passed by, her camera clicking away. At the end of each day she took responsibility for sorting the beds in George so I could rest straightaway if needed. She had matured a great deal since the UK journey and had proved to me that the concerns previously discussed were in the past. It was a pleasure to have her around. Bev and Becs had found a nice little campsite in Kellerberrin with unequivocally clean toilets and a power supply, and we settled down to a relaxing afternoon, Kate massaging my calves and Becs getting straight on with mixing up a fine tuna pasta for dinner.

At 6 p.m. the air filled with screams and wails. I had been searching around George for a beanie hat to combat the chill that comes with country nights, when it began. I cocked an ear, wondering if a child had hurt itself, trying to determine where the noise was coming from. Stepping back from the van I saw Holly 25 metres away from camp, rocking backwards and forwards cross-legged in the sand with one hand to her mouth. At first I thought she'd been bitten by something but then saw she had a phone to her ear. 'Shit.' Nothing comes close to the sound of death. I ran to her, Becs and Bev and Kate did the same. We held her and hugged her as she cried and spoke to her father. Kate fetched tissues and a custard cream, a hoodie to keep Holls warm. Her Granddad had passed away unexpectedly, and all we could do was be there for her. For the first time the team became a family, everyone emerged to let her know we were there, doing what little we could to make things easier.

*   *   *

By morning Holly had made a decision: 'I'm going to stay, he wouldn't have wanted me to miss out on any of this,' she said, determined.

'Just so you know,' I told her, 'if you change your mind we're right behind you.' There was no moping, no histrionics, just the actions of maturity. Holly plugged in her earphones and straddled the team bike, cycling just behind me for 20km or so. At one point I beckoned her up front and pushed along beside her, asking how she was doing.

'I'm OK,' she said smiling. 'It's amazing being out here, thanks so much for giving us this opportunity.' I reached out and squeezed her hand as we both rolled along. I was delighted she'd decided not to go home and was so proud of her for dealing with things as she had done.

The headwind I'd skated into since Midland was slowly bending around and for most of the day it was coming in at an angle against my left shoulder. Typically, local knowledge from all corners had told me I'd be likely to have headwinds, tailwinds, side winds and no wind as a regular companion as I approached and crossed the Nullarbor, but research suggested that the prevailing winds at that time of year should be more of a help than a hindrance. As yet I hadn't seen any proof of this but I kept my hopes up as the wind direction changed, the headwind so far had slowed me by up to 4kmph and was ruddying my cheeks.

As the roads stretched east the sun beat down heavily. After lunch I pulled on a luminous peaked hood to protect my fair scalp and continued pushing like a beacon on a skateboard. Small blisters were beginning to form beneath my right toes and began to worry me; there was no way I could allow them to proliferate as they had during BFUK.

As a rule of thumb the population density in Western Australia decreases the further you travel from Perth, and with only one road serving each settlement on our route stories of similar journeys to ours became more commonplace. We were told about people driving golf buggies and tractors, countless cyclists, Japanese men running, and there was even a man in recent myth who had pushed a shopping trolley across the desert. Even though we were still on the Great Eastern Highway the road wasn't leading anywhere but into the outback and I thought of these tales as Legends of the Nullarbor. Another of these legends had been mentioned to us by a few people as we made our way on. 'You'll be seeing The Walking Man soon' we were told. And sure enough, just two kilometres before a town called Merredin I reached him. Jeff Hunston is a Canadian man on a mission. Pushing his belongings on a three-wheeled chariot in front of him, Jeff is slowly inching his way across Australia, taking time away from his family and job back home to walk across the country in sections. This is Jeff's second stint Down Under and having walked between Fremantle and Merredin so far, today's wander is his last for a while. We just caught him! Jeff presented me with a small medal he had made in the Perth mint; he told me it was for people he met who showed an extraordinary kindness or were in themselves extraordinary. And then he made a $A50 donation to BoardFree. He was a wonderful character, full of tales of the road and a natural born adventurer. It's amazing to think that somewhere in the middle of Western Australia a walking man can meet a skating man, talk for a while and then bid each other farewell and continue in the same direction at different speeds. If people have nothing else, they have journeys to embark on.

* * *

We stay in Merredin for two nights, a decision mainly forced by the small blisters on my right foot and a growing tenderness of the weak skin on my heel. The time is used well, the team sorting out the vehicles while I hide away in an Internet café updating the website and writing emails in an attempt to boost fundraising totals. A contact from Perth had arranged for the Western Australian Water Company to drop some bottles off for us, which was brilliant news; it would keep us going across the Nullarbor. There'd been some tension in camp, partly due to frustration about not making more ground and partly due to disagreements about where certain items of kit belonged. Unsurprisingly in close-knit environments like ours there will always be individual markings of territory but the campsite pets, Billy the Parrot and a scraggy baby kangaroo with a vest, seemed to provide some unity at the end of the rest day, but not before Kate reversed Cheech into a tree, denting the rear panel and giving me a slight hernia. Danny cooked up a barbecue feast as I gazed north across the highway towards the railway track. The huge, multi-carriage trains were irregular and few, but when they did pass they took their time, three minutes and twenty-nine seconds, to be precise. A plate of sausages stopped my boring, mathematical games.

*   *   *

'Bodallin,' pondered Marie, the manager of the Internet café in Merredin, 'it must be about seventy kilometres away.' That threw me, that did. I'd planned on Bodallin being the next stop after Merredin but even with the ever-elusive tailwind finally joining my rear end 70km in one day might be asking just a bit much. Ah well, we'll have to make do with camping just off the road tonight. And that was how the plan for the day went. Up early and on the road before 8 a.m. (even with a 5:45 alarm it's amazing how long it takes to get ready), we'd managed 25km before the other vans caught up. The road drove on through WA, past the site of the commencement of the famous Rabbit Proof Fence that had been constructed in the early 1900s to keep rabbits off Western Australian pastoral lands. There was no sign of the fence now, just an information post surrounded by thousands of buzzing flies a little way off the road.

The highway continued into a channel bordered by three-metre high bush. For 10km this channel undulated, the roads smooth and the wind finally edging behind me. I coasted along with barely a push and lifted my arms out wide. It felt like heaven. At one point a basking lizard stood in the middle of the road, almost a foot long and green as grass. I bent down as I rolled by with barely a metre separating Elsa from the little dinosaur and then, just as I thought the encounter was over, the critter started at the vibrations of my board and hightailed it, colliding square with my back wheel. My heart stopped, a cart-wheeling gecko spun off towards the side lane and, to my relief, landed on its feet, staring at me nonchalantly. Simon, riding the bike just behind, swerved a little to avoid a bad ending, and we continued on our way. Later Kate was riding the bike and swerved as a Road Train passed. She lost balance as the front wheel dropped into the gravel at the roadside, and fell. Becki was there almost instantly, relishing her position as Head Nurse and patching up Kate's bloody elbow and knee marvellously. I skated off feeling guilty, because although I'd been at Kate's side to comfort her, a voice had been whispering in my head that I should be frustrated at another delay. I realised, without being able to do anything about it, that fatigue was starting to play its part in my mindset.

In the early afternoon I pushed over the 50km mark and was starting to feel the strain. Remembering Marie telling me that Bodallin was 70km from Merredin I pulled the vans over. 'Guys, let's start looking about for a place to camp, the next Roadhouse is about twenty kilometres away so it looks like we're going to be stuck by the roadside tonight.' Not far down the highway there was a wide lay-by peppered with bushes. I looked around as Dom filmed some horses in a nearby field. The place didn't feel right. 'No shelter here, let's move on a bit.' And just around the corner, much to my surprise, was a sign saying Bodallin, 2km! We rolled into the Roadhouse right on the 59km mark and were utterly dismayed to find No Overnight Camping signs everywhere. Always a group to try it on, though, we approached the lady who worked at the station and she said it might be OK to stay, although it was really up to the council. Twenty minutes later a white car drove up and two women and a man got out, handing us $A25 in donations. Then the chap spoke, 'Would you like to stay here tonight?'

'Mate, we'd love to,' I replied, not knowing who the hell he was. 'Good, it'll be OK then, I'll let you,' he said, tapping my shoulder gently. 'Are you from the council then?' I asked, and he nodded.

'I have a meeting with them tonight, I'll let the rest know.'

Off he drove and left us to it. The wall along the side of the station was riddled with spiders. Some of the team watched fascinated as a pair of redbacks attacked an earwig, it didn't have a chance. Those team members who weren't watching were reading in the vans, trying to pretend spiders didn't exist. I lay on George's bottom bunk, typing up my diary for the day and chuckling at a story from earlier:

We ate lunch at Carabbin Roadhouse where two large skinks hovered around the toilet block. Over a foot long and very plump, one of them guarded the Ladies entrance. A little local girl ran over and answered Bev's questions:

'Does it bite?'

'No.'

'Is it a bluetail?'

'I don't know, I'm only five years old.'

The next day was a breeze, literally. A strong tailwind pushed me the 45km to Southern Cross by midday despite the roughest roads yet. With four days scheduled to cover the 190km to Coolgardie I was determined to retrieve the time lost during the unplanned rest stop in Merredin. Choosing to rest for the entire afternoon in Southern Cross, I was preparing myself mentally to reach Coolgardie in three days, not four. Also, the free afternoon gave the team time to obtain supplies for what we had had coined 'a warm-up for the Nullarbor'. The road between Southern Cross and Coolgardie was empty except for two small roadhouses, we were heading into the outback.

The first day of September was a miserable one. A blanket of grey spanned horizon to horizon as the roads dipped and rose like waves, glistening from the constant drizzle that permeated my shorts, t-shirt and gloves. Dom rode with me on the bike, braving the weather when he could have easily sat inside in a dry vehicle, and I was grateful for his company as we reminisced about the UK journey. A roadhouse called Yellowdine was the only defining factor of the day. With two large trucks parked across the road, a lady behind the counter warned us about this end of the Great Eastern Highway. 'There are two separate gangs of Road Train drivers,' she said. 'They hate each other and it's not unknown for one truck to turn around and chase another for kilometres. It's like a battlefield out there.' It sounded like an old wives' tale to me and in a sense her story tempted fate, because only one Road Train passed us that afternoon, a two-trailer carrying hundreds of sheep, and the only ominous thing about it was the awful smell and the blast of wet, sheepy air that plastered our faces. Dom, still on the bike, rejoiced sarcastically,

'No showers for three days, yeaahh!'

We spend the night in a dirt clearing just a few metres behind a line of scrub that borders the highway. It's the first time we've 'roughed it' on BoardFree Australia but we're all in good spirits. As the sky darkens and the Road Trains rumble by I type up my diary:

Snuggled onto George's top bunk, a fair distance from any kind of civilisation, I realise two things. One, that today I skated past the 400 kilometre mark, and two, very unlike BoardFree UK, we haven't been making a big deal of the one hundreds. 100km down, 200km down, 300km down. None of that. I think at one stage I told Dom and Dan that I'd passed the 200km mark and got no more than an unimpressed grunt in reply. And here, camped in a clearing 40 metres off the Great Eastern Highway with Southern Cross 52km to the west and Coolgardie some 135km to the east, I can understand exactly why these mini-milestones aren't overly significant. It's because Australia is a bloody big place.

The next was a day of extremes. I woke up grumpy, a night of tossing and turning and interrupted sleep didn't bode well for a day in which I hoped to skate close to 70km. 'It's my birthday!' squeaked an excited voice – Kate's wide eyes shining blue just inches away signal the second BoardFree birthday in a week. The usual early morning crew was on the road by 8 a.m. Although the sun was out when we woke up it had disappeared behind clouds, which always threatened rain but never quite delivered. Instead, a cold wind blew from the north east, right into my face. The going was hard. It was one of those mornings when I got angrier and angrier with every push. Why hadn't the team woken up when I asked them to? Did they have no respect for me? Why were some of the documentary team still back in camp and missing some outstanding scenery? Why wasn't anyone waving from their cars this morning? Why did it feel like I wasn't making any ground despite hard pushing? Horrible moments, these, and they always pass. But for a while they're poisonous and just expend more energy. After 15km I pulled the Jackaroo over and sat on my board, hugging myself, exhausted and inconsolable. Kate gave me some food and a hoodie, Dom and Dan tried to make things better by telling me it had all been uphill so far and that I was doing really well. I hadn't noticed any uphills, I just wanted a nap.

'I'll go another five kilometres and then have a sleep in George,' I told them, and we moved on. A rest area, usually a wide lay-by marked by yellow waste bins, was signposted for a kilometre up the road and I pushed on towards my shut-eye. Then a white utility vehicle pulled up alongside me containing two men with beards. The driver leaned over and said,

'We're working on the pipeline about three kilometres up the road, when you get to us we'll sort you out with some bottles of water.'

At the lay-by I delayed my nap. 'Let's push on until we see these pipeline guys, they're only a couple of k's down the road,' I said to the team, 'after then we'll have a kip.' Kate trundled off to the toilet. By now she was proficient at standing up and urinating like a bloke, her skills had earned her admiration from all the other girls, as well as the title 'Queen of Shewee!' There was no place to be shy and withdrawn on the team, at some stage we were all going to see everything and our inhibitions had flown out the window long ago. If Kate and I both needed the toilet, we tended to stand side by side and go, although I realised quickly that she still had some directional trouble and took delight in peeing on whichever of my shoes was nearest to her. Before carrying on, it was time for Kate's Birthday Box. She opened it up to reveal bubbles and beads and a skipping rope, which she gave a good workout right there and then amidst a shower of bubbles.

I pushed on. It was almost 10km and more than an hour of skating before we reached the worksite. The effort was well worth it, a box of water and a bag of goodies awaited. Steve, the guy in charge of traffic control and one of the chaps who drove alongside me earlier, was a super bloke and had instigated the generosity. He showed us the break in the pipe that they were working on, describing the machines that men lay on in order to get deep within the pipe to unblock it. The work they were undertaking was unthinkably difficult in dark, wet conditions yet in stifling heat, flies absolutely everywhere. I felt incredibly lucky not to be in their position and was a bit embarrassed when the workers started offering compliments about the journey. Before we left Steve told me there were some road works on the Nullarbor before looking me up and down and shaking his head. 'Man,' he said, 'all I can say is man, you're hard as nuts.'

Just around the corner we passed an emu and four chicks, which scurried into the bush when we came close. Kate was celebrating her birthday on the bike but didn't have to go far before we found a good place to pull over. I was just about to put my head down when Steve drove up in his ute again. We chatted for about half an hour as he relayed some great stories about Road Trains and the wildlife and his life as a traffic control worker in the outback. Before leaving he emptied his cooler of drinks and handed them over, and even gave me a stray orange from the passenger seat. He told me about a place to stay tonight, 'About ten kilometres up the road there's a beautiful look-out spot, a small version of Ayres Rock, the views from up there are incredible. You should check it out.'

Not long after 5 p.m., in the middle of nowhere and skating through an avenue of tall, graceful trees, I crossed the 500km mark. 'Only another five thousand five hundred to go!' said Simon, keeping up his role as cheeky bugger of the group. I was longing for the end of the day when a black car passed. I waved but received no response, and felt a pang of annoyance that they hadn't waved back, or honked, or at least done something. Although other vehicles had passed without communication, this one felt different. Maybe it was because it was all black with tinted windows, maybe it was because I was tired and feeling irritable, but my hunch that this wasn't your regular passer-by was confirmed seconds later. A few hundred metres up ahead I saw the car stop and someone get out. 'What are they doing?' I mumbled to myself. As I pushed on I watched as a figure walked around and then climbed back into the vehicle. It drove away. 'Why the hell would a car just stop in the middle of the road?' I asked myself, and thus began a process of deduction that I have to put down to complete and utter fatigue.

I felt sure that there was only one explanation for the black car's behaviour; the occupiers had clearly felt this was the right time to test out one of their remote control bombs. They'd pulled over, planted one by the side of the road and driven off to a safe distance, from where they would detonate the explosive as I skated past. 'Don't be a dickhead, Dave,' I told myself, 'why would they want to blow *you* up?' But despite my question, I felt sure I'd hit the nail on the head. I mean, why else would they have stopped? I couldn't be sure exactly where they had planted the bomb, so moved over to the opposite lane just in case. As I cautiously approached the suspect area I scanned the flat, red verge for signs of a foreign object, holding up my palm to Cheech and pointing down, signalling for Danny to stop where he was while I looked around. If someone was going to get blown up here, it sure as hell wasn't going to be my team. God knows what they were thinking. It's bizarre enough driving after a bloke on a skateboard, let alone being warned not to go on as he skates along in a crouch position, looking scared. And then my eye caught sight of something in the middle of the left lane. I made a beeline for it, my heart pounding, sure this was the end. But it wasn't the end, it wasn't a bomb, it was a rock, a simple rock. And underneath it was a ten-dollar note. What a great way to donate!

Shortly afterwards I finished for the day, another 66km down, and we drove back to camp. The spot Steve had earlier recommended was indeed spectacular. Our vehicles parked close together at the edge of a clearing, which was dominated by an enormous rock. From the top we could see for thirty or forty kilometres over dense forest, it was a place just to sit and be silent. Later, down below, we were polishing off our supper when a silhouette hopped along the top of the rock two hundred metres away with the sunset glowing orange behind it, our first wild kangaroo!

* * *

I'd finished the night before beside a green triangle signpost, one letter – the destination – followed by a distance. Every five kilometres they stood at the roadside, sometimes glinting in the sun, sometimes hidden behind leafy branches, always endlessly taunting and highlighting the slow pace at which I was travelling. Five by five I had counted down since leaving Southern Cross for Coolgardie, from that first triangle that read C 180 all the way through to C 70. Whether they were there or not they never failed to play games with my head. Skating past C 110 when I expected to see C 105 was a blow but sometimes, usually when a sign had been removed or I had simply missed one in the haze the inverse occurred. The elation of being 5km further along the road than expected was always greeting by a cheer, a pumping fist, a series of harder-than-normal pushes. Stood by the C 70 sign I knew there were thirteen more of these to pass before I reached Coolgardie that evening, bringing the journey back to schedule, earning a day of rest for everyone.

The sun beat down, the heat countered by a blissful cool breeze. The clouds above sat on a light shade of grey as if the sky was a watercolour painting, and for much of the day the bush grew further back from the road than normal, five-metre stretches of rust through which lizards skittered into the shadow of trees. For the first 30km all of the vehicles stayed close, spirits high as I ate into the second 500km; Bev sprinted alongside me as I careered towards a water break. All at once the scenery changed, the roadsides opening up into clear fields spiked with skeletal dead wood, blackened from a recent fire. Kate was riding beside me again as a tour bus passed, the driver pointing at me as he spoke into his microphone, the faces behind him squashed against windows, flat noses and waving palms directed at the moveable attraction on a skateboard. I realise I'll be part of the show for a little while longer, at least until I push beyond the desert. In Perth the distance signs read Coolgardie 580km, it was a daunting prospect, the length of Scotland along just one road. But now we were in lesser double figures, an emu and her chick bumbled around on the road as Coolgardie 29km was advertised, the giant birds arrowing their necks forward as I approached, speeding into the bush with Catherine-wheel legs. Behind me the silver tarpaulin covering Cheech's roof rack reflected the sunlight into my eyes, looking for all the world like a bulbous alien spacecraft.

Exhaustion turned to exhilaration when Coolgardie's western reaches appeared. A 70km day, the longest yet, had completed the three-day mission from Southern Cross but meant one other thing; it was goodbye to the Golden Pipeline. In a strange, new country and in the middle of an original, groundbreaking project, I had taken heart from the pipe's constant presence. I was going to miss it as we turned due south towards Norseman.

*　　*　　*

The well-earned rest day predictably became a day of activity. Coolgardie Primary School welcomed us as I strode past a No Skating sign to give a talk to dozens of tiny people. Then a drive to Kalgoorlie-Boulder, the heart of the Western Australian goldfields, 40km north east of Coolgardie. Two radio interviews first, one for Radio West and another for the ABC at their Goldfields-Esperance studio. Producer Pippa Doyle introduced me to David Kennedy, a lovely guy with one of those crisp radio voices that sets you at ease immediately. We chatted for ten minutes as the team waited behind the glass, and afterwards Pippa and David promised they'd keep in touch throughout the journey.

It was a sad afternoon, news filtering through as Kate and I sat in an Internet café that Steve Irwin had died while filming a sea-life documentary off the coast of Cairns. Six years earlier I became fascinated with programmes featuring this gregarious, passionate Australian who jumped into rivers and wrestled crocodiles and crawled on all fours to within inches of the world's most poisonous snakes, and was an all-round nice guy as he did it. Steve Irwin may have been an easy Aussie stereotype to some but to me he defined a happy person. Someone who loved what he did so much his personality was infectious; he lived life to the full and was a true ambassador for his country. He will be sorely missed.

*　　*　　*

A quick interview with Triple J was dominated by a poor telephone signal the next morning, and soon afterwards I was back on Elsa. Before we left the campsite a neighbour had strolled over and handed me a copy of the local paper, the *Golden Mail*. And there I was taking up the entire front page, brilliant! At Coolgardie the Great Eastern Highway ends and highway 94 continues south towards Norseman under the title of the Coolgardie

Esperance Highway. It was a tough day; the inexplicably inconsistent wind had turned full circle and was now straight into my face once again. All the jokes about BoardFree turning into a horror movie – one Australian Internet skateboarding forum had nicknamed the journey The Wolf Creek Skateathon – weren't so tongue in cheek as I rolled passed an ominous-looking shack in the woods, which looked exactly like one of the sets from the *Wolf Creek* film, where a group of young travellers end up being preyed upon by a manic serial killer. In reality, the only true horror was the road surface. It was hellish, so bad that I still had to push on the rare occasion that the road led downhill. I dropped into a dark mood and kept my head down, knowing this was one of those days I just had to get through no matter how hard it was.

The end of the day, though, was a different story. Chewing on a cooked breakfast in the Coolgardie Roadhouse the day before, the team had been approached by two men who introduced themselves as the headmasters of two schools in Kambalda, a district 40km south of Kalgoorlie. They offered accommodation in return for a talk at each of the schools and we happily agreed on the deal. Fifty-seven kilometres south of Coolgardie I finished the day at a fork in the highway. Kambalda was just a short drive into the bush. Just as I was pulling my luminous jacket off a ute pulled up. The driver climbed out, walked over to us and asked, 'Would you like to go a kilometre underground?' Delirious with fatigue and having spent the whole day absorbed in my own horror movie, my face was probably a picture of terror at the guy's question. 'Well,' he continued, unperturbed, 'I work in a nickel mine a few kilometres down the road, we heard about you on the radio and thought you could do with a break.' That sounded a lot nicer. I took his card, shook his hand and jumped into Cheech promising to call him the next day.

Russell O'Neill, the head of Kambalda High School, gave us a classroom to sleep in for the night, and much to our delight, the run of the school. There's something wonderful about travelling without a rigid plan of action. The flexibility and spontaneity of life on the road means that each day we're open to a huge number of wonderful possibilities. I've always been in love with the notion – and practice – of waking up in the morning not knowing where I'm going to rest my head the coming night, and today was one of those days which highlighted the benefits of not calling ahead to arrange official accommodation in a particular place. The team was delighted at yet another tick on the list of unexpected places to stay. Several years on from our last taste of a school classroom, the sexes bonded and grouped stereotypically: the girls remained in the Home Economics department as the boys raided the sports locker and played gleefully in the gym. It was a wonderful night, the ability to momentarily relive an aspect of our youth draining the strain from the journey.

* * *

The next day was just as unusual. Following my first talk at the High School the most touching moment of the morning occurred as a girl chased us as we left, brandishing a fifty-dollar note with the words, 'What you're doing is amazing, I'm so sorry I don't have anything else.' It was the equivalent of £20, from a teenager, and Simon and I looked at each other, amazed.

'They're a generous bunch,' said Russell, tapping his shaven head. 'All of this came off last month and they raised almost fifteen hundred dollars because of it.'

The next talk, at Kambalda Primary School, was to much younger pupils. The question and answer sessions are always the best. Towards the end I decided to ask the kids a question, the first to answer correctly got to ask me the final question of the day. So I asked, 'How fast do you think I go down on a steep hill?' A bunch of hands went up, I chose one belonging to a cheeky female face towards the front.

'Very fast,' she replied, much to the amusement of the adults in the room. 'Well that's a good answer,' I told her, 'but I'm looking for a figure, can anyone else have a guess?' Again, hands galore. I chose one.

'Faster,' came the reply.

Back on the road and fuelled by cookies the High School's Home Economics class had baked in what had been our bedroom for the night, I closed the gap on Norseman by another 40km. The distance was largely uneventful except for a pit stop at Widgiemooltha Roadhouse, a run-down petrol station manned by a large, disinterested bloke who was plain rude. 'I just don't see the point in people doing this kind of thing,' he moaned about out-of-the-ordinary journeys for charity. He wouldn't even let us eat our homemade sandwiches inside. We were the only ones there.

We'd been given directions to the Mincor Mariners mine, and I pulled Elsa up at the end of the correct dirt road that led off from the highway. I'm not sure any of us were expecting what was to come. Set a few hundred metres from the road and hidden in dense forest was a small village featuring two hundred or so prefabs; self-contained, en suite rooms, a dining hall, wet mess (bar), recreation room and ablution rooms (toilets). For about five minutes we all felt quite out of place but then Gabby, a friendly yet efficient lady – the type that takes shit from no one – showed us around, gave us keys to two rooms and left us to it, saying, 'I'd have given you eight rooms if we had them available.'

We showered, changed and wandered into the dining room where we tucked into a multi-course dinner and helped ourselves to at least three servings of pudding. Gabby walked in and told me that there was a short event on in the wet mess at a quarter to eight, 'It's called the Golden Spanner and basically it's a chance for the boys to take the piss out of each other for their antics on the site. You should come on over.' So we did. A ripe old fella named Foss (short for Fossil) took centre-stage and promptly began dishing out items like hats and rucksacks to people who had earned them, for such reasons as missing shifts due to drunkenness. He even plugged BoardFree, taking the chance to ask why it had taken me so long to get here from Perth, handing me a Mincor baseball cap and inviting the gathered crowd to give some money to the cause. They duly did, adding over $A250 to the $A325 we had raised in the schools earlier in the day. Overwhelmed and pinching ourselves at our completely random luck, we retired to vans and en-suite rooms to get a good night's sleep in preparation for a tour of the nickel mine the next morning.

*　*　*

The man stood and operated a deafening handheld drilling machine for fourteen hours non-stop, three-quarters of a kilometre underground in sweltering conditions. We had been watching him for just a few seconds and were already exhausted when he turned, and only then I recognised through the dirt spread across his face that we had played pool against each other the previous evening. Naivety I suppose, but I was taken aback by the conditions normal, everyday people subjected themselves to for money. It's an incredible lure, the pay is certainly fitting of working in such an environment and there are no outgoings when one lives on camp, but even the long holidays wouldn't get me down here. The BoardFree team, each kitted up in overalls, boots, helmets and head torches, lingered in a cave surrounded by the eerie howl of machinery screeching in the depths of the earth. It was an eye-opening experience and we were grateful to the people who showed us around; the professionalism of the operation was never in question. Paul, the man who had met me shortly before we drove to Kambalda two days earlier, made a donation from the proceeds of the camp's soft drinks machine and bid us farewell. The kindness of strangers, even out here in the middle of nowhere, continued to be astounding. 'If you need anything,' Paul said, 'just call.'

*   *   *

I woke with a start. Outside, the rain hammered against the roof and overhanging branches brushed violently against the side windows. The late start after leaving the mine had only allowed me to skate 30km further south, and we had made camp on a dirt track just off the highway. I was confused by waking in the middle of the night. Once I was asleep only morning usually got me up, but this time was different; the blankets beneath me were sodden. My eyes widened and I sat bolt upright, smacking my head on the wooden bars supporting the top bunk and clenching my bladder shut in an instant. I'd been urinating in my sleep, pissing myself. I lay back down for a couple of seconds, wondering if this was really happening, then propped myself up on my elbows and glanced across at Kate, her blonde head lying motionless on the pillow. Determined not to wake her I pulled myself out from under the sleeping bag and grabbed a towel, spreading it out over my side of the mattress. Still needing to finish my pee I crawled down to the end of the bunk, slid open the door and knelt upright, relieving myself through the door as rain drove in against my bare chest. I finished, pulled on some clothes and lay down on top of my sleeping bag. I'd been plagued by stomach cramps, fatigue and a loss of appetite since leaving Perth, but couldn't help wonder just how tired I needed to be in order to wet the bed. I was back to sleep in seconds, haunted by thoughts of whether I should tell anyone what had happened.

We were on the road early, as usual letting a few of the team stay behind. An hour later Kylie stormed up. Becki wound down the window, 'George isn't starting, the video cameras were left on charge all night and have drained the battery.' Kylie took over as my support vehicle, Simon joining Becs and Bev up front as Dan, the most mechanically minded among us, drove Cheech back to camp. It was a nice change having new people on the road and Becs and Bev enjoyed their new role too. Si was his humorous, laid-back self, always good company and totally passive. He and Dan were the emotional constants in the group, everyone else's moods seemingly rotating around the solid axis they provided.

I was pushing along head down when I heard a hushed voice hissing at me from the van behind. Looking up, I saw an emu in the middle of the road, rushing off in that familiar, awkward gait when we drew closer. Suddenly I felt all silly and decided to give the others a laugh. Without warning I ran off my board and chased the emu into the Bush, head down with arms trailing behind in my very best emu impersonation. I bashed around off-road for a while and then ran back to the van, only taking my human shape outside Becki's window. The others were wetting themselves and it struck me that in the space of just a few hours all present had done the same, Becs, Bev and Si just didn't know about my little episode last night!

Two hours later George had rejoined us. 'I called Paul from the mine,' Kate told me. 'He drove down and fitted a brand new battery from his car. He was awesome.' It transpired that Dom had been responsible for leaving the chargers in overnight and he looked sheepish as Kate continued, '. . . and when Paul put his hands on his hips and said "that's a typically girly thing to do, isn't it?" Dom didn't say a word and let me take the blame.' I pushed the final 10km to Norseman getting more and more worked up about Dom's idiocy. Had we been in the middle of the Nullarbor it would have caused a lot more upset than just embarrassment and a few hours' delay. One thing was for sure, there weren't going to be people like Paul around to help us out if similar errors were made on the Plain.

I pulled to a stop at a junction just north of Norseman, where the Eyre Highway branches off. I glanced down the road before pulling into a filling station, knowing full well that it wasn't just any old road. This one led across the Nullarbor. A bearded traveller in a clapped-out motor home warned us that he'd heard Road Train drivers talking about us over their CB radios. 'They must have passed you on the Great Eastern,' he said, 'some of them think you've got rocks in your head and have complained to the police.' He strutted off, pleased with himself having given us the willies.

A patrol car pulled up and a policeman stepped out. 'What are you doing?' he asked, which seemed a fair question, if not a little obvious.

'I'm skating across Australia,' I said, simply.

'Right,' he said, 'did you get permission to do this before you left Perth?'

'Oh yeah,' I said, 'the police in Perth were fine with it.' I was being a little extravagant with the truth, but it did the trick.

'Well that's all I need to know,' the patrolman said, his face turning from frowns to smiles as he slapped a hip and climbed back into his car. He drove away with a final comment, 'Good luck on the Nullarbor!'

I breathed a sigh of relief and turned to Danny, 'Mate, let's face it, we've travelled seven hundred and fifty kilometres without being stopped, he would have looked a bit silly had he arrested me.' I just hoped that as we continued the distance clocked up would form some kind of protection against pernickety officials, however strict the transition would be from outback law-enforcer to east coast cop.

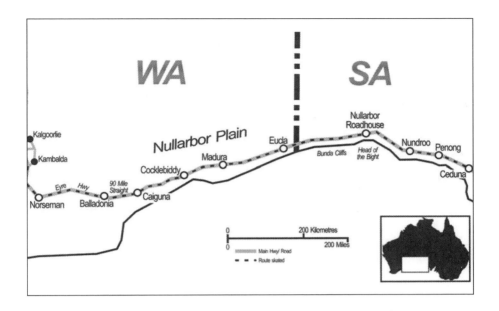

17 The Nullarbor Plain

11–29 September 2006

There's a very hairy caterpillar halfway up our front door. It's about five inches long, fat as a swollen thumb with a face like a baboon. 'How do you think it got there?' Kate asks me. 'Did it fall off the tree and land on the door?' I laugh out loud but she doesn't stop. 'Well that's how they get places,' she stresses, 'they fall off plants.' Outside, rubbish is strewn across the ground. Kate heard a thrashing sound earlier and growled from the bed, 'It's the crows!' She rushed to the door and sure enough, a large black crow walked pompously away from a pecked rubbish bag. Kate shut the door, grinned and victoriously put her fist in the air, 'Yes! I knew it! Crows!' She's on one today.

We're staying in Norseman's Great Western Hotel. Pat, the manager and her husband, Russell, who compiles the local newsletter and is running a piece on BoardFree, are kindly putting us up gratis. We've been here for two days. Becki and Bev had been clearing shelves at the supermarket while the team juggles the logistical challenge of repacking the vehicles taking into account several cubic feet of newly donated water. Russell was happy for us to stay until we were ready. He had been a friend and guide since we arrived, showing us Beacon Hill, which overlooks the town and the salt lake that borders its north and west sides, Lake Cowan. In the other direction, to the east, there was nothing but trees. The land reached out to the horizon with barely any undulation, a green blanket as far as the eye could see. The thought that this was where we were going should have been terrifying, but this was it. The Nullarbor, the Plain so many had said I couldn't cross. I couldn't wait to get going.

'How are you coping with the skating itself?' Dom asked me earlier during an interview. 'Physically, how are you feeling after skating seven hundred and fifty kilometres in two weeks?'

I rested my chin on my hand, sighed deeply and replied, 'I realised a couple of days ago that I'm now used to being constantly in pain. My muscles ache, my joints ache, my back aches, my feet ache. I'm perfectly able to carry on, but at the same time it's not healthy just to accept this constant pain.' Rest days, I was learning, were just another part of the journey.

*　　*　　*

It was time to go, we've got a desert to skate across. Dom and I flare up shortly before leaving Norseman the next morning. His financial contribution to BoardFree Australia remained unseen and he still hadn't paid me his share of costs from the BoardFree UK journey. Dom was a fun guy to have around but often sank into heavy moods, sniping unnecessary comments at other team members, especially Becki. I put it down to a clash of big personalities. As we prepared to leave the Great Western his insistence in keeping his tripod in an already full Cheech went completely against a recent request I'd made. It was, I thought, common sense that the tripod should be kept in another vehicle, as he'd never need it when driving along in the car behind me on the road. But still he brought it into Cheech, complaining it would get damaged in another van, his tripod filling a seat which was needed for the short drive back to the start point. When he slammed the car door in my face it was the last straw. 'You fucking prick!' I yelled.

The racing bicycle had been tied onto George's bull bars, but the tyres hung inches from the ground. It was asking for trouble, a small pothole would buckle the wheels and render the bike useless, and I channelled my frustrations into untying the bike, asking everyone to think a little bit harder about what they were doing, and then, as there were no spare seats left in Cheech, I jumped on the bike and led the vehicles out of the compound and down the road to the petrol station. Just what you need, Dave, I thought as I pedaled furiously, a nice little cycle ride before a forty-mile skate.

Tensions were put aside briefly for a pre-skate interview. I stood beside a sign that pointed east to Balladonia and Adelaide. 'This is it, the beginning of the Eyre Highway. We're going to be on this road for over a month now. This road alone is longer than the length of Britain, it's going to take us across the Nullarbor. We don't hit another town until the seventh of October, it's the eleventh of September today.' I looked at the sign, turned to look down the stretch behind me and then refocused on the camera. 'Let's do it,' I said, walking away. I had always been comfortable speaking into the camera but certain questions always tailed off into other things and usually I tended to ramble on a fair bit. The argument we'd had earlier meant that Dom wasn't saying much at all and that, coupled with what was a truly critical moment in the journey, made me feel as I walked away that I'd just given the most honest, concise piece to camera that I'd ever delivered. Whatever the situation, I wasn't going to let the start of this stretch be ruined by pigheaded quarrels. I'd been waiting for this for more than a year and wasn't willing to bow to the fact that some people I'd brought on this adventure were contributing more to my mental stress than necessary. One kilometre down the road I skated past a direction marker. It was the most horrifying, soul-destroying sign ever constructed. Adelaide 1986. From then onwards the 5km green triangle markers at the side of the road bore a much lesser significance and I shook my head at the thought that when I finally rolled into Adelaide having covered those 1,986km I still wouldn't be halfway to Brisbane. You know it's bad when you're travelling by skateboard and the signs give you a distance larger than the year you were born.

We were heading into the unknown, a place with few supplies, little shelter and a distinct lack of Internet. The Nullarbor wasn't just a challenge, it was a black hole in the journey as far as spectators were concerned. I assumed it would be at least a month before I could update our progress on the Internet and made this clear on the BoardFree website before leaving Norseman, writing a blog that ended with 'see you on the other side'. With our minds on the task in hand, it must have been an impossible situation for our family and friends watching from afar, knowing we were going dark and had weeks of potential danger ahead.

We'd prepared well, though. Becki and Bev had their stressful moments in Norseman but had embarked on two epic shopping trips, emptying the local supermarket to ensure that we had enough food to be completely self-sufficient across the Plain. Poor Kylie heaved under the weight as a new pattern emerged. With no towns or physical markers to go by, Bev and Becs had nowhere to fundraise or to drive ahead to in order to organise accommodation. They became a more constant part of my day, a growing white dot at the side of the road that I'd pass with a wave and which would then overtake me in turn, an uncompetitive jostling for position that I knew I could never win.

Fifteen kilometres out of Norseman I sat at the side of the road and cleared the air with Dom. With every push any unresolved issues manifested themselves, taking my mind off the skate and churning my thoughts into a soup of anger. It wasn't healthy and the key was to take a breather and act on it. I told him he needed to sort the money out and not ignore it anymore. He apologised and that was that. The bottom line of the conflict, though, continued to bother me, and I could attribute it to others on the team too. I was starting to feel a little alienated from the group, with Kate the only person behaving consistently around me. Perhaps the distance that was forming could be attributed to my moods. Fatigue was playing its part now, and smaller things began to hit my radar of irritation. Things like Holly playing with her mobile rather than taking photographs, like Becki treating Bev as if she were a child with orders and unnecessary putdowns, like Dom and the money he owed me. Or when one of the documentary team was reading a magazine when I passed the van they were sat in, it took the piss! Here I was skating my arse off and the cameraman was reading *Empire*, please! I was aware that I was becoming difficult company sometimes but also had the distinct impression that there was a glaringly obvious reason for this, I was exhausted!

That evening we camped in the bush after the nearby Fraser Range Lodge had turned down a request for free camping sites, and I called a team meeting. It was the first of note since the morning we had left Perth and I wanted to get across a few points. I asked the team to be aware of what I was going through and that if they weren't willing to do what I was doing – which wasn't just the skating, it was the managing of day-to-day operations, updating the website and mediating tiffs among other things – then they weren't to give me any shit.

'Guys, I'm in constant pain, I'm going to be grumpy an awful lot, please just bear that in mind if something gets on your nerves,' I told them. At the same time, I understood that everyone was feeling the strain in their own way. Most of the team were several years younger than I was and this was their first real challenge, their first taste of a true journey. Although I was enduring far more physically each day everyone else had their own roles and were ultimately going to experience their own frustrations, their own fatigue. We all had our moments of stress, and I knew the key to getting us through this was to make the most of it and quash arguments as quickly as possible.

'We need to be aware of how travelling like this can affect us,' I said. 'If you have a problem with someone else on the team then deal with it immediately. If you can't deal with it between yourselves then come to me and I'll deal with it. If it festers it's going to cause real issues, please don't let things get out of hand. We're in the middle of something amazing and we musn't forget that.'

*   *   *

For people travelling from west to east along the Eyre Highway Balladonia is the first roadhouse on the Nullarbor, and I had my sights firmly set on a good shower when we awoke after the second night in the bush. There was a catch though; I knew we would encounter roadworks before the day was out. How severe they were and how much of the road they affected I didn't know, and the surprise element was almost intriguing as the 21st day of BoardFree Australia commenced. I pushed off in celebratory circumstances, twenty Australians from a 4x4 cross-country tour were in attendance having pulled their vehicles to the side of the road to make donations and shake my hand. We had left Perth three weeks earlier and covered almost 900km, being stopped several times each day by passing motorists for photographs, donations or just a friendly chat. Nothing had changed since we joined the Eyre Highway, not many vehicles took the route but those that did contained some wonderfully generous folk who never ceased to lift my spirits. The Nullarbor Plain had its crosses to bear though, the temperatures were hotter than ever before. Even before mid-morning I found myself skating in heat of over thirty degrees; it sapped my energy and made my litre water bottle seem pitiful, but there was always a new one being dangled out of the window by Kate or Danny when I'd taken my last sip.

Skating long distances in the heat doesn't contribute much to one's patience, either, and I found myself furious on more than one occasion. I had to resort to screaming my lungs out when Si, who was driving along in the opposite lane with Dom hanging out the window camera in hand, blocked traffic attempting to overtake us. The fact that an upcoming hill was a blind spot that could have harboured a Road Train steaming in the other direction didn't say much for their judgement. Not long afterwards, Dom and Becki got into one of their petty spats and as I tried to intervene Becki turned her back on me and stomped off to Kylie. That in turn gave me the hump and I pushed the next 5km cursing her rudeness, cursing Dom for instigating the whole bloody thing and cursing myself for not demanding that the pair of them got on the bicycle and rode for a while, just to see how it felt to exert themselves a little bit.

I was still wishing the same when a predictable incident occurred a few kilometres on. Simon drove up a small incline to get back on the road and buckled the front wheel of the racing bike, which again had been tied so low to the ground a hamster could have reached up and spun it. Kate was especially distraught, showing a great deal of bottom lip at the fact that previous warnings about tying the bike hadn't been heeded. The damage meant that there was now no way for the team to exercise during the day, causing upset throughout the ranks and meaning there was one less outlet for any frustrations.

One by one large yellow signs bore bad news about the road ahead – anything between 40km to 60km of disruption was forecast. My nightmares were compounded when the signs ended and the works began. Only one word came to mind when I skated over a hill and came to a stop two hundred metres later, faced with a road that was no longer concrete, just potholed dirt. 'Fuck.'

Whatever the surface, there was no choice but to deal with it. A British guy who worked for the engineering company responsible for the roadworks agreed to guide me through. The disruption meant that traffic was only allowed to travel in one direction at a time and he wasn't willing to let me skate through alone, especially with hulking great Road Trains around. There hadn't been much rain for a week and the dirt road was compact, if nothing else, although the timing of a water tanker that pulled in front of me and started spraying liquid across the track couldn't have been less appropriate. I skated along with difficulty, determined not to walk if I didn't have to. At some points, though, I was forced to pick Elsa up and leave the road. Infuriatingly, these occasions coincided with the sections of works that had one lane of tarmac. I wasn't allowed to skate on it for safety reasons, they told me. With vehicles backing up behind and others single-filing in the opposite direction they couldn't afford any delays. 'And besides,' said one of the site managers, 'we have to make sure you're safe.' So they banished me to walking along the side of the road, where giant steamrollers trundled and forced me to stand aside a little way into the bush. I couldn't help have doubts about the manager's safety concerns, after that.

Dom jumped out and joined me for a bit, sometimes to film my reaction at the situation but mainly to give me company. We walked for several kilometres, excruciatingly close to the tarmac lane that ran smoothly on the other side of a mound of soil. For minutes at a time the lane was empty as the turnaround in traffic found its place in the lights, but I didn't want to make any trouble so bit my tongue and continued on foot. Eventually, after 25km, I grew restless. 'How you feeling, mate?' Dom asked me.

'No skateboarding allowed,' I said, drearily, wandering along with my luminous yellow hood still covering my head. 'In some parts, if there was skateboarding allowed we wouldn't be able to do it anyway because there's too much mud and there's too many stones and there's too many potholes. And it gets even better; you see the concrete up ahead?' I said, pointing forwards as I walked past Cheech. 'I'm not allowed to skateboard on it.'

'Are you not skating that bit Dave?' asked Kate, who had been sat with Dan and Holly in Cheech for hours as I made my way.

'I am bloody going to skate it, yeah,' I said defiantly, tired of walking. I put Elsa down and skated the rest of the way with cheering workmen saluting as I passed. Emerging from the final roadblock and passing the final yellow and black signs, I looked back to see the words Road Closed. Absolutely shattered, I took in some fluids and chocolate at the roadside, Kate hugging me passionately despite my bearded, dusty face. Time was getting on and I was expecting another 15km until we reached Balladonia, so I nearly cried with relief when just 4km later I pushed uphill and arrived at the Roadhouse. I could barely walk and collapsed into a camping chair. Becs thrust a bowl of soup into my hands as a local cat rubbed against my legs. It's not easy, this skateboarding business.

*   *   *

Almost as soon as we had left the outskirts of Perth the roads had begun a steady process of becoming longer and straighter. Where once I would have split my day into short legs by targeting the next bend as a reward to push towards, I was now forced to create a new focus. Sometimes it was a noticeably large tree, others a 5km distance marker – which was perhaps still out of sight – or one of the support vans parked a few kilometres along the road, just visible as a dark shape with a dash of yellow. Not far out of Balladonia the road couldn't have got longer or straighter. The 90 Mile Straight is Australia's longest stretch of road without a bend, the start indicated by a large rust-red sign, which was disappointingly covered in mindless graffiti. By now, though, 146.6km didn't seem like a huge distance and I saw the Straight as another mini challenge, just as the roadworks had been the day before. I was more interested in the irony of another signpost a hundred metres further on, a yellow diamond with a black kangaroo warning drivers to be aware that they weren't the only creatures on the road. Just beyond the sign was a dark, still body covered in flies. Roadkill was a growing everyday occurrence and kangaroos were the main concern. Up to fifty a day lined the road, figures assisted by the animal's tendency to head straight for lights at night-time.

Dead roos come in varying conditions: full and seemingly untainted bodies lay prone on the verge, while in the road there would be inconsistent streams of blood, lumpy with destroyed organs and bone, piles of fur, nothing else. I couldn't ignore the death. It provoked a consciousness of my own legs still moving and of the potential imminence of plight in such a desolate land. I wondered how each accident had happened as I skated past, trying to work out which direction the kangaroo had been hopping in and where it had been struck, and by what type of vehicle. One disturbing image stayed with me; a large kangaroo at the roadside near Coolgardie with its head missing, a neatly severed hole at the top of its neck that didn't look at all like the product of a road accident. There were questions everywhere. Depending on the wind direction I morbidly took motivation from the bodies. A strong headwind would tell me that there was roadkill up ahead before I saw it. The stench of death is sickening and far stronger when you're exposed to the elements and near to the ground, where a cloud of hot air hovers, strengthening the scent. I pushed harder and faster to try and get past each corpse, covering my mouth with my sleeve if the kill was just a few hours old and the insects and eagles hadn't yet found time to hasten the decomposition of the body. When the wind was behind me I experienced the only catch 22 of a tailwind, the repellent smell of a dead kangaroo hanging on the air for up to half a minute after I had passed it. All I could do was push on as fast as possible, knowing there would be more kangaroos lying up ahead.

They weren't all dead, though. To avoid squatting in the bush the girls had bought a toilet stool, which was effectively a toilet seat with legs. This contraption immediately gained a nickname, 'Pete the Seat', and it turned a toilet break in the outback into a front row seat at a nature reserve. Halfway down the 90 Mile Straight I wandered fifty metres into the bush, finding cover behind a small copse of trees that rose above the waist-high savannah. Out of the corner of my eye I saw a kangaroo hopping towards the road, disappearing out of sight behind the scrub. I put my head down as I sat, waving the flies away and not thinking anymore about the roo until it jumped into view from behind a bush no more than ten metres away. We faced off, just staring at each other for fifteen seconds before it took flight, and I made a promise to myself that I'd take a camera to the toilet from then on. Not long after, I was faced with a similar, more dangerous predicament. This time in dense tree cover, I made use of Pete the Seat at the edge of a small clearing, a hundred metres across the road from camp. Then, just a few feet in front of me the vegetation stirred. Snake! I didn't move, didn't even breathe, as a King Brown slithered across my viewpoint from left to right. Eight or nine feet long and as thick as my arm, it was a terrifying, humbling sight. I watched it go and finished up, hurrying carefully out of the forest and back to camp. Yet again, I'd forgotten to take a camera to the toilet.

It took two and a half days to skate the length of the 90 Mile Straight. Danny helped me along, taking his blue and white customised rollsrolls out of George for the first time and pushing alongside me one evening. 'I'll buy you a bag of lollipops if you can make it to the end of the day, mate,' I jibed, not for a second believing he would. Nevertheless, it was great having someone else on the road with me, eight wheels rattling along the highway rather than four, and I knew that Dan was doing it at least partly to keep my spirits up. I'd had a bit more practice at skating than him, though, and after a while a gap opened up between us. Dusk was falling and I was determined to reach the distance marker I'd set myself before it got too dark, so I waved cheerio to Danny and sped off, passing Bev and some other travellers who were cheering from a rest stop where we were making camp that night. Two kilometres later I reached the sign, did an end-of-day interview with Dom and was about to jump into Cheech when I saw Danny skating up the road. 'The little bugger!' I said to Dom, who still had the camera on. 'I thought he was going to stop at camp but he's done the whole thing!' Danny was absolutely beat when he reached me but I gave him a big hug, 'I'm fucking proud of you mate, and I owe you a bag of lollipops.'

The 90 Mile Straight was witness to another BoardFree achievement; I crossed the 1,000km mark with the words, 'Three weeks of pushing, three highways, one long-gone city, quite fitting that we've crossed this first milestone on Australia's longest stretch of straight road.' The team marked the occasion by scrabbling around and collecting enough stones and bones to write 'BoardFree 1000km' at the roadside. We left a water bottle stuffed with BoardFree leaflets and a little note to mark the reason behind the memorial and as I put it on the ground Simon spoke.

'I'm actually quite sad,' he said, 'it feels like it's all coming to the end.' With that he sat down in George and I stepped back onto Elsa.

'Don't worry Si,' I said under my breath, 'still five thousand kilometres to go.'

* * *

The Nullarbor is a mystifying, beautiful place in which to spend a prolonged period of time. Prior to the journey tales of the Plain had mainly involved warnings about the heat, the trucks, the animals and the boredom. But once we were there, slowly moving through the middle of it, the Plain was so immense it was easy to accept your insignificance. The realisation was peaceful and humbling, and I lost count of the number of times I was pushing along, my right foot entering my vision at the beginning of each push, and then lifted my head to see endless flat land on both sides. Back in Swansea when this dream first came to me I tried to visualise what it would be like to stand at the side of the highway, knowing that the only way I was getting out of there was on my board. And here I was living my dream, and each time I stared out over the countryside I knew that I'd made the right decision. That leap of faith at the beginning, quitting the job and creating a very real difference between a life full of ideas just spoken and a life full of ideas acted upon, whatever happened from hereon in I knew I'd given it my all. Skating through the desert sure felt better than sitting at a desk between nine and five.

We started to develop a very real sense of space. If something happened every seven days it was very much a regular event. At intervals, certain straight stretches of the highway had been painted up as makeshift airstrips for flying doctors and when pushing between the end-of-runway markers I couldn't help but keep a keener eye on the skies. Wedge-tailed eagles circled overhead majestically, their bodies about a metre in length with a wingspan of over two and a half metres, feathery trousers visible from a great distance. We saw a wedge-tail at the roadside feeding on a dead kangaroo, a hulking great bird with piercing eyes, not as big as an emu but with far more presence.

Alongside nature was the omnipresence of man. While preparing for the journey I had found pictures of the Nullarbor taken from an aeroplane. These images of the spinal Eyre Highway running parallel to the coastline of the Great Australian Bight were awe inspiring, but they were just a snapshot. Now, there in the heart of those images, I realised the wide-open flat spaces were constantly traversed by humans. Of course there were Road Trains, blitzing through the emptiness with their commercial loads, and I could never get over the humour and irony of the Over Size trucks which carried boats across the desert, these pristine craft, sometimes as wide as two lanes, floating noisily along one of the most desolate highways in the world. Then there were cars, which would have slotted quite happily into an inner-city traffic jam. And the motor homes, mostly driven by the middle aged, or the Grey Nomads as they were known. In Australia once the kids had flown the coop it was time for the parents to take advantage of their freedom, and many of them swapped buildings for wheels and went on an adventure. Those members of the Grey Safari that stopped to chat were split into two well-defined groups: some who were full of praise and compliments, and those who couldn't for the life of them fathom why a fair-haired pommie bloke wanted to push a skateboard across Australia. One of the latter, a withered old lady from the east coast, looked me up and down and uttered the immortal words, 'With that accent you'll need plenty of sun cream.'

*   *   *

The 90 Mile Straight came and went and ended at Caiguna, which was followed immediately the next morning by a bend in the road. It was a warm, calm day and I decided to spice things up a bit. A game on the project website had encouraged people to set dares which I needed to complete en route, in return they would make a donation. The game was called, ingeniously, Dare Dave. Swansea University's alumni office decided that I should bounce one of their branded beach balls along a kilometre stretch of my route, and I decided that it was time for this next challenge to be achieved. And thus began a curious sight, a man draped in yellow riding a yellow skateboard through a desert as he bounced a blue and white beach ball on the way. It was surprisingly fun despite a passing Road Train blowing the ball out of my hands at one stage, and it was over all too quickly. Still, I think the team especially savoured the break in the monotony.

When the headwind became so strong that Elsa was stopping before I'd finished a push I waved Cheech on and skated behind it, using the Jackaroo as a shield. Whatever small slipstream was gained from this was immediately countered by the effort of concentration needed to remain safe. I would skate between one and five metres away from the rear bumper, as though an invisible elastic string was constricting and expanding. With one eye on the ground between Elsa's front and the car and the other looking straight through Cheech's windows at the road ahead, I turned this into yet another game. Cheech travelled consistently at a pace not far off 12kmph, which was close to my average top speed, and it was my duty to keep up, wagging my index finger when I needed the vehicle to go a little faster. This formation also placed a huge amount of stress on the driver, their concentration split three ways between keeping up a consistent speed, watching my signals from behind and also maintaining a eye on the road ahead. Whoever was sat in the passenger seat helped keep watch out of the windscreen and in the rear-view mirrors, but it wasn't always possible to cover all angles at once.

I was sailing along, pushing fast without the debilitating headwind to worry about, when my board stopped dead. Automatically I started running, somehow keeping my balance despite the shock of Elsa's disappearance from her usual position beneath my standing foot. Had my right leg been at the very end of its pushing arc I would likely have fallen, but the impact had still slightly twisted my ankle. But I was far better off than the cause of the incident. For days we had been witnessing Shingleback skinks crossing the road in what always seemed like a curious migration. These foot-long lizards were harmless creatures, capable of a good open-mouthed hiss when scared, but they were gentle by nature and I'd become fond of their presence. Unfortunately, one had eluded the gaze of both Danny and Kate in the front of Cheech and by the time they saw it disappear under their front bumper it was too late. Elsa hit the skink head on, and had broken one of its legs. I hurried twenty metres back along the road as fast as my ankle could carry me, and when I inspected the skink and saw its damaged leg and blood trickling out of its mouth I burst into tears. I'd skated over 60km by then and for most of the afternoon had been battling into a headwind. I was exhausted and couldn't quite deal with what had happened. Dan, Kate, Dom and Holly stood around as I carried the skink off the road and sat down. I was talking to it, 'Sorry mate, I'm so sorry, I really am sorry . . .' and slowly it crawled underneath my bent legs.

'It's saying it's OK, it understands,' said Holly kindly as tears ran down my cheeks. I couldn't help it, the journey wasn't intended to cause harm to anyone or anything but I knew that ultimately I was responsible for this. Had I not been here this skink would have happily walked on with all legs intact. I decided to carry it a little further away from the road and see how freely it was moving. Thankfully, it was still able to scramble away quite quickly and we had no option but to continue. With a broken leg the chances of its survival were lessened; I hadn't a clue what I would have done had the skink been unable to move. But from then on I became more wary on the road and made it my mission to save any skink that happened to be on the bitumen when I passed. Countless lizards found themselves being transported without effort across the highway from then on, and I'd like to think I prevented more skink squashings than I ordinarily would have had I not struck one myself.

*　　*　　*

Each night I took some time for myself and walked to the road. I likened the sunsets on the Nullarbor to sunsets in the middle of the ocean. The land was so flat and vast that there was no obstruction to the natural line of the horizon, and in its final minutes of each day the sun glowed orange and red and sank so quickly its vertical movement was almost visible with the human eye. Once its death throes had ended the Nullarbor sunk into darkness with only the moon and stars as faded beacons. Then began the desert's light show, the overnight Road Trains throwing up a ghostly semi-circular glow that shimmered in the distance. You could see them long before you heard them, and it was between ten and fifteen minutes before the still air began to vibrate with the noise of engine, wheels and rattling cargo. As the lone beast roared past, its carnival of lights bordering the cargo giving the impression of an incredibly noisy horizontal Christmas tree, the game began again in reverse as the lights faded slowly into the outback. The desert night was pitch black at first, but there was always light if you looked hard enough.

On the 26th day of BoardFree Australia I had my second wind. I was feeling physically strong after almost a month on the move and had been liberated from the pain of small blisters on my toes by the sheer freedom of skating along the Eyre Highway. I hadn't travelled further than 74km in a single day before Cocklebiddy, a lonely red-roofed café, bar and motel slap bang in the middle of the Western Australian outback, but with two days scheduled to reach the next roadhouse I pushed off from there with another personal challenge on my mind. By the end of the day I had skated 90km in seven and a half hours. 'You have to see this,' Kate told me, skipping with excitement and leading me around a bend. The jubilation of smashing my longest-day record didn't compare to what awaited. The team stood at the top of a cliff, the highway running down a slope behind us towards the roadhouse, and I realised we had reached an escarpment. Passing travellers had mentioned the Madura Pass but I hadn't been expecting the sweeping Roe Plains, dotted with acacia trees and stretching flat as a snooker table as far as the eye could see. It took me straight back to Africa and the Great Rift Valley: elephant and wildebeest wouldn't have looked out of place here. It was beyond me how people had the nerve to say that the Nullarbor was boring, the vista was a fitting end to a long but ultimately satisfying day.

The next two days were spent in the shadow of the escarpment and I contented myself by imagining I was now skating along the floor of the Rift Valley as mobs of kangaroos bounded magnificently through the bush alongside the road. William Clive, an old friend of mine, had set me another Dare Dave challenge, which involved racing a form of indigenous Australian wildlife and I eyed up the kangaroos, hoping one would conveniently hop parallel with me for a while to give the impression of a race. In fact, I was looking at the wrong animal.

Two hours out of Madura an emu sidled up from the right and I grabbed the minicam from Cheech. The bird started running but just as quickly veered off the road and pulled up to walking pace again. Everyone in Cheech sighed and we waited with bated breath to see what it would do next. I started chatting into the minicam, 'What I'm going to do is wait until he's on the road and then we're going to race. I can almost guarantee that he is faster than me, but also that he's scared . . .' and then it went! Head down and legs spinning, the emu sped off. 'He's running! He's running!' I said, my voice changing pitch with excitement. 'Let's have it, let's have it!' I pushed off on Elsa as the emu legged it along the roadside about thirty metres off to my right. I could hear laughter behind me; Kate and Bev were hysterical, breathlessly shouting 'Go on Dave!' between giggles. The emu's tail feathers were bouncing along with every step. It skipped around bushes seemingly determined to keep parallel with the highway but was clearly oblivious to the excitement it was causing. We raced side by side for about eighty metres before the bird gave up, and I claimed victory: 'Crossed the finish line, Cornthwaite wins, emu loses!' And then, unbelievably, the emu started running again! 'Come on Cornthwaite!' I yelled, pushing on. 'You've got this bird Cornthwaite, you've got this bird!' As a Road Train thundered up behind, the emu stopped at last and I pulled over for a final piece to camera. 'What we are looking at my friends, is a defeated emu! Wandering lonely in the scrub knowing full well that he was beaten in a fair race! We have just raced an indigenous form of Australian wildlife, William Clive that is your Dare Dave, I'll be having thirty pounds please, Sir! Signing out . . .'

The border with South Australia came up in no time, but not before we were passed by a group of twenty cyclists who were peddling between Perth and Sydney to raise awareness of AIDS and HIV in Africa. They pulled over and invited us to share a sandwich lunch, and we chatted for a little while about the differences between cycling and skateboarding across the Plain. They were travelling much faster than I was but it was a boost knowing that there were other people living their own dreams out here. They disappeared quickly into the distance after lunch but promised to follow our progress on the website. Another man, this time in his seventies, caught us a few kilometres before Eucla. We had heard about him, tales of a man unprepared for the wilderness who was cycling from Perth to South Australia without adequate provisions. He seemed to be doing well, though, and hurried off on his way as if he didn't want to get too caught up with other people. In the same rest stop four other travellers came to say hello. One of them, a jolly lady named Elsa, seemed to be the humorous brunt of endless teasing from the others. 'His board's called Elsa,' a tall man with a moustache and walking stick exclaimed, pointing at me, 'we should put wheels on you and see how well you'd travel!' They were a great bunch hailing from Brisbane, and Elsa herself kindly extended an invitation to stay with her and Bosse, her husband, once we arrived in Queensland. We thanked them and went on our way, motivated by the blue sea that slowly filled the horizon up ahead.

This was the Great Australian Bight, and a scenic stretch of cliff-edged coastline that signalled just how close we were to South Australia, our next State. The wind by now was strong to my rear and I made myself as big as possible to catch any benefit from the gust, stretching my arms out wide and being blown for several hundred metres at a time. After all of the hard work pushing slowly through headwinds it was a wonderful feeling knowing that nature can sometimes help and not hinder our progress. Shortly before I scaled a long, steep road leading back up the escarpment to Eucla the wind lashed a permanent dust cloud across the road. It found its way into every pore, my sunglasses not doing a thing to protect my eyes. I disappeared into the cloud, Cheech behind me with all its windows closed, and emerged fifty metres later having travelled that short distance without any sight at all.

Eucla, the only stop on the Nullarbor that could have been classed as a village, had a fixed population of fifty people. The hotel and campsite cater for many more transitory visitors, but there is a police station, a medical centre and a museum heralding the settlement's former importance as a site for the telegraph station that once enabled communication between Western Australia and the eastern states. I'd skated for eleven days without a break, travelling 720km from Norseman, and we had earned a much-needed rest day. Repacking the vehicles, washing clothes and soaking in clean, modern showers were all necessary distractions from the nomadic existence we had become used to. The team ventured down to the ocean on our day off, taking photos in the sand covered ruins of the Eucla telegraph station and running along the beach and up sand dunes. Holly and I couldn't resist a dip in the ocean, only finding out later that the waters were prime hunting grounds for Great White Sharks.

Almost two weeks in the outback had numbed the team's fundraising instinct and I called everyone together, preparing them for what was to come. Although simply getting across the Nullarbor in one piece wasn't an easy task, I felt the need to instil a sense of reality; soon our time in the middle of nowhere would be over and fundraising would become a main priority. With an easy catchment area Eucla was a testing ground and I was unsettled that no initiative had been taken by the team towards making the most of that. Following the meeting everyone jumped into action, the team splitting into two and leafleting the entire camp, gaining a few donations. Although there were still several hundred more kilometres to go before we hit civilisation again I knew the time would fly by and I wanted the team to be able to fulfil their duties without a regular kick up the backside. Yes, the days were fairly long, but however hard the workload was I took the opinion that if I was doing the skating everyone else could do their bit; all I could do was set the example and give the team something tangible to capitalise on.

*   *   *

Revitalised by our rest day, potential achievement hung in the air. The road was beckoning and so was our first border. Twelve kilometres on from Eucla I reached South Australia and passed into the new State with some words to echo my only previous skateboard-related border crossing, the Scotland to England passage during BoardFree UK four months earlier. 'I'm pretty sure I've just become the first person to skateboard across the width of Western Australia, how bizarre is that!' Western Australia had been over 100km longer than the entirety of BFUK yet I'd managed to push the distance in three fewer days. My feet were blister-free, Elsa was rolling smoothly and we hadn't had nearly as much rain as the UK had offered up. I was now ready to start claiming some of South Australia's kilometres. First though, Danny changed Elsa's wheels and bearings in the Border Village petrol station as Bev, Becs and Holly posed with a giant kangaroo statue outside. Tacky postcards and dodgy cassette tapes were snapped up, and then it was time to go.

From the first push I knew the remainder of the day was going to be memorable. The roads were as smooth as marble and a strong tailwind had picked up; both combined to send me east. Si stood there open mouthed, his camera trained on Elsa and I as we floated uphill without pushing. Ten kilometres into South Australia the sea rolled in to my right, blue as a clear sky, and we took advantage of each scenic lookout point to have a breather and gaze out over the ocean. From our vantage point above a sheer cliff we stood together as two whales swam down below, a mother and her calf. I'd been hoping to reach Head of Bight near the end of the Nullarbor Plain by mid-October, before the last of the pod of Southern Right whales swam south from the spot on their annual migration to Antarctica, but 200km away from the Head none of us had expected to get this lucky. We saw seals from another lookout later, another highlight in a day which was peppered with support from passing motorists. One man handed Becki a half-full bucket of coins, another lady leant out of her car window and lost grip on the coins she held out to me, dropping them on the ground. I scrambled around on the road like a beggar in

Above: A short rest surrounded by worn out shoes before the final push into central Adelaide.

Left: Seven stitches in my heel kept me on crutches and off the road for ten days after I stepped onto a protruding shard of metal during a photoshoot.

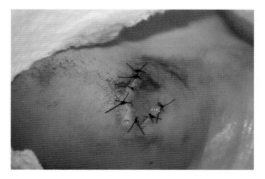

Below: Skating off the ferry after crossing the Murray River at Wellington.

Above: Bev, Becki, Simon and Holly wrap up warm on the Victoria border. We'd spent six wonderful weeks travelling through South Australia, but crossing into a new state was always an exciting prospect.

Right: On the first morning in Victoria conflicts led to me leaving the team to sort out their differences in Nelson. I fully expected to continue onto Brisbane alone.

Right: Thankfully resolutions were made, the team caught up and Simon recorded my thoughts in atrocious weather near Portland.

Above: The visitor information centre at Port Campbell had a welcome message for us on their door as we made progress along the coast.

Above: Skating the length of the Great Ocean Road in less than summery weather just added to the dramatic location.

Right: Laura Hatwell joins the team in Melbourne, offering two more arms to our fundraising efforts.

Above: Alan Fletcher, or Dr Karl Kennedy as he will be known to fans of the soap opera *Neighbours*, was a great supporter of the journey and had plenty of time for us after a gig in St Kilda.

Above: At the end of our visits to specialist schools which made use of services offered by Sailability in Gippsland, I always skated around with a high-five for everyone involved.

Right: My brother Andy joined us in Sale and proceeded to cycle alongside me for 70km the next day.

Above: After skating 4000km across Australia, was there ever a better photo opportunity?

Right: A 76km push across the Great Dividing Range between Orbost and Cann River led to the blisters on my right foot swelling. There was no choice but to jump in the vehicles and head to Sydney for a week of fundraising.

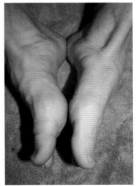

Below: In a state of depression after driving along the mountainous road in southern New South Wales, I was only persuaded to continue to Brisbane by Bev as she sang the BoardFree song with the Sydney Harbour Bridge in the distance.

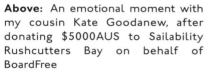

Above: An emotional moment with my cousin Kate Goodanew, after donating $5000AUS to Sailability Rushcutters Bay on behalf of BoardFree

Top Right: Back on the road, the efforts of skating 60km each day along the NSW south coast frequently led to Kate comforting me at the roadside.

Above Right: Simon lifted the mood by posing as me for a studio interview in Mallacoota. Meanwhile, his doppelganger was still skating along the highway!

Right: Kate receives a pile of coins from a generous passer-by, we raised thousands of dollars from on-the-road donations like this.

Above: I take my final push before breaking Jack Smith's distance skateboarding world record.

Above Left: My Mum and Kate celebrate during the world record procession at Sydney Olympic Park.

Above Right: Simon cycled the full 42km between Corindi and Grafton, despite a faulty bike and intense heat.

Left: Leaving Sydney wasn't easy, the steep hills towards Hornsby were hard enough for Cheech the Jackaroo to scale, let alone my weary legs.

Right: Cult Australian musician Ash Grunwald tests out Elsa at the side of the Pacific Highway en route to Ballina. Ash later invited the team to a gig in Coolangatta, where I joined him on stage to promote BoardFree.

Above Left: Another big hill on the Pacific Highway, my right calf bulging as a welcome change in road surface arrives.

Above Right: Just 3km from Brisbane I take my first big fall of the journey. Stunned, I lie at the roadside as the team and a local physician tend to my injuries. Thankfully, nothing more serious than heavy bruising and friction burns.

Left: Having endured taunts about the Ashes from Australians throughout the journey, it seemed fitting to end the penultimate day of the journey outside the famous Gabba stadium.

Right: The reception in Brisbane's South Bank once I had crossed the line was astounding, a truly fitting end to the 5823km journey.

order to add to our collection. A coach load of travelling pensioners were a tough catch for Becki and Bev – the ones who took leaflets made use of them as handheld fans – but it was funny to watch from afar the confused elderly reactions at the girls' BoardFree sales-spiel.

The only negative incident of the day occurred when I was forced to run off my board. Incomprehensibly, Dom had positioned himself and his tripod right in the middle of the road, making overtaking impossible for a couple of caravans behind Cheech. One of the vans decided to pull into a rest stop but the other continued and when it passed me I apologised profusely to the occupants, who weren't best pleased. Dom was still in the road despite my shouts, and as I looked back at him I lost my bearings and Elsa ran into the roadside gravel. Danny pulled Cheech to a quick stop, and I spent the next 10km wondering whether there was anything I could say that would make the team heed my constant requests to consistently wear reflective jackets and put the project's reputation before individual needs. Besides that little incident the day was positive, and culminated with another BoardFree record broken. Shortly before 6 p.m. I skated over the 100km mark, in my delight rushing past Dom who was hoping to get an interview. Instead, I just wanted to keep pushing, finally pulling up at the 103km marker and ending the journey's longest day so far.

A day and a half later, another 90km covered, I arrived at a signpost: NULLARBOR PLAIN. WESTERN END OF THE TREELESS PLAIN. Although the name Nullarbor is widely attributed to the vast, semi-arid space spanning the empty land between Western Australia and South Australia, the true Nullarbor Plain is actually far smaller. Travelling along the Eyre Highway there are only 25km between the western and eastern markers, but there it becomes distinctly clear why the Plain is named after the two Latin words *nulla* and *arbor*, meaning *no trees*. Barely 2km on from the sign marking the western end of the treeless plain the Nullarbor Roadhouse provides a base for the area's most famous tourist attraction, the Head of the Bight and the whales that commune there. I had a present for the team up my sleeve and set about organising it as soon as we arrived. Just behind the roadhouse is a short runway, the launch pad for Whale Air. I had a chat with the resident pilot, a bubbly lady named Caroline Disney who seemed thrilled at the opportunity to do some low-level flying. 'I'd like to give the team a treat,' I told her, 'but it would also make some great shots for the documentary. Would you be able to track close to the highway if I were skating along it?'

'Shouldn't be a problem,' Caroline said, making the appropriate calls and getting the go-ahead from her boss to give us a discount as well. I wandered into the café next door, bought Danny the bag of lollipops I'd promised him after his long-distance skating exploits on the 90 Mile Straight, and sat down with the team. 'Anyone fancy a little flight?' I asked, grinning.

Half an hour later Kate, Dom and I were soaring into the air and heading east above the highway. To see the Nullarbor Plain from above was a real privilege and confirmed just how flat and expansive it really was. Typically, though, I couldn't take my eyes off the road, a silver trail running straight as far as the eye could see, with just a small kink near the roadhouse. We turned south as a side road left the highway and blazed towards the ocean. The Plain ends here spectacularly, the limestone it rests upon drops without warning some ninety metres into a cauldron of white water, creating the mighty Bunda Cliffs. The night before we had made camp at the far end of a scenic lookout and had woken that morning to watch the sunrise break out of the ocean, the cliffs slowly becoming more pronounced as the sun climbed skywards. Now though, we were flying directly overhead, Southern Right whales basking in the turquoise sea, mothers and calves side by side, their perfectly shaped tails clearly visible from several hundred metres above. And then the splendour of the coastline, nibbled cliffs with balustrades of fallen rock at their feet, all concluding at the same altitude when the Plain sweeps away like a tabletop, blotchy with the yellows of sand and the greens of bush, dark shadows cast by clouds inking the surface like giant birth marks.

I held Kate's hand as we stared down and she turned to me beaming. 'This is the most beautiful thing I've ever seen.' She kept pointing, spotting whales and maybe a seal, exclaiming in her special way, blown away by the view. As the flight came to an end and we neared the Roadhouse I began to feel deflated, as though standing on dry land would never be the same again. As soon as we landed Kate and I rushed to Cheech. The rest of the team would have their turn now and as they flew I'd be skating along the highway, continuing my journey while up above they'd be filming and taking pictures, recording BoardFree from a whole new angle. The next 20km were a breeze, it didn't feel like any effort at all. The Cessna swooped overhead as I pushed on, then it banked towards the coast and Kate and I pulled over for half an hour, waiting for the next flight to come along and track us. Just before the end of the day I rolled past the marker for the eastern end of the Nullarbor Plain and started to wonder what all the fuss had about. People had said it would be impossible for me to skate across the Nullarbor and I'd managed to do it in just one day!

*   *   *

The next day we didn't get back on the road until early afternoon. Despite the cost of the flights with Whale Air I thought it was only fair to give the team a closer look at the whales, so we drove to Head of Bight and spent an hour on a specially constructed walkway that allows visitors to stand as close to the ocean as possible. The size of the creatures was hypnotic, even from fifty metres away I could make out the barnacle-like markings on each head, the gaping mouths, the gentle splashing of tails which were wider than cars. I was getting itchy feet by the end, determined to move on and somewhat annoyed by the fact that only Kate and Becki thanked me for paying. I hadn't taken the team there for the thanks; I did it because I wanted them to feel valued, but instead I felt like they were along for the ride. Perhaps two tours in two days was a bit much. A close encounter with a Brown snake just outside the toilet block put things in perspective, though. About six feet long and insanely fast, it wiggled in between the rocks lining the footpath as a warden gave chase with a long stick. As I left my cubicle he barked at me, 'Stay back there, you don't want this thing close to you, not with thongs on.' Like the whales the snake was fascinating, but standing and gawping wasn't on the agenda. I followed orders and stood well back until the snake had been caught and deposited far away from the site.

Ceduna was close now, the town that marked the official end of the Nullarbor Plain. After an hour of skating the treeless plains were replaced with heavy vegetation and forest. The rough road frustrated and tired me but adrenaline was dragging me along. Almost without warning we became haunted by clouds of March flies, as big as the end of a thumb and boasting a proboscis that could deliver a vicious bite through the top of my shoe. For two days the team stood on permanent guard, armed with magazines and flip-flops. It was too hot for the vans to drive along without the windows open – my budget hadn't the might to cope with buying air-conditioned vehicles – but open windows let flies in, invoking a constant flurry of arms and high-pitched screams. I wasn't so lucky, these March flies were keeping up with me even at 10mph. It was terrifying and I skated with the expedition's only fly swat at stand-by. Passing cars must have thought we were both hilarious and mad, three vans full of swiping, twirling bodies, and a skateboarder crouched at the ready with a fly swat.

At Yalata, the site of a former Aboriginal-run roadhouse, a distance marker for westward-bound traffic told me that I'd skated 1,001km since leaving Norseman sixteen days earlier. We were now 275km into South Australia and the promise of civilisation tempted us on. George had been suffering with mechanical trouble, occasionally failing to start once the engine had been switched off, so Kate and Becki had gone ahead to Nundroo, the next roadhouse, to see if they could get it fixed. It was a long day with awful roads, the temperature was into the mid-thirties and I was wilting seriously. We pulled over for a break, still swatting March flies and amusing ourselves with a game of makeshift baseball involving sticks and stone. I usually had half-decent eye to hand coordination but failed on each swing to make contact with the stone. Eventually I gave up, sat on Kylie's rear spoiler and sucked at my water bottle. Three hours later the signs for Nundroo began, the roads smoothed out and George appeared, racing towards us. The girls got out smiling.

'We sweet-talked a mechanic and managed to get the van fixed,' Becki said.

'And you boys have a treat in store tonight,' said Kate, eyes twinkling. 'The roadhouse restaurant at Nundroo serves up kilogram steaks, and if you eat one you win a t-shirt.'

Safe to say, it took me all of three minutes to cover the last 2km. The lure of steak has always been a good way to get me to do anything, unfortunately the same can't be said of Danny. Dom, Si and myself all managed to polish off the dinner plate-size hunks of meat but Dan was more creative, slicing eyes and a mouth out of his and holding it up in the air like a mask, much to the distaste of a passing waitress.

*   *   *

The countryside became less arid as we left Nundroo behind, gently undulating hills populated by farmsteads and windmills. The foot-high yellow grass that had lined the highway for days was still present and was clearly a haven for snakes, as a new type of roadkill joined the highway platter. I rarely saw the snakes until the last minute, but even the dead ones which were flattened down by tyres had their mouths ominously wide open, heart fluttering distractions from my mission. I crossed paths with a young guy from Canberra, named Winston. He was cycling across Australia and still had the Nullarbor to come, but the wind had turned since I crossed the border and after we bade farewell to each other I pushed off into a headwind as Winston sailed west with barely a pedal.

We spent our final night on the Nullarbor in the wheatbelt settlement of Penong, a village defined by dozens of authentic windmills, which pump the local water supply from an underground basin. Skating into the village I was somehow oblivious to the windmills, my head down in bulldozer mode. It was a zone I was finding myself in more and more frequently and was my way of getting through some parts of the journey. Going through the motions without thinking was a great help, it blocked out any pain or emotional niggles I was experiencing and had the duel bonus of carrying me further along the highway. Bev was in tears when we arrived in Penong, 'I'm so sorry Dave,' she said, 'I reversed into a tree and smashed Kylie's rear window.' Bev had been a rock all journey and I hated to see her so upset. After Kate had backed Cheech into a tree in Norseman I'd berated her for not being more careful and wasn't going to make the same mistake again. I gave Bev a hug and told her not to worry. 'I'll pay for it,' she said, but she didn't have to and I had no intention of letting her, accidents happen.

The next morning I daubed my cheeks and nose in yellow and blue war paint, with Dan attaching similarly coloured ribbons to my helmet and to the right side of the vehicles. The Aussie Rules Football Grand Final was coming up that weekend and was to be contested between Sydney Swans and the West Coast Eagles. Some West Coast fans would be driving across the Nullarbor from Perth to watch the game in Melbourne and we wanted to show our support, hoping that the fans in return would stop and make donations. It took a while to get going because of a second vehicle failure in two days. Kylie, her rear window gaffer-taped in place, was now refusing to start, so Becs and Bev stayed behind to address the problem.

My head was heavy from the long push across the Nullarbor and I was feeling a fair bit of strain as I pushed into a strong headwind. This, added to the stress of George and Kylie's mechanical troubles and the costs associated with remedying these, sunk me into a deeper mood as the day went on. The countryside changed as the Eyre Highway edged closer to the sea again and I found myself growing increasingly frustrated with Holly, who was hungover after a late night in Penong and opted to sit in Cheech and play with her mobile phone all day, rather than take any pictures. Holls had been great all journey, working hard and taking some astounding shots, but even after that I struggled to accept that she should neglect her duties, especially on a momentous day such as this.

When I found myself thinking in this way I almost always kept the thoughts to myself. I understood but couldn't control the moods that the fatigue was bringing upon me, and although I was capable of continuing physically the emotional conflict that I enacted on myself furthered my exhaustion. I was very aware during these times that I wasn't easy to be around and that I was capable of being very blunt to the team, and tried to repress any anger I had as best I could, knowing that an outburst would affect everybody. These periods came and went several times each day, but just as one incident would piss me off another would fill me with delight. A car sped by and soon afterwards a young man rolled down the road in the opposite direction, on a skateboard! He was from Belgium and wanted to skate a little of the way with me, having picked up one of our leaflets in an earlier roadhouse. I was overjoyed! His girlfriend took pictures after a 2km push, her shattered boyfriend shaking his head at the task I was undertaking. Eventually, after much imbibing of water, we shook hands, hugged with mutual respect and continued towards Ceduna on our respective wheels.

The town sat on the coast at the very edge of the Great Australian Bight, the Bunda Cliffs a long distant memory. In the other direction across the bay, giant silos marked the port of Thevenard, seeming to me to be like an odd recreation of the Acropolis in Athens. Before I could pass into Ceduna our vehicles were stopped at a Fruit Fly inspection point, a reminder that Australia was incredibly strict about the quarantine laws, which disallowed the transport of fresh fruit and vegetables from state to state. We were cleared and waved on, the gate opened and I skated beneath it into Ceduna eighteen days after leaving Norseman. We had finally crossed the Nullarbor.

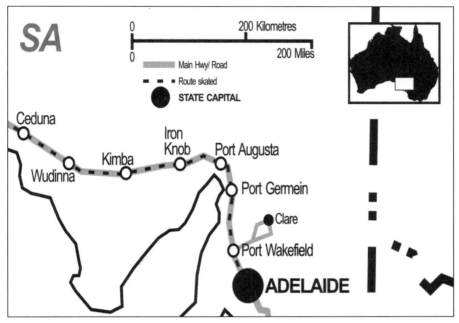

18 To Adelaide

29 September – 27 October 2006

Crossing the Nullarbor had been on our minds for months, for some of us over a year. Now, having skated those roads and beaten the obstacles – descriptions of which filled warning messages sent to us before the journey – there was a real sense of achievement surrounding our efforts. We had arrived in Ceduna eight days ahead of schedule, a happy coincidence as that weekend happened to host a local annual festival, the Oysterfest. I called two days of rest for the expedition and we set about enjoying ourselves, helped along by the receipt of a package full of CDs sent from Western Australia by Sonny Rolph, a musician we had met in Balladonia. Sonny had made notes about the team and subsequently returned to his studio and recorded a song about our journey. He appropriately entitled it 'BoardFree'. The BoardFree boys all followed through with a promise we'd made each other in Norseman: it was time to shave into our heavily bearded faces and walk away with what can only be described as a Gringo. Kate wasn't at all impressed with my new moustache, which headed due south as soon as it reached the sides of my mouth.

A carnival was due to trawl through town and Becki spoke to the organisers and, quite humorously, they agreed to give BoardFree a spot in the procession, so I jumped back on my board and gently pushed through town, the team rushing around making sure everyone in the surrounding crowds had a leaflet. Along with the emu race and bouncing a beach ball along the Eyre Highway, rolling along between a float covered in purple-wigged girls and a small herd of Shetland ponies being led by scouts and guides was surely one of BoardFree's most unusual moments. The Oysterfest swells Ceduna's resident population of 3,000 to nearly 10,000 over the long weekend and the girls take advantage, deciding to leaflet the crowds for two days, shaking buckets and raising several hundred dollars. After the loneliness of the Nullarbor our heads were spinning with people but there was a drive and energy to the team that I hadn't seen before. We were ready for the next stage, the long push to Adelaide.

The final 500km stretch of the Eyre Highway lay between Ceduna and Port Augusta. I put my head down, and after two hours of skating from Ceduna we passed another milestone, the 2,000km mark. The day continued, hot and dry as I ate into the Eyre Highway. A new bicycle, purchased in Ceduna in order to give the crew some exercise, had a baptism of fire today. Dom started, Bev continued, Becs had a go and Kate pedaled for 10km. And then, as I decided with shadows lengthening to push hard for another 30km and finish a day ahead of schedule, Dom patted his paunch and declared, 'I'm going to try and do the rest with you, I've got some steak to burn off.' So he did, and spurred on by an enormous Brown snake that slithered across the road we reached Wirrulla having travelled 94km in nine hours. 'The Town With a Secret' read a curious sign as we pulled off the highway, an eerie calm and a distinct lack of people magnified by two looming grain silos, which cast our campsite – a disused tennis court that we shared with no one – in shadow. A large Huntsman spider eyeballed me as I showered but I didn't care, I hadn't expected to reach Wirrulla until the next evening and had started a personal battle to take my mind off the distance ahead; I wanted to get to Adelaide ahead of schedule and relished the opportunity to push my limits. The next day was shorter, a sensible 47km to Poochera, where we rested for the afternoon, baking in the heat and humidity which was searing indoors and out.

There were 600km to go until Adelaide, our second Australian city, but having passed the 2,000km mark 600km seemed almost dainty. Ridiculous, maybe, but the team had started to enjoy life on the road more than rest days. A clockwork-like eagerness to experience what lies around the next corner seems to be wound up every night and released the next day. Each evening as I updated the route map with another white dot and a slight lengthening of the red progress line, I felt a sense of achievement; it was becoming an addiction, an obsession to make more ground. I skated 72km the next day, Kate cycling almost 50km of those with me. We were making good time and were getting lucky with accommodation too. In Wudinna the manager of the settlement's Hotel Bar gave us two rooms at his motel on the eastern edge of town and also offered us a free dinner in his restaurant.

'It's the least I can do,' he said shrugging. 'I can see your team is doing a good job and God knows you've taken on quite a challenge.'

Simon provided us with an eagerly anticipated present before dinner. He had finished the latest video which would sit on the website as a visual guide to our time on the Nullarbor. His editing improved with every video and we waited with bated breath for each instalment. For ten minutes we watched in silence, memories of the whales, the flights and the endless roads coming back to us. At Mundrabilla Roadhouse Bev had played a song written by Holly and Dom, and like Sonny's song it was called 'BoardFree'. Bev, a talented musician with a voice like falling rain, performed it brilliantly. Si had ended the video with a three-minute montage of clips shot between Norseman and Ceduna, and the BoardFree song provided the soundtrack. By the end of it we were all blinking away tears, already the Nullarbor seemed so far away.

Over 100km of open road lay between Wudinna and Kimba, the next town on the highway, and I felt a challenge boiling in my blood. Unlike the day we crossed into South Australia, though, the wind direction wasn't favourable and if the previous day's roads were anything to go by Elsa and I weren't in for a smooth surfaced treat. Still, if I was the type to make things easy for myself I wouldn't be pushing a skateboard across Australia, so I rolled out of Wudinna with only one goal in my sights, a new longest day. Fifteen kilometres on we reached Kyancutta and I called for the minicam: it was time to make some observations about this stretch of the Eyre Highway.

'Every town since Ceduna seems exactly the same. We're just coming to a place called Kyancutta, as usual to the left there's a road, which goes across some disused railway track. To the right there are some pretty obscure general stores, and then, the *piece de resistance* for a place like this, the silos.' I pushed passed the silos, across the shadows they shed on the road and then, unexpectedly, I saw something that was unusual for one of these settlements. 'And now the road veers off to the east, we've turned a full ninety degrees,' I said to the camera as the Eyre Highway enacted a right-angle turning to the left.

I moved the camera around so it looked back from where we had come, and focused on Dom who was riding directly behind me.

'That's the first turn in two thousand kilometres!' he shouted, his bike wobbling with excitement.

Either side of an undulating road the countryside turned vaguely British, sheep and horses stared at me as I glided by and I half expected an olde English pub around every corner. Instead, the day was peppered with random events. Dom ran up to me holding a dead frilled lizard by the tail, its stiff body swinging in the wind. The driver of a van stuck a chubby middle finger up as I moved over to let her pass, a totally unnecessary act as I'd pulled off the road out of kindness: yet again I raised my water bottle in anger and nearly lobbed it after her. Another woman drove by waving a five-dollar note out of the window and then panicked as two cars appeared behind her. She threw the note, which, being paper, didn't gain any velocity and flapped around in the wind until I caught up with it. I had been doing an on-the-road video blog at the time and I looked at the camera and grinned. 'Apparently word has got around that I must be crazy to be doing something like this, too crazy even to talk to.'

David Attenborough's audio book *Life on Air* had kept my left ear company for the past few days. The man has led a fascinating life and today, as I listen in to Disc 8 of 17, he talks about flying to Nairobi with a co-cameraman to film a documentary about a lioness who was adopted and reared by a German Baroness in northern Kenya and whose subsequent story became known as *Born Free*. The lioness was called Elsa, and Attenborough recalled the moment when he woke up from a siesta with the hairy, sweaty underside of a big cat's jaw looming over him, 'If I had sat up with a jolt,' he recalled, 'my head would have collided with her.' As Attenborough finished his sentence I looked down at Elsa, the one who keeps my feet company everyday and bares the name inspired by this wildly tame lioness from Kenya, and tapped her with my left shoe. 'That's my girl,' I said, and pushed on.

Somehow I found myself rolling into Kimba before the day was out. The town, which boasted a sign claiming it was halfway across Australia, had one other redeeming feature, an enormous statue of a galah, a red-bellied bird that had been a regular, somewhat smaller sight on the expedition so far.

Absolutely shattered and wanting to eat and rest, a now familiar trait of fatigue began to harp from camp. Stuck for days on end with each other there was little escape from the group, and although we each had our permanent responsibilities Becki struggled with this more than the others. Her role was demanding and two-fold, with both cooking and fundraising as priorities, but Becs often believed she was doing more than anyone else, even me, and demanded thanks and recognition for her efforts unlike the others. Just as Kate soaked up my moods Bev took the brunt of her best friend's wrath, but the team was starting to sicken of the constant griping. Every mealtime Becki issued half an hour of barking orders, demanding that Bev fetch this and fetch that, that Bev was looking in the wrong place and that she knew she was doing so.

The situation came to a brief head in Kimba, where Bev and Becs hadn't managed to find a place willing to offer us free accommodation. It wasn't a huge issue as the town had a central picnic spot where camping was possible, but in a local hotel bar where the team were due to eat dinner Kate decided to give the accommodation hunt another go. Becki had tried the same hotel already but Kate spoke to a different person who then agreed to put us up for the night. Becki was furious. She accused Kate of undermining her and made dinner an uncomfortable affair with snide comments and heavy breathing. Later that night, safely tucked up in beds rather than the bunks in the vans, Becki's upset continued. I was exhausted, worn down as much by Becki's response as by anything else I'd encountered on the journey, and for days had tried to distance myself from her as much as possible so as to avoid the knock-on effects. I'd skated 104km, the journey's longest day, and Becki was actually moaning *because* we had accommodation: there was no logic to her behaviour and therefore no logical solution. Kate stormed into our bedroom as Becki howled down the corridor. 'I'm fucking sick of this,' Kate spat, 'she is so out of order.' I slept badly, wondering what I could do to rectify the situation and not coming up with any resolution that involved Becki remaining on the team. There was a crisis point coming, I just had no idea when.

The 104km day had taken it out of me and it took two days to cover the 87km between Kimba and a place which somewhat immaturely had been on my horizons for longer than most of our Australian stops. When Phil was still a BoardFree team member in late 2005 he researched our route and had noticed a little place set deep into the Eyre Peninsula. 'Dave,' he said, holding a hand to his mouth to stifle a little chuckle, 'we should pay a visit to this town, it's called Iron Knob.' A historical moment it wasn't, but I managed to muster a tiny amount of childish glee when I skated into the village, and felt obliged to have a photo taken next to the welcome sign just so I could send it home to Phil.

Iron Knob was, in fact, abandoned. There was barely any sign of life due to the closure of the local mine, but luckily the owner of the roadhouse took pity and offered us accommodation in the motel. The man, whose extreme kindness made up for his lack of articulation, called himself Chug. His wife appeared now and then, but his son Jacob, who at three years old was absolutely fearless and proved to be more proficient at skateboarding than I was at the age of twenty-five, filled me with hope. Here was a poor family, making ends meet in the best way they knew how, through struggle. But they were kind to the end, admiring of what we had done and refusing in every way possible to accept payment for the shelter or food they provided. Jacob climbed trees and fell, rode my board and fell, grazed and bloodied his knees and arms, but smiled continuously. 'Show me a kid his age in the UK who would fall without bawling his eyes out . . .' I said to those members of the team who sat by the tree from which Jacob dangled like a monkey, '. . . and I will eat my longboard. This is one tough cookie.'

Chug's elder son, Michael, was in his early teens and was determined to have a race on the boards before I left. I obliged the next morning, giving him a one hundred-metre start in a three hundred-metre race, and only just beating him because he lost his balance and ran off the board. He was beaming as I put an arm around his shoulders and ruffled his hair. In just a few hours we had become part of a family I'm sorry to say we probably wouldn't have looked twice at had we been travelling independently. The opportunity to meet people like Chug, his wife and his boys, and the according generosity that they and so many others had shown to us throughout the BoardFree journeys, gave me a faith in humanity that I hadn't previously been aware of; it made me all the more determined to plug on whatever the cost.

In the middle of the afternoon on Tuesday 10 October, having battled against a crosswind so strong it blew me off my board twice, I pushed into Port Augusta and off the Eyre Highway. For an entire month I had skated the length of just that one road, travelling almost 1,700km through two States, eastwards across the Nullarbor Plain and the Eyre Peninsula. It was time for one rest day, and then a new journey would begin. It was time to head south, to Adelaide.

*   *   *

Port Augusta was a shabby town with a couple of shiny spots to keep people happy. One of these was the Big4 Caravan Park, a clean and well laid out campsite in which we were kindly given parking space and two cabins in which to spend a well-earned rest day. With a population of 15,000 Port Augusta was the largest urban area since Perth. From now on, at least for the most part, the lonely outback roads are past, and the steady whoosh of cars will again become commonplace. Another reality check: we have mobile telephone coverage again. At ten to seven on Monday morning – our rest day – the *Knight Rider* theme tune rang out for an interview with ABC South Australia. In the early afternoon I chatted to Jess from Flow FM, which has good coverage throughout much of South Australia. Later I spoke to Triple J for another of their national BoardFree updates. Robbie Buck and his co-presenter had been openly incredulous about my chances of skating across the Nullarbor but now, with the Plain behind me the tone had changed just a little bit. 'If you are in a car this afternoon spare a thought for Dave Cornthwaite. Here is a bloke who has just made history. He is the first person ever – as if anybody else would do this – the first person ever to skateboard across the Nullarbor in his quest to skate from west from east.' As Robbie finished his intro applause picked up in the studio.

'Who's clapping in the background?!' I asked, bemused.

'Ah, that's Dools,' said Robbie about his co-presenter.

'It's me, sorry Dave, I'm a believer,' said Dools dryly.

'He was a doubter to begin with but after you've done that . . . I tell you what, congratulations man . . .' said Robbie.

It was always fun talking to Triple J, knowing that word of the journey was getting around Australia, and Robbie reading out the website address at the end of each interview sent thousands of people online to look at the pictures, maps and videos we'd uploaded. I hoped that now the donations would start rolling in as well.

The next morning, I'd been back on the road for all of ten minutes before ABC Tasmania called in, and to finish off the media flurry I was on the phone at 5 p.m. that evening speaking to my old friends at BBC Radio Cumbria. When I had visited their studio during BoardFree UK I was about 350 miles into my long-distance skateboarding career. Just south of Port Augusta, with over 2,500km skated in Australia alone, my feet were looking considerably better than they did for much of BFUK, and despite a transitory tummy bug that the team was passing around I felt fit and strong, if a bit achy. It also looked likely that a couple of toenails were on their way out, but I could deal with that, and despite everything my pace hadn't slowed. Sixty-five kilometres south of Port Augusta I pulled into Port Germein, a delightful little fishing village that once boasted the longest jetty in the southern hemisphere. In need of relaxation some of the team ventured down the mile-long jetty to crab until the sun disappeared into a remarkably calm Spencer Gulf.

We lunched the next day in Crystal Brook, Dan having cycled with me the whole morning along smooth roads. With every push Adelaide drew closer and the wind was again behind us. There were less than 200km left to the city that had always been our halfway marker, but I got the feeling as a large proportion of passing vehicles honked horns in recognition of a journey they had already heard about through the media, that the urban experience was going to be an entirely different matter compared to the first, desolate half of the journey. Kate rode with me for the afternoon and we were soon joined by another cyclist, a Canadian teacher named Rob who had upped sticks from his home in North America to follow his dream: he wanted to cycle around the world. Rob had been riding his bike for five years through the United States, South America, Africa, Europe and Asia, and here he was in Australia on what was perhaps his last leg. Unsurprisingly he was now a storyteller, tales of being knocked off his bike in China to being chased by an elephant in Botswana seemed ingrained into his communication, and once the day was over we talked about writing travel books and following dreams, living life and pushing boundaries. I'm not sure that we'll contact each other much after we go our separate ways, perhaps we're too similar to be good friends, but I hope Rob writes his book – behind his showmanship there was an important story to be told. He wasn't afraid to throw away his security blanket and jump across the garden fence, and I get the feeling he's become a better man for it.

Rob cycled with me all of the next day, as did Kate. The 76km between Redhill and Port Wakefield was full of extremes; blisteringly hot tailwinds made pushing unnecessary for kilometres at a time, 38–39°C temperatures were throat-strippingly unbearable, sending the cold water in my bottle warm in two minutes flat. My usual average speed of 11–13kmph rose to an average of 19.6kmph, salt lakes and wheat fields blurry to the sides of Highway 1 and the skies shimmering with the haze of bushfires to the east. I broke my personal speed record on one hill, somehow managing to correct a wobbling Elsa right at the top before speeding down and reaching 65kmph at one point. I've had my chips here, I thought to myself, bending forwards and crouching low for stability, racing up the other side and then down again. I didn't fall. I hadn't yet. I didn't intend to do so at all – the ramifications, especially at that speed, weren't worth thinking about.

Kate was exhausted once we reached Port Wakefield and slumped into a roadhouse seat. She'd done amazingly well, and tailwind or not 76km was no small achievement. We bade farewell to Rob who continued on to Adelaide, and then we jumped into the vehicles and made our way to Clare. Back on the Nullarbor during that long first day in South Australia I had been rolling along only to see a waving figure across the road, stood beside a motor home. As I passed I realised that although I didn't know the man he was wearing a BoardFree t-shirt. For some reason I didn't stop – perhaps it was the amazement – but Becki later told me that the man was named Ken, and he and his wife had heard one of my radio interviews with ABC Goldfields. They had pulled over next to Kylie, bought a couple of t-shirts and offered to host a BBQ for the team when we neared the Clare Valley region just north of Adelaide. It was an offer too good to refuse. Ken and Yvonne were members of the Clare Lions Club and had invited several of their club members and friends along to join in the celebration, so we drove north east from Port Wakefield to find Ken on the Clare outskirts, happily wearing his BoardFree t-shirt.

It was a bonny evening, the first we'd spent in an authentic Australian home. The BBQ was a true testament to the Aussie tradition and we gorged ourselves on sausages and good conversation. I even allowed myself a couple of beers and drifted off to sleep feeling more comfortable than I had done in weeks. The next morning I had a cameo push through the streets of Clare, which of course wasn't on the route. An article in the local paper had sparked an interest though and Becs and Bev rushed around with collection buckets as Simon and Dom filmed, Holly snapped and Dan and Kate trundled nearby in Cheech. Several dollars to the better, it was time for some skating proper and the BoardFree convey pulled out of town.

Before Port Wakefield, though, we lost George. The van had broken down and wasn't in a good state. Ultimately, the vehicles needed to be working in order for the project to continue and my hopes of reaching Adelaide by the end of the day were scuppered by the breakdown. As Dan, Holly and the other mechanically minded people on the team jumpstarted George with Cheech, I took my mind off the stress by making friends with an inquisitive horse from a neighbouring field. 'Horses don't break down, vehicles break down,' I said into the minicam, framing myself and the horse, which I named Mrs Fred, in the shot. 'I'm glad I don't have a vehicle,' I uttered in a contorted voice on behalf of the horse. 'Mrs Fred has taken a bit of a shine to our dilemma here at the side of the road, and hopefully she'll turn out to be a lucky horse,' I said, timing it perfectly as George's motor chugged into life. 'We're off!'

The afternoon was a strain. Bev and I had a run-in over the installation of Kylie's new rear window, silly really because Bev tried to pay for it and I wouldn't let her. We were all tired, getting on each other's nerves, and my mood wasn't improved by a traitorous headwind: only yesterday it had been right behind me! We stopped for the night in a small place called Dublin and made camp by the local oval. Holly and Dom asked to talk to me; their patience with Becki's temperament had reached breaking point. 'It's ridiculous,' Dom said to me, 'everyone is walking on eggshells when she's around. Something needs to be done.' In a way it was slightly easier to stomach that everyone felt the same as I did about Becs, but it was also a recipe for disaster. Dom misused the communal support and let fly at Becki, putting her in floods of tears but knowing that he wouldn't get in trouble for it. The BoardFree walls were crumbling down and, too tired to deal with what was a gargantuan problem there and then, I just wanted to get to Adelaide and give everyone some time off. Maybe then the atmosphere would calm.

George failed to start again the next morning so after another jumpstart from Cheech I sent Dan and Becki ahead to Adelaide to find a mechanic and fix the problem. Thirty-five kilometres north of Adelaide we were joined by Jo-Anna Robinson, a photographer from the *Sunday Mail*. She snapped away for the weekend paper, offering to show us the sights and recommending some hotspots as I edged closer to the city. Jo left us for the final stretch but took two passengers with her, a mother and son who had broken down themselves just south of Dublin. We had been happy to give them a lift, but they surely hadn't been expecting to hitchhike behind a skateboarder!

A representative from Sailability Port Adelaide named Chris Tippett had offered to look after the team, arrange for our vehicles to be serviced and provide accommodation for the duration of our stay in Adelaide, but several missed calls showed that he was an elusive figure. I'd given his number to Becki and Dan, but when we met up on the northern outskirts of the city they were stood besides George, sullen-faced.

'It's been really hard,' said Becki before I could say anything, and I knew instantly that she was in another mood. I really wasn't going to put up with it.

'What's happened, do we have a mechanic?'

'Not yet, we wanted to wait for you to make a decision.' I looked at her, feeling the frustration bubbling up.

'How can I make a decision if you don't have any information?'

'Well, we just didn't want to . . .' she tailed off, '. . . and Chris Tippett hasn't been helpful so we didn't know what to do.'

'Right,' I said, glad that I'd sent ahead two people to get a job done, and they hadn't done it. 'Get hold of some mechanics and find out how much it costs to One, tow, and Two, fix. That's all I needed from you guys.'

'But Dave, we don't have any numbers,' Becki said, shoulders hunching in that familiar way. I knew I was going to have to deal with the fallout of ticking her off, but frankly the lack of initiative astounded me; why have a support team if they're just going to hang around for me to do the job? I glared at Dan and Becs, quite aware that it's difficult to be in a position of authority when you're very sweaty and wearing a luminous vest over your t-shirt, but I gave them a verbal push anyway.

'Guys, have you found a Yellow Pages?' They looked at me blankly, as though a book full of telephone numbers was the most outlandish idea ever. Their heads moved from side to side. I wasn't using Please or Thank You anymore. 'For God's sake go to the shop and get a book, then call some mechanics and find out prices, like I asked you to do this morning.'

I stomped off to get some water from Cheech, boiling at George for breaking down and Becki and Dan for wasting a morning. Chris Tippett from Sailability Port Adelaide certainly hadn't been helpful, but I couldn't do anything about that. For now we needed to get George mended and complete the skate into the city by half past one in order to meet the TV cameras. The clock was ticking and we were running out of time. I was reluctant to commit to getting George towed before Chris Tippett got back to us, so decided that we should leave the faulty van where it was and jump into the remaining two vehicles. I was pissed off at the delay and not being able to skate into town, and needlessly took it out on Kate for organising the media call too early. 'We could have done with another couple of hours,' I bitched, realising while speaking that I was being completely unfair. Kate couldn't have predicted the delay and she was all too often the verbal punch bag for my fatigued irrationality. On the way into Adelaide I tried not to look outside, not feeling like I had earned that privilege yet. Instead, I began to draw comparisons between Becki's behaviour and my own and wondered just how sick of me the team was, too. Disappointingly none of the stations had followed up on the media call and there were no TV cameras waiting.

We sloped back to Cheech, only to find that it wouldn't start. The regular jumpstarts had worn down the battery and now, unbelievably, we had two broken vehicles. The irony that we had just reached the City of Churches and that God was most certainly not on our side was palpable. Three hours later, after a series of jumpstarts and tow trucks, a weary BoardFree expedition found themselves being shown around Port Adelaide Sailing Club by Chris Tippett, who hadn't been able to help us that morning because he'd been painting his new boat. The accommodation he had promised us was actually the floor of the Sailing Club and a Yellow Pages was thrown down on a table with no further suggestions for mechanics. He left soon afterwards with barely a word, and it seemed strangely like he had just wanted to get us into the club, and that was it. I was furious, feeling quite rightly that my team deserved a little more respect than we'd been shown.

Needing to rectify the situation I called Deirdre Schahinger, who ran the other Sailability Club in Adelaide and who had also offered us accommodation. Deirdre was very helpful and incredibly apologetic for the way we had been treated and promised to come by the next morning and do what she could. Half an hour later she called again. 'There's someone at the gate for you.' Confused, I went downstairs and welcomed in Chris Riordan. Chris suffered from cerebral palsy and at first I struggled to understand him, but it quickly became apparent that he had been sat with Deirdre when I called and felt it necessary to drive straight across town to apologise on behalf of Sailability in person. He was a brilliant guy, full of wisecracks and witty to the core. He was in training for the Paralympics and clearly had a great deal of motivation behind him; his presence lifted everyone at a time when we all needed lifting. Until Chris Riordan turned up, Adelaide was a very lonely place for all of us.

I decided that two things had to be done the next day; I needed to skate through the city and finish on the southern outskirts in preparation for the next push, and then we had to find some decent accommodation so everyone could have a bed for the remaining four days we planned to spend in Adelaide. Dom, Holly and Dan woke at half past four the next morning and we drove Kylie to Gepps Cross, where I had finished the day before. We were up early to beat the traffic and I was on the road by quarter to six. The city was empty, a huge contrast to the stretch of highway leading into Adelaide which piped tens of thousands of vehicles north and south each day. With clear streets it took just an hour to roll through the centre, down King William Street and across Victoria Square. A swaying man, on his way home from what had evidently been a night filled with liquor, started singing as I passed, 'Kick, Push, Cruuuise,' he crooned drunkenly, a song by Lupe Fiasco in which the skateboarding connotations were evident. I had to stop and chat to the guy, who kindly donated his last dollar then landed flat on his backside when he tried to step onto Elsa.

By 7 a.m. our day was done. I'd skated 19km through Adelaide and picked my board up in the foothills of Mitcham. Looking back, the high rises sprouted out of a green, luscious city, and I had the distinct feeling that the bad luck from the past two days was about to change. One hundred metres from finishing I'd pushed past a sign for Thorpe Street and found myself wondering whether I'd want the team to take a picture of Cornthwaite Street had the shoe been on the other foot. The answer, emphatically, was yes. So, just down the road we all jumped out having decided to take a funny photo next to the sign, just for our very own cameraman, Simon Thorpe. I'd taken my shoes off so waved away Dan and Dom's request for me to join them on a wall, from which they were going to jump for the picture. 'No way guys,' I said, 'I'll kill my feet if I jump from there with socks on.' Instead, I clutched onto the sign's pole and jumped up beneath it. Holly was never one to rest on her laurels, and by now we were used to her taking a picture and following up with a request for one more, just for luck.

After the second photograph I felt something was wrong, like I'd trodden on a stone. It was much worse. My left foot had landed at the base of the signpost where a sharp piece of metal had twisted out of the casing. Blood oozed through my sock and I immediately sat down in the van, where the damage became more evident. A large flap of skin hung from the bottom of my left heel, dripping blood onto the road beneath. Dan acted immediately as I held my head in my hands, feeling sure that my body weight had driven the metal spike straight through to the bone. I was white from the pain and as Danny bandaged up the wound Dom and Holly captured the moment through their lenses. Of all the people to hurt their foot, it had to be me, I thought as Kylie raced through the city to the Royal Adelaide Hospital. My board hadn't been anywhere in sight.

Five hours later I was back outside the hospital with seven stitches in my heel and orders to remain on crutches for two weeks. None of us could believe what had happened. Having planned to be back at Port Adelaide before the others got up we had taken our only key to the compound. Kate had gone ballistic when she found out I was hurt and I got the impression she and Holly had shared some heated words over the phone. When we finally made it back to the sailing club Kate was inconsolable, hugging me and berating me all at the same time. As my partner all she'd wanted to do was be by my side at the hospital; she had even tried to climb through a window of the club that led out onto the road, but it was too small. Chris Tippett wasn't helping matters, wheeling his chair over to Kylie and laughing at my mummified foot. 'Now you know what it's like to be disabled,' he said.

Once he had gone Becki told me that earlier, when informed that I was in hospital, he had remarked, 'I better tell everyone the bad news.'

'About Dave's foot?' enquired Simon,

'No, about the plastic on my boat spoiling the paintwork,' came the reply.

* * *

The entire situation was laughable. I was usually so careful and not at all accident prone; my foot injury was incredibly bad luck. The persistent vehicle breakdowns and the disappointing treatment we'd had at Sailability Port Adelaide was just salt in the wound. Deirdre Schahinger was waiting at the club when we got back from the hospital and offered to accommodate the whole team temporarily in her own home. She paid for George to be towed and arranged for her mechanic to service it and Cheech. She was brilliant, an angel when we needed one, as was Bob, her husband. They took us under their wing and made us welcome, just what a team of weary travellers needed after a seven-week push across the Australian outback. As ironic as it was that I'd skated 2,700km across the treacherous Nullarbor without injury and had finally been brought to heel by the base of a signpost, there was no use moping. Perhaps an enforced rest was just what we all needed to heal physically and emotionally before the next leg of the journey.

The media, however, found the accident hilarious and those predators that had doubted BoardFree Australia's likely success rubbed their hands as the journey was put on hold. The phone rang endlessly for days, and we quickly realised that this was just a new hook that we had to play to our advantage. The drama was unfolding: not only had I negotiated the Nullarbor but now had to overcome a serious injury before continuing. I dryly repeated the 'British skater hurts his foot and everybody wants to talk' line interview after interview, willingly hoisted my bandaged foot for thirty second grabs for the evening news, and – begrudgingly – posed for two hours with models from a lads magazine who flung themselves around dressed as cheerleaders, and then conveniently removed their tops and jiggled their pompoms for the camera.

Living in each other's pockets for two months has driven us all stir crazy. The wound in my heel doesn't mend quickly and more permanent accommodation is sought for the team in town. Meanwhile, Kate and I remain in the spare room at Bob and Deirdre's, working away quietly during the day on things that weren't a priority on the road – website updating, new designs for team clothes and route planning from Adelaide to Brisbane. I secure a new helmet sponsor in Protec, Circa send shoes to replace the four pairs that have worn away so far and The Magic Touch deliver a box of BoardFree baseball caps for us to sell in exchange for donations. Meanwhile Kate keeps the media circus going, arranging more than twenty interviews during the first week in Adelaide. The team capitalise on the growing BoardFree brand, venturing out into the Adelaide malls and raising hundreds of dollars; not much in a big city you might think, but try handing out leaflets and asking for donations in a constantly moving crowd and you realise that it takes a bit of tactical nous to make city dwellers dip into their pockets.

Deirdre and Bob put on a BBQ for the team and lay on a feast, a stark reminder that their hospitality has made an awkward start in this city a thing of the past. Chris Riordan joins us at the meal; he's an inspiration. He asks me what keeps me going when my legs are tired and the sun is beating down and the road is rough. Chris is focusing on the mental challenge that lies ahead for him as he prepares to go for sailing gold at the Paralympics. He says, 'If we walked down the road and back again I would use ten times the energy that you would. I need to find out what I need to do, how I need to think.' He isn't the type of guy who enters for the sake of entering, and his cerebral palsy hasn't diminished a quick wit and humble, realistic nature that will send him through to the next Paralympic Games as a shining example of exactly what Sailability is capable of achieving.

As each day ticks by I get more comfortable. It's a dangerous situation, juggling an absolute necessity to rest with the knowledge that sitting around breeds complacency. I get out when I can, watch Adelaide United play a couple of games at the Hindmarsh, revelling in the football, especially in the first game where I watch from a corporate box as Romario, the great Brazilian goalscorer, turns out for Miami. He is chasing his one thousandth career goal, a total unheard of in this day and age, but typically I miss him get one closer to his target, hearing a roar of celebration in the ground from an office buried deep within the stadium. I'm halfway through a radio interview with some halfwits from Sydney, and my heart sinks as the presenters at the other end of the line carry out one of those piss-taking interviews. Usually I'd be delighted to laugh along with the jokes about my big right leg and the fact that by the end of the journey I'll be walking around in circles. But not when I'm missing a goal from a footballing legend! Jo-Anna and Renato, the photographer and journalist who put together a great article for the *Sunday Mail*, join us for a second game four days later. Afterwards we sneak into the corporate lounge and meet a couple of Adelaide's players. In the UK Premiership players are inaccessible to all but a lucky few, but here the players were happy to stop and chat for a good while. Bobby Petta, formerly of Celtic in Scotland, was friendly and humble. But my personal highlight was meeting 'the other Cornthwaite on Google', Robert, who plays at the back for United. Funnily enough, he said he'd been approached a few times by people asking if he was related to the guy who was skateboarding across Australia.

Ten days after jumping on a metal spike I found myself back at the Royal Adelaide having my stitches removed by a lovely English doctor. The gash on my heel still looked open and messy, but the doctor understood my haste to get back on the road. She told me that it still needed a few days and that it was up to me to determine when I could safely begin skating again without the threat of reopening the wound. Dom had been with me in the hospital and had his camera ready when we jumped back into Cheech, who was waiting outside with Kate and Dan. I decided it was time for a little joke. 'So how did it go?' Kate asked, looking disconcerted at my glum face.

'Ummm, not good,' I said, not looking her in the eye and leaning my head against the window in mock sadness. 'The doctor said the stitches hadn't done the job and that the injury hadn't healed sufficiently. She had to put some more stitches in and said it would be unwise to start again within the next two weeks.' There was complete silence from the front and Dom was doing his best not to burst out laughing, his forehead running with sweat. Kate and Dan looked utterly gutted, as they were as desperate as the rest of the team to move on. I couldn't hold it anymore. 'Guess it's lucky that all that was a complete lie, eh!' I laughed. 'The foot's fine, we'll be heading south in a couple of days!'

Despite the good news there was a long haul ahead. Even though the stitches were out the injury was still fairly painful, and being my left foot it was the one that would bear constant pressure on the board. The delay meant that we had several days to make up on roads laden with traffic. They said the Nullarbor Plain was impossible; rubbish. We'd done the easy part; luckily we'd been given the chance to rest before the hard graft really kicked in.

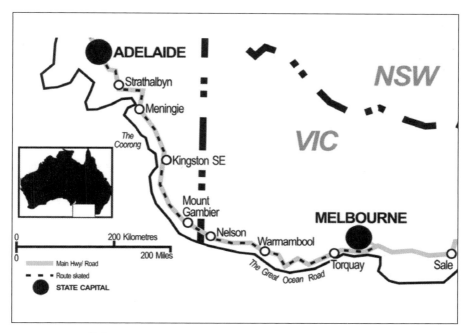

19 Tension

27 October – 16 November 2006

Thirteen days in Adelaide should have provided an ideal scenario for fatigue to abate and emotions to plateau, but it hadn't. Where excitement would have been the ideal response to getting back on the road a total repack of the vehicles provided a platform for Becki to play up again. I stood with her and Holly on the Schahingers' patio, shoes and clothes and other kit strewn across the lawn behind us, and asked Holly to fill up the empty water bottles. It was the first time water had been discussed and Holly had asked for something to do, but Becki somehow took umbrage, waited until Holly was inside, and strutted after her without a word to me. I watched as she flung her arms in the air beside Holly, animated to the core, and although I couldn't hear what was being said Holly clearly wasn't having any of it. Becs stomped off through the house and Holly looked through the living room at me, shaking her head. It was nonsense and I felt sick to the stomach that Becki was still struggling to cope.

'She told me I shouldn't be filling the water bottles up,' Holly said to me soon afterwards, 'she thought the water would be off by the morning and that there was no point doing it today.'

I felt myself boiling up, yet again helpless to deal with Becki's irrationality and attempts to undermine. Having spent much of the fortnight away from the others it was starting to become evident that I'd misjudged team morale. If anything, the delay had allowed the emotional wounds opened up during the first half of the journey to fester, and I started to take a long hard look at the way I was managing the project. Ultimately, if things were falling apart then it was up to me to put them back together, and I really should have put my foot down and taken Becki aside immediately to pull her up on what she had done. A culture of misinterpretation and blame was forming, and for the time being it was me, not Becki or anyone else, who needed to make a change. On the morning of Saturday 28 October it was time to move on. Deirdre and Bob stood at their doorstep as we drove back to the spot less than a kilometre away where I had finished, foot still intact, thirteen days earlier. A news crew from Channel 7 was there to greet us, and filmed Becki and me as we prepared my feet for the off. Two homemade butterfly stitches spanned the chasm on my left heel, which was stained inky red from the iodine treatment I'd been using to dry it out. I hadn't pulled on a shoe, let alone stood on my board for almost two weeks and this was the moment of truth. It wasn't unreasonable to expect that the wound would be incredibly painful for a while, not least because my left foot was stuck to my board while moving and there wasn't much I could do to prevent downward pressure upon it. Biting my lip I took a few cautionary pushes for the sake of the camera and then gave an honestly optimistic interview before it was time to leave for real. I stood at the roadside giving myself two minutes of peace as I looked down at the city skyline. We had only meant to stay in this city for four days, but despite the unfortunate circumstances surrounding our arrival I'd fallen in love with Adelaide, we'd been thrust together through adversity and I had torn feelings about leaving. Torn feelings maybe, but there was only one choice, and I was ready for the road again.

Whether it was time for me to be on the road or not, though, was another story. Only a full day of skating could give me an accurate picture of how my foot was coping. Eager to blast through the complacency that had been built up during the rest, I donned blinkers and pumped my fist at Dom as I set off past his camera, 'Come on! Here we go!' Immediately I started to climb. The Adelaide Hills that bordered the city's southern side were larger than anything Australia had thrown at us so far and I leaned forward at an angle, feeling my left heel stretch as I pushed at walking pace up a horribly steep incline. For an hour and a half the hill went on, sweat pouring down my temples as I pulled

over every two minutes to let traffic pass. The short breaks were welcome as my
fitness had understandably taken a hit. Needless to say, it wasn't the ideal land
over which to ease myself back in to the journey, and although my thighs
burned and my feet pulsed I was glad of the challenge; if my injury could stand
up to this it could stand up to anything.

We lunched in the scenic town of Stirling, which reminded me in many
ways of Aviemore, my stop on the fourth day of BoardFree UK. By then the
back of the Adelaide Hills was broken and the remaining 40km to Strathalbyn
was still hilly, but mainly downhill. We arrived by 6 p.m., Becs and Bev having
found accommodation for the team in a campsite and a room in a hotel so I
could have a bed. BoardFree was the third main item on the Channel 7 news,
a comprehensive report ranging from my interview to footage from the
Nullarbor that Dom had supplied to a quirky little graphic that showed a skateboard following my route across Australia. We were ecstatic, Simon so much so
that he cheered during the piece, despite the fact that Dom was filming the TV
so we could get a copy of the report for our website. My foot was hurting but
didn't seem more damaged than at the beginning of the day; we were truly back
on the road.

*   *   *

The Channel 7 piece served us well and for the next three days as I pushed
through the wine regions of the Fleurieu Peninsula and the flats of the Coorong
National Park cars pulled over on a regular basis, handing over small donations
and congratulating us on crossing the Nullarbor. One woman, an incredibly
friendly lady named Jo, pulled over with a look of dawning awareness. 'Are you
the guy who has skateboarded from Western Australia?' she asked, before
hugging each of us in turn, telling us young people were wonderful and there
should be more people like us. 'Here's my number,' she said, handing me a
piece of paper, 'when you get to Melbourne give me a call, I'm sure we can put
you up.' As she drove away I looked down and saw that the piece of paper was
joined by a $A50 note.

Shortly after Wellington the road met the mighty Murray River, which was
nearing the end of its 2,575km journey. Naturally, I couldn't skate over the water
and the meeting introduced a new method of transport into the BoardFree
equation, a ferry. I skated aboard, knowing full well that the next two hundred
metres of the journey wouldn't count towards the world record attempt. As
occupants of other cars on the ferry climbed out to have pictures taken with Elsa
and I, pelicans glided inches above the surface, landing with a splash as their feet

extended and bills dipped in. I skated off the ferry, leading the cars and drawing camera flashes from the vehicles waiting for their turn to cross the river, and 2km later reached a junction. From here we would turn ninety degrees to the right and head south on the B1, the road that would take us almost all the way to Victoria.

As I skated south through Meningie and Policeman's Point the road gave direct views over the Coorong National Park. The Coorong is a wetlands ecosystem harbouring a great variety of birds, animals and fish in its waters. It is best viewed from the air, a privilege we were to have only through our guide books, which show a magnificent stretch of coastal beach fronting the Southern Ocean, at the same time doubling as a 200km spit of land which protects a 140km long lagoon that is rarely wider than 4km. The Coorong is a place in which to sit quietly and watch, but we were on a mission and sadly our eyes were largely focused on the road south.

Near Salt Creek I met for the second time a Korean man who was pedaling a bicycle around Australia. I had overtaken him the day before and here he was, in front of me again, heavily bearded and laden down with sacks and bags. Out of one of these, his rucksack, emerged a dirty yellow teddy bear; I presumed it was this extra weight that enabled me to pass him! As I skated past him I waved and he waved back, smiling and laughing to himself. The day before when I first overtook him he hadn't said a word, but now we were friends, both travelling towards Victoria under our own steam without knowing each other's names. Not long afterwards the girls had spread a toilet roll across the road, it was time for me to roll past the 3,000km mark. At the last second I ducked down, limbo'd the makeshift tape and pulled to a halt. We celebrated with two swigs of beer and a good bit of hugging, and got back on the road as the Korean man approached in the distance; it'd be rubbing it in if he was overtaken for a third time by a bloke on a skateboard.

At Kingston SE, the Coorong now behind us, we were entertained by the local Lions Club who threw a BBQ and then pulled me up to the front of the group for a little talk. Once I had finished the BoardFree tale one of the members spoke up, announcing that travelling across Australia from west coast to east coast was a formidable feat. His grandfather had been one of the first men to drive across the country, he told me, and he left us in no doubt that Elsa would go down in history as the first skateboard to make the journey. Finishing off, quite ominously, he said, 'Make sure you keep the board safe, someone'll nab it if they get half the chance.'

I was made aware of something else before the end of the night. 'Did you see the crayfish when you came into town?' I was asked.

'What crayfish?' I said, confused. Everyone burst out laughing.

'Dave,' said Holly, 'there's one of those giant things here, how did you miss it?'

It appeared that I had once again been in 'the zone', and the next morning we took a team photo for posterity, all of us stood beneath a red twenty-metre high crayfish that I had managed to ignore. 'At least you're focused,' someone said, but I couldn't help wondering what else I'd missed along the way.

* * *

Three days and 175km later we were in the Blue Lake City of Mount Gambier being served up a feast by Doug and Jill Thorne, who seven weeks earlier had happened upon us at Caiguna Roadhouse on the Nullarbor. The most memorable moment of our first meeting was Doug's mocking of Dan's hair. Sat with a beer in hand Doug had glanced first at me and then at Danny, his eyes slowly rising up to Dan's mohican before proclaiming, 'You need some scissors on that, snakehead!' The japes were followed up with an exchanging of cards: 'Call me when you get to Mount Gambier,' said Doug, 'I know some people from the TV and I reckon we can get you on the news.' Sure enough, the local news crew had paid us a visit earlier that day and Doug had extended an invitation to come round for a BBQ. After being greeted by various guests and family members I was delighted to find that the photo album from their recent trip was lying open on the coffee table, and there we were, pictures of Cheech, Elsa and me. Dom saw it too,

'Makes you wonder just how many photo albums you're in, doesn't it mate?'

Kate hadn't been feeling well for days and had opted to give the Thornes' BBQ a miss and stay in bed across town, as she had done for the Lions Club get-together in Kingston earlier that week. I was worried about her, but it seemed that stress rather than a virus was mostly to blame for her condition. Niggles between team members had proliferated from the day we left Adelaide and after a week back on the road everybody was exhausted, which just heightened the tension. Things were getting silly. Three days earlier Danny, who had been teaching himself to play guitar, was snapped at by Becs because of the noise only for her to pursue a tickle-fight with Bev that resulted in fifteen minutes of high pitched, hypocritical screaming. Elsewhere, since coming off the Nullarbor Holly had spent hours texting and calling people on her mobile phone, which didn't do much for my sleep patterns as she regularly returned to bed in George hours after the rest of us, pulling the door shut with a soft but definite crunch. To me, unsettled once again in the dead of night, the sound of that door closing equalled despair and frustration; everyone was in this for themselves now; any team spirit we once had was somewhere back along the road.

On the same day that we left Mount Gambier I crossed into Victoria, our third state. Danny changed Elsa's wheels as the rest of us mulled around, far too disassociated from the new milestone that should have seen our spirits soaring. Instead, 3km later we arrived in Nelson, finding accommodation quickly in the village's only campsite. When the vehicles parked up everyone dispersed, slinking into the cabin, heads down, the lengthy and it has to be said, immature silences now too profound to be confronted head on.

I was left to carry my kit in myself. Trudging slowly, barely being able to lift one foot ahead of the other, I was longing to lie down. Through the door I saw that wasn't possible, three members of the team were spread out on the only double bed in the cabin. They looked at me as I entered, then returned to whatever they had been doing. After all this time these people still have no idea, I thought, helplessness brewing. Needing an escape Kate and I drove to the coast, the torrid sea boiling onto the beach, a perfect reflection of the fractured atmosphere within the BoardFree camp. We spent the next two hours arguing. Kate and I sat in the front of Cheech together, howling about the situation. Kate was frustrated at things like food and bickering and the difficulties of driving behind me. I was frustrated at her, because I felt she, along with everyone else, had been absorbed into concentrating on the irritating, yet insignificant crumbs of disillusionment. It was all so pathetic; the problems all tiny but unresolved hunting together like piranhas to take down a bigger, wounded beast. I pounded the dashboard with my fists, fury taking over as our escape from the group highlighted the very inescapable position we were in. I had no control. For the first time in my life pressures had come to such a head that I was Jekyll to my everyday Hyde. Kate cried, I sobbed. 'I have to do something to change this,' I said, 'I have to leave everyone behind.'

'Don't do that,' Kate begged, 'don't go.'

'I don't think I have a choice, babe,' I said, finally giving her the hug she had needed all afternoon.

My mind was made up that evening. Becki continued to nail little comments into the back of Bev's head. There was no need for it, but it had become usual, expected, and nobody had done anything about it. And then the last straw as I lay in bed finally. The TV blared as Dom berated the singing acts on screen. 'You're fucking shit, you fat cow! You've got no talent, get off my television. You're shit!' Simon wobbled on a chair with one crooked leg. Dom had stood on it earlier as he jiggled with the TV aerial, buckling the leg in the process. Reporting the accident to the kind people who had allowed us to stay for free never crossed his mind. He did as he always did, neglected responsibility and shoved the chair to the side for someone else to sit on, then pulled up a fresh one. I sank into a tortured sleep, Dom still swearing at the TV behind the curtain, Becki's irritability pinching my nerves, mini-heartache at the stress that Kate and I were under. She lay across the bed, the space between us shouting at me to do something to resolve this mess. I had no choice. There was only one way out of this.

The next morning I packed a rucksack and called everybody together. We sat there in the cabin, a fever upon us. Whether or not there was a cure available, I didn't know, in fact I strongly doubted that the situation was redeemable. But this was it now, the only solution, my last shot. I told them that I was leaving because I no longer had a support team. 'All I know is I'm fucking exhausted and I don't feel that I can get any mental rest because the whole team is bitching, constantly,' I said, sat at the bed with my bag beside me, 'I'm going to Brisbane, with or without you guys. But you're not going anywhere until you've worked out what you need to do to settle your differences and find some social decorum. When I've gone, you stay in this cabin and talk to each other and decide whether you want to carry on or not. You need to realise you're all in a privileged situation here. Try and remember why you applied for this in the first place, and then decide whether that initial enthusiasm still applies.' In between my sentences there was silence, everyone stared straight ahead. I repeated my main point before standing. 'I'm going to Brisbane, it'll take me longer and it won't be as effective, but I'll get there, with or without you.'

As I prepared to go Dan and Kate stood by me. 'We don't want you to be on those roads alone, are you sure you don't want one of us to drive with you?' asked Dan.

'You both need to stay here.' I kissed Kate, and left.

*   *   *

The rain was falling heavily as I set off, luminous jacket pulled over my rucksack to aid visibility. For the first time in weeks I felt some relief at acting on the troubles that had infected the team, but any relief I had was obscured by loneliness and anger. I'd made my point in the only way I knew how, by pushing on. But I was overwhelmed with emotion and screamed into the forests as the rain ran down my helmet onto my nose. I ran hot and cold, an icy wind ripping inside my layers, meeting the heat of exertion at the seams. I felt like tearing my clothes off and skating naked, lusting for liberation from the mess this had become. But I kept them on, because I've never liked the cold. Seven white parrots crossed the road ahead of me and continued to do so. For 30km they flew from tree to tree as I pushed through the rain, logging trucks blaring their horns as they rushed up behind me, thundering giants that had no intention to pull around me, passing just inches to my right so close that I could see the knots in the fallen trees they carried. They blew me off balance and left me drenched in thick spray. I was deafened by the rain and the thoughts in my head and found myself moving on instinct, searching the roadside for sheets of cardboard or wood that I could crawl beneath for shelter.

I continued to scream out loud, alone in a strange place, haunted by my part in this strange, bitter story. I had played a big part in the conflicts but I wasn't facing them head on, as perhaps I should have. Kate had suffered most. She was a two-way sponge, soaking up as much of the team's conflicts as she could before they got to me, but at the same time she had to deal with my moods, my stresses and my exhaustion. I'd changed as a person as the mental difficulties of travelling with a group slowly broke down my strength, which was already brittle from physical wear and tear. I'd become an awful person to be around, grumpy, argumentative, demanding. I hated myself, for being this way, for losing control. I was becoming an empty shell, rationality and calm disappearing in streams of tired frustration. Kate wasn't the catalyst for the anger that grew within, but we had begun to argue more and more, winding each other up like wild animals in a cage. Trapped souls, always eager to touch and show remorse for the foolish, unexplainable fights, but unable to speak fairly and honestly to settle things completely. We had all been reduced to unhappy, circling beasts and as I pushed 40km beyond Nelson I was alone but for the seven white parrots, which continued to squawk their support from nearby trees. I was sure I wouldn't see the team again. I wouldn't blame any of them for leaving. They could have the vans. They could drive to the airport and fly away to happier shores. It had all gone so disastrously wrong and this wasn't my dream anymore. I was lost in fury and sadness and despair, berating myself for bringing together this team of honest, brilliant people who had each fallen prey to conflict for which I was ultimately to blame – a sorry, soaking man, rain dripping from his beard, pushing a skateboard along the Portland Nelson Road, two and a half thousand kilometres to go to Brisbane. I'm in this alone now, absolutely shattered. But fuck me if I'm going to give up having come so far.

Two honks of a horn from behind. As the sounds reach me my arms are raised to the sky in the middle of an angry remonstration to everyone and no one to explain why I was pushing a yellow skateboard in the middle of an Australian forest. It's the vehicles, one after the other; Cheech first, then George, then Kylie. Headlamps flashing and faces within. I push slowly as they converge at the side; they hold me one by one. I'm sobbing as they do, and I wonder if they can tell the difference between my tears and the rain. No one spoke as we clustered together and I couldn't help but break the silence: 'The roads are really shit around here.'

Kate pulled out a poem and read it out loud, smiling at me as she paused before each line:

> *When things go wrong, as they sometimes will,*
> *When the road you're trudging seems all uphill,*
> *When the funds are low and the debts are high,*
> *And you want to smile, but you have to sigh,*
> *When care is pressing you down a bit*
> *Rest if you must, but don't you quit.*

'Come to the van,' she said. And we all squeezed in out of the rain. 'We've all been talking,' Kate continued, 'and decided to tell each other what was bothering us so we could get everything out in the open, and then we went around and told everyone what we loved about each other, and the only person we haven't done this to is you.' So they did, one by one each person said their piece. Dan said I was the strongest person he had ever met and called me an inside-out armadillo. Si had turned BoardFree into a cheesecake, and I was the plate the cake sat on. It was obvious that things were settled and I cried as Kate wrapped her arms around me, the rain pattering on the roof as I shivered away the morning's emotions.

*   *   *

The rain fell for several days as I pushed east via Portland and Port Fairy, the sea once again visible from the road as Melbourne drew closer. Victoria, for all of its beauty, had given us a wet greeting, reminding us all of home as we left a dry South Australia – our transitory residence for a month and a half – behind. Home, I think, featured more often in each of the team's thoughts as the journey progressed. It was easy to look back now and wonder at the distance we had covered, but with hindsight it felt that the time was disappearing faster than we could understand. In a way, I suppose, it was. One answer came in the form of political clock changes. When we flew into Perth in mid-August we were a mere seven hours ahead of the United Kingdom. Now, with two inexplicable 45 minute changes, first at Caiguna and then at the Western and South Australia border, then some daylight saving chucked in for good measure and a final 30 minutes when we crossed into Victoria, we find ourselves eleven hours ahead of the UK time thanks to one final daylight saving hour lost back home – which came when we gained one last week.

I edged around the bend towards the penultimate stretch of the journey, gaining pace as certain pressures had dissolved following the Day of Resolution, otherwise known, quite simply, as 'Nelson'. One-on-one issues were now being dealt with head on and everyone was back on their game, playing each day out with enthusiasm, raising money like never before and helping me cover ground that was inconceivably far away at the beginning of this escapade. By the time we reached Warnambool BoardFree had raised close to £11,000, a long way from my initial figure of £50,000 but still a fair achievement, especially with three major cities and a considerable proportion of the Australian population remaining on the route.

The Great Ocean Road began in Warnambool, a 400km stretch of winding coastal road, which held treasures that more than outweighed the fact that it wasn't the most direct route to Melbourne. The Great Ocean Road is the world's biggest war memorial, built by soldiers who returned from World War I as a dedication to their fallen comrades, but it is also renowned as one of the world's most spectacular coastal drives. Tourists flood to view spectacular rock formations near Port Campbell – sights such as the Loch Ard Gorge and the Twelve Apostles – but after our journey so far, after the way we had travelled and the moments we had experienced, I wasn't overly taken by the large monoliths of rock that emerged from the ocean, stacks of rock that hinted at years of erosion that was eating away at the land. Instead, I revelled in the experience of the land as a whole, travelling through such a beautiful place and skating along smooth roads, which swept around cliff faces and dipped and climbed as the waves crashed below. It rained almost constantly, causing some disappointment at the loss of scenic impact for our film and photography – the postcard pictures we had seen of the route were bathed in sunshine and looked truly spectacular; but the moody grey skies and torrid waters showed the Great Ocean Road in a most dramatic light.

The people on the way were just as memorable. Caroline Disney, who had piloted the small plane that gave us such an incredible point of view over the Head of Bight and the Nullarbor, was now based in Peterborough conducting air tours over the Twelve Apostles. We popped in to say hello and then as I continued east Caroline launched her Cessna into the sky and gave us a fly-past. That afternoon I rolled into Port Campbell only for Becki to lead me by the arm to the town's Tourist Information Centre. 'This was here when we arrived!' she said happily, pointing at a newspaper article about our journey that had been stuck to the office door along with a note that wished us good luck and encouraged people to donate. I thanked the people inside, who were delighted to see us, and we all clinked glasses at a packed local bar later in the evening, raising over $A600 in cash donations. From Port Campbell Simon made a superb effort, pedaling the bike almost 15km over some sweat-inducing hills, but he wisely jumped back in the van as I climbed for four hours towards Lavers Hill, along narrow, damp roads which were steeper than those that had led out of Adelaide.

It took a day to skate from Lavers Hill to Apollo Bay, the final 20km directing me through the altitudinal inconsistency of the Otway National Park. Parrots and wallabies stirred the undergrowth until I emerged on the final run down to the sea, the sole of my right shoe wearing thin as it steadied and slowed my pace on the final steep decline.

Apollo Bay was a beautiful place, glorious in its simple sweep of a blue bay surrounded by a comforting wall of green rolling hills. We ventured into the surf, revelling in the blue waters and clean waves thanks to the donation of two surfboards from a sponsor based in southern Queensland. Chris Cleator from Real Wiiings had provided two boards for the team along with a collection of Real Wiiings – innovative four-inch paddles that attach to the wrist using a Velcro strap thus enabling the wearer to paddle faster whilst using less energy. With the ocean such a regular feature of our remaining journey around the coast the opportunity to warm down in the water after a day of skating often kept me going on long hard days. Sure, the added exercise probably contributed to my overall fatigue, but mentally it kept me strong, despite a regular propensity to wipe out spectacularly on even the smallest waves.

Our final two days on the Great Ocean Road took us along arguably the most scenic stretch of coastline on the route, through Lorne, where tensions briefly surfaced due to a difficulty in finding accommodation, and then onto Torquay, capital of the Surfcoast and home to the famous Bells Beach. With Melbourne just a sniff away we gave ourselves a morning off and toured around Torquay's Surfworld Museum, which contained a detailed collection of memorabilia from surfing history. There was also a collection of old skateboards, which of course were an offshoot from the early days of surfing, and before we headed on the museum's manager took me to the side and said he would be proud to exhibit Elsa once BoardFree Australia had finished.

On 16 November, Becki's birthday, BoardFree Australia took its second ferry trip, travelling some 10km across the mouth of Port Phillip Bay from Queenscliff to Sorrento. Melbourne sat on the north-eastern shore of the bay, and as I completed a long, tiring 70km day Kate, Becs, Bev and Simon drove ahead to the city to search for accommodation. We had a five-day rest in the capital of Victoria to look forward to, and just two and a half weeks after pushing out of Adelaide I picked Elsa up and jumped into Cheech. My left heel was still in some pain but the wound was looking far healthier than it had done, despite having to endure the pressure of skating 1,058 kilometres. Mentally, however, that distance plus the emotional trauma suffered by team conflict meant that a rest was truly needed. All said and done, though, there were some things in Melbourne that we had good reason to be excited about; BoardFree Australia was about to be given a new lease of life.

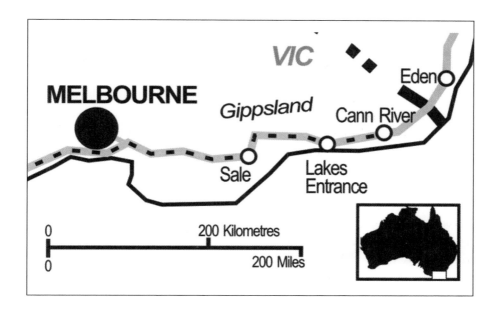

20 Gippsland
17 November – 28 November 2006

It had been a torrid time for the accommodation team in Melbourne. Tired and sick to death of rejection, they had no luck in finding shelter and Kate's voice was worn and tetchy when I called her from the outskirts. Unlike arriving in Adelaide I was experiencing the traffic entering Melbourne from the safety of a support vehicle, but the aggravations of urban life were just as tangible from Cheech's passenger seat and I felt for the four who had been rushing around the city all day. Luckily, we had one final option. I called Jo, who had passed us on the road two weeks earlier near Wellington and had offered a single night's accommodation. Unfortunately she wasn't in the city at the time but urged me to call her boyfriend, Jon, who thankfully said we were welcome to stay at his place. While there was obvious relief at finding accommodation I always felt slightly uneasy when the entire team descended upon a stranger's home, eight extra bodies – as we knew all too well – could be entirely suffocating and I was always at odds with myself in these situations, trying to find a truce between needing rest and not wanting to outstay our welcome. Jon, though, was a relaxed, friendly host. When he said 'make yourself at home' he truly meant it, and he became an honorary team member that first evening as we celebrated Bec's birthday in a St Kilda restaurant.

The next evening, a day bisected by television and radio interviews behind us, the team donned their official hooded tops and made their way to Melbourne Airport; it was time to pick somebody up. Six months earlier, a stranger to all of us had been bitten by the BoardFree bug. As I slowly made my way south from John o'Groats to Land's End, Laura Hatwell got wind of the journey through the media and started to piece together her own BoardFree journey. She got herself a longboard, taught herself to skate and then, just as the Australian expedition was setting off across the Nullarbor, Laura skated 25 miles from Glasgow to Loch Lomond, raising over £500 for BoardFree's charities in the process. Her organisation and commitment to the cause had been impressive and as BoardFree's profile started to grow in Australia I began to wonder whether we could harness Ms Hatwell's unwavering enthusiasm. A unanimous vote in Port Augusta had sealed it; Laura was to join the team from Melbourne onwards, offering an extra pair of hands to our fundraising efforts and alleviating some of the pressure from Becki and Bev's shoulders.

Two days later we were back at the airport to welcome another face to the team. Pat Midland was to join us for the rest of the journey, reuniting with Dom to ensure that the final stages of the documentary went smoothly. In the meantime I wasn't resting as much as I should have been. The stresses of the past weeks had caught up with me, I was looking gaunt and my mouth was full of ulcers. Another, larger ulcer had been sat on my bottom lip for ten days, opened up by the sun and healing far slower than it usually would have. My body was slowing down and holes in my immune system were evident but I was determined to ensure that my fundamental intentions for the journey remained on track. Hours were spent in front of a computer as the hunger to fulfil my self-set obligations to Link, Lowe and Sailability and to every member of my selfless team became all-encompassing. Laura was getting stuck into fundraising around the city with Kate, Holly, Bev and Becs, and it was a difficult initiation. City living tends to close off most people and it's always noticeably harder to exude donations out of the urban bustle, but the money continued to flow in, and will continue to do so with the team working this hard.

Our last night in Melbourne was a treat. Actor Alan Fletcher, who holds a legendary status among British students thanks to his long-running role as Dr Karl Kennedy in the soap *Neighbours*, is also the lead singer for The Waiting Room, a band who mix their own quirky tunes with rehashes of iconic rock and pop songs. When they're not touring, the band take up a regular residence at the Elephant and Wheelbarrow in St Kilda, and Alan invited the team along to the gig to show his appreciation for their work. First though, three other *Neighbours* stars were part of the entertainment and wandered around meeting the predominantly British crowd. As they did, singing and dancing competitions were laid on for the crowds, and remarkably BoardFree came away as a two-time winner! Bev blasted out a rendition of the *Neighbours* theme tune, leaving the other singers for dead. And then Dom stepped up to the dancefloor, kicked his shoes away and finally out-jigged the competition, despite the overly homoerotic efforts of a drunk, shirtless chap who somehow managed to push Dom all the way to the end. It was all, though, a starter for the main course. A year earlier Alan and I had briefly met after a Waiting Room gig in Cardiff, and I had given him a BoardFree t-shirt to say thanks for his support. Even so, a year on in Melbourne, it was a huge surprise when he paused halfway through a set to walk to the side of the stage, pick up that very same t-shirt and then put it on before relaying a little story to the eager crowd. 'Last time I was in the UK there was this mad bloke pushing a skateboard the length of that little island. Well now, I'm pleased to announce, he's here in Melbourne having pushed his board across the country from Perth!' He introduced me, beckoned me out on stage and we had a bit of banter about the journey, the crowd down below roaring with appreciation. Afterwards, he found time to meet everyone on the team before we headed out into the night, thrilled at the positive reaction from the crowd and glowing from perhaps a few too many beers.

Alan Fletcher's generosity and respect for the project filled a hole somewhere in all of this. Suddenly, the morning after, the permanent aching in my legs didn't matter so much. We had experienced several disappointments en route so far – it's to be expected having travelled half way across the world plus another 3,800km with such great expectations – but they were totally insignificant beyond the moments themselves because the team continued to believe in what they were doing. The support from celebrities who were willing to clear a busy schedule and show their respect, in addition to the smiles we had left behind on the faces of those Sailability members who had taken the time to appreciate our efforts, was more than enough fuel to push us on towards the east coast. And the east coast, after everything we'd been through, wasn't far away now.

*   *   *

Gippsland, pronounced with a hard G, stands squarely between Melbourne and New South Wales, a drought-ridden region bisected by the busy artery of

Highway One, which meanders east via Gippsland's main urban offerings. Motivated by our city break, encouraged by the ever-growing support from passing motorists and tempted by the nearness of yet another State, we were slung-shot out of Melbourne and sped along the highway. A small family in Bayles stood outside their general store and applauded as I approached, ushering us all inside with orders to take a cold drink of our choice. One $A50 donation later I was back on the road with a wave of thanks, another meeting driven by generosity. Despite smatterings of blister appearing on several toes, I was averaging over 65km skated per day, adrenaline boosted by continued media coverage and the company of a crew from ITV, who followed us one morning for a piece on the evening news.

The heat was increasing as summer approached and as some compensation for the heat I donned a cobber, a material neckwrap that maintained its coolness thanks to polycrystals sewn into the fabric. The regular temperatures of thirty degrees plus were magnified by the mustiness of the land, it was one of the driest seasons on record and farmers were feeling the pinch. By the time I'd reached Sale, 300km east of Melbourne, Laura had slotted into a regular position in Cheech, charged with the duty of ensuring that I was continually fed and watered while on the road. She always had a spring in her step and rarely stopped singing, traits that I struggled to deal with at my lowest moments when all I craved was peace and quiet. In truth, though, I hadn't done as much as I should have to ease Laura into the team and in my fatigue and blinkered focus I was slowly paying less and less attention to the team's needs. In Laura's case this must have been especially difficult as she hadn't yet become accustomed to my slow, distanced attitude towards managing the team. Despite this, spirits were generally high despite occasional squabbles, and laughter frequented camp. Holly recounted driving past the bodyguard of *Neighbours* star Dylan in Melbourne, whom we met one night for a brief spell before he was ushered away by his enormous Maori guard. Holly, being Holly, decided to call the guy 'the Kiwi Bouncer', a nickname that totally confused Kate, who in what is possibly her blondest moment yet thought Holly had seen a bloke bouncing fruit along the road. Simon, meanwhile, continued to be so laid back he was horizontal, and was by far the most lax team member when it came to updating his online blog – I had skated over 3,000km since he last made an entry.

The girls had secured some accommodation at a fairly rundown campsite in southern Sale. It had a lovely setting though, despite the shell-like carcasses of cicadas that hung off the outside walls of the cabins. Danny cooked up a grand

BBQ in the cooking hut, and we all munched away in high spirits, buoyed by the presence of the koala curled up in the tree above our vehicles. The evening light glinted through the trees, which lined a dark river that ran quietly behind the site, and I looked around at the team, partly in shadow and partly in sun, and felt happier than I had done in quite a while. There was a smile on every face. After dinner we all decamped to town, where we settled in a bar as the girls rushed around with their collection buckets.

Dom and Pat had remained in Melbourne for a few days to buy another van and we were waiting for them to turn up. What I hadn't banked on, though, was the person they had brought with them. When my brother walked in, arms swinging like a monkey and mouth grinning in a wide arc below a pair of aviators, I hugged him and blinked away the tears. 'You little bastard.' I cleared the lump in my throat. 'What the bloody hell are you doing here?' Yet again, the support of my family had gone beyond expectation and here, in the middle of a dry Victoria, I couldn't help but remember the moment where I choked back the tears in Manchester as I squeezed my bro farewell en route to John o'Groats. Half a year and several thousand miles of skating later here he was, completely on his own steam, doing his bit to push the team and me forward a little further.

* * *

The flat land separating Melbourne and the Great Dividing Range in eastern Victoria caused my shoes to wear down at the sole, and bit by bit the lack of cushioning beneath my toes started to have an effect on my feet. Bad blisters started to form, too slowly for me to notice as blister pains had become a regular feature of each day.

The towns of Traralgon and Sale offered up opportunities to visit Specialist Schools, home to children of various ages and disabilities who have the opportunity to sail with Sailability. On consecutive days I followed a brief talk with a 'High Five Roll' along lines of pupils, meeting hands with everyone and realising that Sailability's work goes far further than just an entry to sport; it's a chance for people – youngsters especially – to develop a sense of independence and physical individuality. At first glance most people wouldn't believe what these kids are capable of in a boat, their achievements – not necessarily rewarded by medals or trophies – increase awareness of disability among the able-bodied. We handed over several hundred dollars in contributions to Sailability clubs at Wellington and Gippsland before skating on, Channel 7 broadcasting a report of one of our visits across Victoria, which only served to drum up more support and donations further along the road.

My brother cycled the full 72km with me from Sale to Bairnsdale, and the following day ran shuttles towards Lakes Entrance, drawing lines for the rest of the team as they had a long-time concern confirmed: the Cornthwaite family might be physically fit, but Dave certainly wasn't the only crazy one. We rested for a day in Lakes Entrance, a beautiful little town beached on the man-made channel between the Gippsland lakes and the Tasman Sea beyond. Sheryl Lawler, manager of a quaint holiday village called Kickback Cottages, had written to me after hearing an earlier radio interview and invited us round for dinner. She and her friend Jodie laid on a BBQ feast for the team, which was memorable for the after-meal entertainments: Simon trying out a child's scooter and Holly happily honouring a request from one young guest to autograph a skateboard.

Sheryl's hospitality was very welcome but I felt unable to fully relax; ahead was the long road to Sydney and one rest day never seems enough when 800km of hills are looming. The condition of my feet also stressed that a longer break was needed and on Monday morning – as I pushed east under the glare of television cameras responsible for world-wide news reports thanks to the Australian-based SNTV – the aching in my feet, ankles and legs didn't bode well. The Great Dividing Range was coming closer, an imperious spread of mountains which stood guard, cross-armed and stern, protecting the east coast as the final major obstacle to my becoming the first person to skateboard across the width of Australia.

* * *

In Orbost, some 130km west of the New South Wales border, I prepared for two big days by trapping a huntsman spider that lurked in our cabin, the rest of the team either peering edgily around the door frame or fleeing as fast and as far away as possible. Several months Down Under certainly hadn't cured certain team members' arachnophobia, and it was all I could do to contain my prankster urges as I deposited the four-inch square critter a hundred metres away from camp.

The troubles with the team that riddled our passage through southern South Australia had abated. With future journeys in mind – not to mention my hopes about writing a book about the inception of BoardFree – the team was never far from my thoughts. My life was at its easiest when everyone was on form, operating to their full potential and enjoying themselves. Of course, even so far into the journey tiffs and moods broke out regularly and when stuck in a vacuum it took a while for the temperature to change again. On the road I mulled over every detail of this journey, wondering whether or not I'd have a team this large for future treks, questioning whether or not glum faces meant they'd lost enthusiasm for BoardFree or that there was just a low moment in the offing.

We had passed over the 4,000km mark and the sheer scale of the journey was now almost harder to conceive than it had been when we left Perth. I spent between five and ten hours on the road each day, swinging my right leg but using up more energy with my brain, which was slowly losing processing speed as fatigue set in. My physical capabilities were almost completely dependent on my mental attitude. Everything hurt, absolutely everything, and the only way I could take my mind off the pain was to dwell on other, more menial issues as I pushed on. Kate and I tended to argue when I was off the road, my behaviour was becoming choleric and I was uncomfortably aware of the moments when I was losing control, yet had no way of holding myself back. Kate had been my mainstay throughout, giving me a solid platform away from the others. She had supported me through thick and thin and quit her job to join the team; and despite my pleas that she should only do that for her own reasons we both knew that she was there for me, so we could be together, so she could help me deal with the hard times. Now, somehow, the seams were tearing slightly. We had been travelling for over three months with barely any respite from each other or the team and I, with no rational grounds for my actions, was starting to take that out on her. So, when Pat announced that he was going to drive on to Sydney in order to rent a room and make a good start on editing the documentary, Kate asked me if she could go too.

The injury delay in Adelaide had built up an irretrievable hole in the journey's schedule, and pre-organised fundraising events in the Sydney area were fast approaching. Missing these was not an option, so at some point at the end of November the journey would have to be put on hold so the team could drive north for a long weekend, attend the events and then drive back. We had three or four days of skating left before the drive, and Kate reasoned that she would be more effective in raising the media's interest if she was based in Sydney in the run-up to the events. Also, although we didn't discuss it, we both suspected some time apart might do us, as a couple, the world of good. So I squeezed her goodbye, and my brother too because he needed to go on to Sydney to meet his girlfriend, and they climbed into Pat's new van and drove away.

I felt alone. The team rallied around, aware that with Kate gone they'd have to fill the void of emotional support, but as I plodded on I felt a little like I'd been abandoned. I hadn't of course; with Kate on the ground in Sydney much more would be done to pave the way for our arrival, and I couldn't ignore the fact that she needed a rest. For months she had been picking up my pieces, keeping my spirits up, playing errand-girl when I was too tired to even fetch something from across the room. All this plus her media duties had exhausted her, but my rationality left when she did. Every push increased the jealousy I felt towards her just because she was speeding towards Sydney. I had forced conversations with myself, convinced that Kate was now on a holiday and wasn't interested in organising any media coverage, that she was planning to sit beside Sydney harbour with a gin and tonic as I pushed my way across the Great Dividing Range in sweltering heat. I missed her and cursed her, all at the same time, these tormented thoughts not doing much at all for my mental state and sending me again and again to the roadside, where I curled up with my head between my knees, silent as the stillness amplified the rhythmic throbbing that emanated from my feet.

I had started over the Great Dividing Range, climbed for hours without any perspective on where the next hill was or how steep it would be, trees towering above me, swaying in the dry, lifeless breeze. My skin beaded in sweat, the effect of the heat so near to the road always more evident when the air was still. I stopped frequently, panting heavily, dizzy from the effort, afraid of the loneliness, missing Kate. The team was still there, though, and they put on a show. As I'd turn a bend there would be Simon prancing at the roadside, strutting around in a bikini. Or Holly in a Hawaiian shirt and boxer shorts, which had been stuffed with what seemed like the entire team's socks. At one point the boys were even treated to a topless show: Becs and Holls twirling bras above their heads, breasts bouncing with laughter as I pushed past in amazement. No hill has ever been as easy as that one, there's a lot to say for natural motivation.

At about 3 p.m. and with 30km still to go, we pulled into a roadside café and I bought everyone a cold drink. The couple who ran the place were nice enough, but were hard work. The lady asked questions about the journey, about which leg I pushed with, all the usual things, but didn't seem to care about anything except making her own suggestions for what I should do. 'You should use both legs,' she insisted, 'you'll not make it to Cann River with just one.' The 4,100km I'd managed so far on one leg didn't quite register with her, and I turned for conversation to a pleasant Dutch couple, who had driven in at the same time as us. We nattered for a bit before moving outside to a garden separated from the highway by a row of trees. Holly laid down a blanket and I slept for an hour, Bev curled up beside me, a cool breeze floating down the valley to counter the dry heat of the day.

I opened my eyes, overcome by confusion at heavy sleep in the middle of the day. I wanted more, greedy for rest but knowing I was having myself on. Barely two hundred metres along the road Kylie stormed towards us. Becs and Laura had brought cold drinks having been informed of our slow progress by a group of labourers who Holly had been chatting to when I was napping. My tired, irrational side was angry at them for wasting petrol, but I ticked myself off for being an idiot and thanked them for being so thoughtful.

My inner conflicts were compounded by Dom, who had been quiet and surly since he and Pat had caught up with us four days earlier in Sale. His attitude had changed towards me and I assumed Pat had been involved. Dom still hadn't paid his team contribution. I had asked Pat to sort it out and he duly promised to do so, but his business partner's behaviour didn't appear to be at all remorseful. In fact, Dom had become more argumentative and less thoughtful than usual. During a talk I had given to a Sailability club south of Bairnsdale Dom positioned himself directly between the crowd and me. His choice of placement was baffling and intrusive, barely anyone in the room could see me and after stumbling for a couple of minutes I had no choice but to ask him to move, which he did with a loud, petulant exhalation.

On the road the next day I had walked over to George to find Dom sat in the passenger seat next to Holls, snipping away at his beard with some scissors. I was appalled and told him to get out of the van if he was thinking of making a carpet. I brought up a similar incident at Deirdre and Bob's house in Adelaide, when Dom had trimmed his beard and left the bathroom sink covered in short black hairs, with no attempt made to clear up. 'What kind of thanks is that for their hospitality?' I asked him. He looked back at me shaking his head; Holly just sat there smirking. She had spent more time with Dom than anyone, and knew just how generous he was with his spare facial hair.

A breaking point in our relationship came 20km from Cann River. I had pulled over for a break on a steep, long hill and was leant forward holding my knees, a usual position of rest by now. 'At some point up here I'd like you to pretend to collapse,' he said, 'you know, it's been a hard day and everything, it would be nice to have some drama on film, you really struggling.' I stared at him, not quite believing what he had just asked me. He looked back, his face straight as an arrow; he was being completely serious. I laughed, said nothing and pushed on, absolutely furious. Who the fuck did he think he was? Yes, it was a hard day. Yes, I'd like nothing better than to lie down and rest. But sorry, mate, it's just not me. I wasn't here to put on a z-list acting recital for the sake of the camera, I certainly wasn't going to change the way

I carried myself. When we next pulled over I told Dom. I repeated the words I'd said to Pat when we first met in Hyde Park in April: 'I'd want the documentary to be about the journey, not the journey to be about the documentary.' He didn't seem to understand, shrugged and said he was making a film and that I was making it seem too easy. There and then, any respect I had for him disappeared. His short bursts of aggression and endless thoughtless behaviour were one thing; any of us could be forgiven for our daily ticks when living within a pressure cooker environment like ours, but professionally he had just stepped beyond a line he had been pushing at since day one. His request showed me absolutely no respect and displayed a distanced attitude towards a journey he had been filming for months. That he still had no comprehension of why I was doing this amazed and confused me. It was an incredibly sad moment.

A few minutes later I decided to give him just what he was after, half to shut him up and half to make a point. I dismounted with a wry smile at the team. 'I'm now going to fall to the ground in agony and roll around in the dirt, just for Dom,' I said, matter-of-factly. Theatrically I lifted an arm to cover my face, which was stuck in a fixed grin at first – not quite the expression of desperation. The resulting footage, which Dom eagerly recorded from all manner of angles, would no doubt feature quite heavily in the 'struggle' scenes of the documentary and would, I promised myself, be the only shots filmed of the BoardFree project that were anything but one hundred per cent reality.

Bev cycled with me for the last 15km, taking over from Danny and keeping my spirits up with some tuneful singing and a typically positive outlook. Bev had been a star from the beginning and had worked ever so hard without complaint, yet her energy seemed boundless – although it was probably powered by her insatiable appetite for sleep. The girl could curl up on the ground, in a bed, in Kylie or, frankly, anywhere, and be sleeping in ten seconds flat. Becs was often charged with the duty of waking her diminutive best mate, and it wasn't an easy task!

Seventy-six kilometres on from Orbost, Bev pedaled alongside as I rolled past the welcome sign to Cann River. We'd broken the back of the mountains but the efforts had taken their toll on my feet. Becs had come up trumps with accommodation, as per usual, and I slowly shuffled into the Cann River hotel with a heavy limp, gratefully slumping onto a bed. As the evening wore on my right foot swelled, the blisters that had formed as I crossed central Gippsland hadn't coped well with the day's topography and had puffed out beneath my toes, horribly reminiscent of the injury that gave me so much pain during

BoardFree UK. There was usually a way to prevent blisters like this appearing but in my condition, tired and run down, my body wasn't in the best position to cope, and I was forgetting to deal with my feet in the way I ordinarily might. The mountains had also worn through a pair of shoes that were brand new on that morning. If only I could get a foot sponsor.

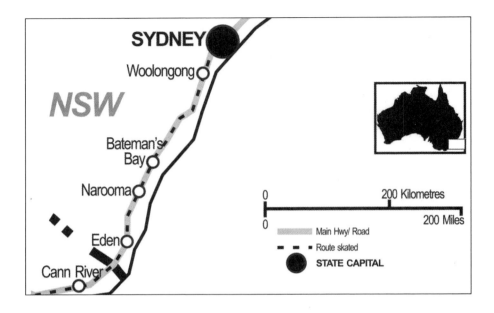

21 | 60 a day
29 November – 16 December 2006

The night did nothing to help the healing. Sole to sole, my right foot cast a shadow over the left. I could barely walk, had to stand on one leg in the shower. That familiar tingling sensation was back; the pulsing of pain around my foot, up my leg. There was no skating on this. We were so close to New South Wales I seriously considered sitting on my board and pushing with my hands, but it wasn't a realistic suggestion. It was time to make a critical call; pushing on could cause serious damage. I needed rest and there was no use us staying in Cann River with fundraising events waiting up ahead. We were going to Sydney early.

I sat up front in George with Holly, devastated as we drove into New South Wales. Up until then I had crossed each border on Elsa and I felt like a total fraud speeding towards the east coast in one of the vans. We would be returning to Cann River to resume the journey within the week, but here I was in New South Wales, and I wasn't on my board. There is nothing worse for a long-distance skateboarder than driving the route he has to skate later. Impossible to avert my eyes from the road I stared straight ahead, clouded by depression as we passed through Eden, meeting the east coast of Australia and the South

Pacific. I saw the landscape, the trees, the blur of buildings as we rushed through settlements, and I saw the road. And the hills. This east coast, it put the Great Dividing Range to shame. There were no flats, it was all up and down, some inclines so steep the vans couldn't cope in the heat. We pulled over time and time again, Holly managing to control George when a rear tyre burst.

It took two and a half days to drive from Cann River to Sydney, and by the time we reached there I was totally, thoroughly depressed. The drive had given me knowledge I didn't want and I couldn't shake it; so used to being driven on by the surprise around the bend, I was now precisely aware of what I had to face if I was to reach Sydney. Exhausted from worry and from the pain in my legs and feet, haunted by the border crossing, battered by the undulation of the east coast. I wasn't sure if I was capable of this anymore. I sunk into depression and withdrew from everybody, slowly becoming convinced that reaching Brisbane was asking too much. I took walks alone and cried in defeat. I was a beaten man.

* * *

Three fundraising events between the first and third days of December served to put my mind back on the job, at least temporarily. Sailability Illawarra, based on the northern shore of Lake Illawarra just south of Wollongong, hosted the first get-together, a fairly unusual fundraiser. We were greeted by Melissa Richardson, who ran the club and seemed fully in control of preparations for the evening BBQ. Originally, there were plans for several hundred plastic ducks to be released into the lake. Each duck was to be numbered, with each number relating to a ticket bought by a member of the public. The ducks would proceed to race, powered only by the wind until one crossed an agreed finishing line, thus winning a healthy prize for the lucky holder of the relevant number. Unfortunately, the team's anticipation at witnessing a duck race was dashed due to the difficulty of ordering so many plastic ducks in one go, so an alternative race was set up. 'This time,' explained Len Snowdon, who seemed responsible for such events, 'there will be several hundred numbered ice-cream paddles, which will race across a small paddling pool with the aid of an electric fan.' Well, all hell broke loose as the crowds bundled in to get a good view of the floating sticks of wood, and unbelievably there was a tie for first place and it was left to me — safely trussed up in a lifejacket of course — to bob for the winning stick. Embarrassment doesn't come close. Len was a cracking fellow, a sailor and a surfer despite the loss of his right arm and leg in a train accident several years earlier, and he epitomised the spirit and character that we had begun to associate with Sailability; it was a pleasure to meet him.

After Illawarra we drove north to southern Sydney, led by Tish Ennis and her husband Jim. Tish had been in regular contact via email since the spring and had organised the second event of the weekend, a Christmas party at Kogarah Bay Sailing club, from where she and Jim ran the local sailing club. The team spent the night in the club, but I drove into the city to Rushcutters Bay for a reunion with my cousin Kate, who I hadn't seen since Christmas, and of course, my Kate. It felt like I hadn't seen her since Christmas, either. My brother Andy was there too, as was his girlfriend Maddy and friend Sharky, and I could barely manage a beer before my eyes started to close. The next day, several hundred more dollars were raised at Kogarah Bay. I was tasked with skating down the pontoon to greet Santa Claus and another chap who was wearing a rather bizarre reindeer head. Santa then jumped onto Elsa and I pushed him up the gangplank and into the dining room, where a short question and answer question was followed swiftly by a delicious meal. Again, though, I was dropping off and at one stage woke just in time to stop my head plummeting into a plate of nibbles. 'Let's get you home,' said my cousin, determined for me to get some rest before the journey resumed. So we went.

The final event of the weekend was to be held at Sailability Rushcutters Bay, just around the corner from my cousin's flat. Kate and I were staying there, and over a cup of tea that next morning I poured my heart out to both of them, explaining my feelings about the drive up from Cann River, laying my thoughts on the table. Few moments had gone by without my doubts churning and I felt like I had reached a decision with myself. 'I'm not sure I can physically reach Brisbane,' I told them, 'just getting to Sydney is going to take so much out of me, I'm not sure I'll have anything left to give after that.' I went on, pondering the pros and cons, wondering whether the team's fundraising efforts would be better suited should we remain in Sydney for a month rather than trekking further up the east coast. When I was done my cousin handed me another cup of tea and Kate gave me a hug.

'I'm going to stand by you whatever you want to do,' she said. 'Only you know whether you're going to be able to live with yourself if you don't go all the way to Brisbane.' Deep down, I wasn't sure how I felt; perhaps I was just making up excuses? All I knew was that a decision had to be made quickly.

As well as the Sailability crowd at Rushcutters, we were joined by members of the Brady and Gardiner families, both bringing their boys along, children with Lowe Syndrome. At eleven years old Connor Gardiner looked half his age. With glasses perched upon his nose with unthinkably thick lenses held in place by special flexible frames, his energy was boundless. Fuelled with curiosity he explored, hugging legs. He made a quick habit of scuttling up to the microphone and yelling into it, his dad, Alex, chuckling at his boy, who couldn't be controlled. The team took turns to watch him as visitors bought homemade cakes and BoardFree baseball caps. And then Connor met Elsa. The two of them rolled around, colliding into ankles and screaming in pleasure. And then, when it all became too much, Connor threw Elsa to the floor causing what was to become my board's greatest injury of the Australian journey. Just a couple of inches of surface covering fell away from one of the wheel wells – I won't deny I had a pang of disbelief when someone showed me the damage! – but it revealed another side to Lowe Syndrome which I hadn't seen before, and who was I to make any judgement? Connor's presence served as a timely reminder that although Sailability was obviously a focus of this journey, finding a cure for Lowe Syndrome was still very much at the forefront of BoardFree Australia's aims.

I had been invited to make a speech, and in it I was preparing to announce that the journey would culminate in Sydney. First though, Bev took the stage to perform the BoardFree song. As she played I stood to the rear of the crowd as she plucked her guitar with the Harbour Bridge in the background, everyone around listening intently. This song had played on so many occasions, but the words this time struck a chord and I welled up as Bev sung:

> *I'm moving on I'm moving on,*
> *I'm breaking out I'm breaking through the barrier.*
> *I'm skating down I'm making ground,*
> *And if Elsa breaks well I'm gonna carry her.*
> *My legs are strong but the roads are so long,*
> *I'm pushing hard but I seem to be getting nowhere.*
> *It may seem hard it may seem tough,*
> *But this is my dream this is no nightmare,*
> *For all of you who say it can't be done,*
> *Well I'll see you when I get there.*
> *When will I get to Brisbane, how long do I have to go,*
> *First Adelaide, Melbourne, Sydney, I'll never give up . . . oh oh no!*

I took the microphone, and spoke. I thanked everyone involved in the event, especially my cousin, Kate. I thanked the team individually and stressed that without them this journey wouldn't have been possible, and that on behalf of BoardFree we were making a donation of $A5,000 to Sailability Rushcutters

Bay. The amount was far larger than any donation we'd made to other Sailability clubs, but it was in thanks to my cousin for being the Sailability representative in Australia, for geeing everyone up, for helping to pave the way for us.

And then I took a deep breath and told everybody how I'd been feeling. How the south coast of New South Wales had filled me with dread, how I doubted that I could complete the journey. And then I told them how listening to Bev play had made up my mind, how the song summed up BoardFree. I looked around knowing that of everyone on the team only Kate knew I'd been considering ending in Sydney; the rest of them just stared, open mouthed. I said it was about my journey, my dream. It just didn't sound right, I told the crowd, if we tried to change the words to 'When will I get to Sydney . . .'. It just didn't sound right! I looked at the graphics and logos all over the t-shirts we were wearing, covering the support vehicles. This journey was from Perth to Brisbane, I said, it was never meant to end in Sydney, so we were going to Brisbane however hard it would be, however big the hills were. Bev may not remember it, but she got an extra big hug from me after that.

A visit to the Triple J studio was our only commitment the next day. It was always nice to meet presenters and producers in person, and on this occasion not least because Robbie Buck and I had only ever had conversations on the phone that were listened to by hundreds of thousands of people. A personal relationship it was not! As we went live the message was simple, we were to return to Cann River the next day and would then begin an eleven-day journey in order to reach Sydney in time for the sixteenth of December. I had skated just under 4,200km between Perth and Cann River, and preparations had begun for a celebration of a new world record. In order to attend that celebration and break Jack Smith's world record for the longest distance ever travelled on a skateboard, I would have to push an average of 60km per day for eleven days straight. With my right foot still suffering from multiple blisters, and knowing full well what the New South Wales south coast was about to offer, I told Robbie that I was about to face the biggest challenge in my life. Gracious as ever, he wished me luck and promised to call again soon.

*   *   *

We decided to drive back to Cann River via Canberra, so as to avoid the coastal highway. I spent the day sleeping on my bunk at the back of George, giving my body its final rest before the road called again. What was to come absolutely terrified me but I was now ready to face it head on. It wasn't just down to me;

it was going to be a team effort. We arrived at Cann River after dark and I sat the team down in the hotel bar. 'We need to get up at five a.m. each morning and get away by seven. Is everyone willing to do this?' I asked. Everyone agreed with a nod, except Dom.

'Only if you get up at the same time as the rest of us,' he said, bluntly.

He had no idea what it was taking for me to walk up the stairs, let alone move at everyone else's pace.

'I'll be up with everyone else,' I said, and shuffled to bed like an old man.

It was horrific being back on the road. Every joint ached. My head pounded. My feet stung. One week of no exercise and I felt rather like I was about to combust. I spent more time sat at the roadside tending to blisters than I did on Elsa, it seemed, and shovelling down chocolate bars in an attempt to gain energy wasn't helped at all by a distinct loss of appetite, brought on by stomach cramps and a proliferation of mouth ulcers. Two hours after leaving Cann River we got word that one of the vans had broken down. Becs drove ahead to the nearest town and returned a while later, leading a tow truck back to our stricken vehicle. The hills continued, endless half-hour climbs rewarded with what I felt were petty downhill runs considering the altitude I'd scaled. Of course, everything levels out eventually, and as I rolled passed the riverside settlement of Genoa and hauled myself into the final 10km of the day I was quite aware that my mind was playing tricks on me. The hills weren't being unfair, they were just easy to blame.

I finished on the New South Wales border having skated 62km. One day down, target reached. George's technical difficulties were being remedied several kilometres off the road in Mallacoota, where the manager of a local campsite had willingly offered us accommodation in cabins. He appeared later that evening and told me he'd taken the liberty of organising a studio interview with the local radio station for 8 a.m. the next morning. I thanked him outwardly, but secretly found the situation troublesome. Mentally, I was dealing with the prospect of the hills ahead by setting myself a pattern; an early start meant a couple of hours of skating in less oppressive heat, and I was also likely to reach the end of the day sooner, which in turn meant more rest. An interview at 8 a.m. the next morning would mean we wouldn't be on the road until 9 a.m. at the earliest, and for once I wasn't willing to make media coverage a priority. It was, after all, a relatively small local station. Instantly I formed a plan and walked across the campsite to the other cabin, where the team were relaxing. 'Guys,' I said, 'we're going to have a bit of fun tomorrow morning.' They looked at me, waiting for the punch line. 'Si,' I smiled wryly, 'your time has come.'

For months I had endured Simon's theatrical impressions. He'd cock his head as another team member would ask him a typical BoardFree question, and then he'd answer just as I would have answered, facial ticks and expressions and all. He was a good half a foot taller than me, but on more than one occasion people had approached Simon thinking he was the guy skating across Australia, so slowly but surely he had developed quite an act. If anyone could play Dave, Simon could.

I hunkered down in Cheech as we drove away early the next morning, hoping that the campsite manager wouldn't be watching. Half an hour later Danny was changing Elsa's wheels in preparation for our third border crossing; all of us laughing at what was unravelling back in Mallacoota. Simon was kitting up, Clic sunglasses, Circa baseball cap and skate shoes. He was wearing a pair of my shorts, a BoardFree t-shirt, and he had my spare board too. He was trudging up the road with several members of his team, through the front doors of the radio station, into the lair of the studio. Let's see just how good he is at being Dave now, shall we. Somewhere on the radio waves in Victoria Dave Cornthwaite was being introduced to Gippsland, or so thought the female presenter. In fact, the real Dave Cornthwaite was pushing his skateboard further and further away from Victoria, having finally made his long awaited entrance into New South Wales.

It was a long hot, day as I skated through the Timbillica, Nadgee and East Boyd State Forests, and then on into Eden, where I lunched with Dan, Holly and Kate by the ocean, celebrating having skated the entire width of Australia. Another 20km remained, a hefty challenge with hills so steep they left my legs shaking. Approaching Pambula I descended at pace, around 45kmph, when I turned back to see Kate pull Cheech off the road. Suddenly without cover, traffic was screaming past my right side, so close I could have reached out and touched wing mirrors. I dragged to a halt, always at risk of toppling when braking at that speed, and ploughed into the gravel beside the road. As I turned in fury to remonstrate with Kate Elsa continued downhill. In slow motion I saw her go, arcing back towards the highway, bouncing up onto the bitumen into the line of traffic. I ran, my heart sinking as a lorry trundled past, I was on the road, my board was between the wheels of the truck, I reached out a leg and placed my right foot on Elsa, dragging her away just as the truck's rear wheel descended. I picked her up and returned to the roadside, my legs buckled and I fell to the ground.

I screamed, so livid that I was hoarse in seconds: 'What the fuck did you pull off the road for, are you trying to fucking kill me?' Everyone in Cheech stayed there for what seemed like minutes. Kate had her head in her hands behind the wheel; Dan and Holly were stock still. Twenty metres away I hunched up, my head in my hands as the traffic continued just metres to my left. Eventually they walked down towards me. Kate cried and I stayed silent, confused and upset at what had just happened, at the shock of running so close to those vehicles, at nearly losing Elsa. Something has snapped in me; I had no emotion left. I just felt sick, empty. My reaction was born out of desperation; but it was unfair. For this was the first time that Kate, who along with Danny had driven the majority of the route from Perth, had put a foot wrong. Although the consequences may have been horrific, that this was the only error either of them had made was a testament to their skill and judgement. I couldn't have had two safer guardians.

That night I stopped. Two days down, still on target, 491km to the world record. We laughed as Dom replayed the video footage of Simon's radio interview earlier that day, at the blood draining out of his face as the phone in the studio rang. He was sure he'd been caught out, but he hadn't and kept enough composure through to the end, even managing to flirt with the presenter a couple of times. I sunk into a restless, haunted sleep, waking all too early with the 5 a.m. alarm, ready to do it all over again.

Day three was a slog, slowly nibbling into the highway that had depressed me so much as we drove north ten days earlier. The road twisted and turned, rose and fell, a rollercoaster of emotion. Through Bega, Anglesdale, Brogo and finally to Cobargo to complete another 76km. We spent the evening 20km east of there in the coastal village of Bermagui, where donations flooded in from drinkers at the local hotel and I chatted to a Canadian cyclist, who in his seventies was heading into Victoria, retracing my footsteps.

From Cobargo Highway One banked north east through the southern reaches of the Kooraban National Park, where dense forest gave way to rolling, Tolkien-like farmlands. Kate jogged alongside me on one steep uphill, giving me a huge psychological push towards Narooma. Physically I was struggling, the blisters on my feet behaving like mercury – slowly they grew and merged with others – and contributing to the pain that surged through my shins, calves, knees and thighs with each push. Without the scope to rest for a day I needed support from the team running and cycling with me, but they couldn't be there all day long and mentally I continued to struggle, as though each big hill was just a nail in the coffin. A car honked its horn and a lad jumped out with a longboard. He pushed up a huge hill with me, a laughing, happy stranger, and raced down the other side before jumping back into a car full of mates, but not before we handed him a BoardFree t-shirt.

We spent the night at the Clark Bay cottages, a tranquil spot hidden away across the Wagonga Inlet from Narooma. Surrounded by forest inhabited by hundreds of species of bird and animal life, I leaned against the veranda railings and chatted to Barny Barnbrook, who had set up Clark Bay as an ideal holiday location designed to cater for all. Each of the site's self-contained cottages were ramped for wheelchair access and rigged up with endless gizmos to make the accommodation completely accessible for disabled visitors. Barny, a towering, genuine guy who also ran the local Sailability club, peppered our conversation with observations about bird calls that echoed through the woods and stories about the parrots and wallabies which frequented the grounds. His daughter, Ame, was a national Sailability success story, spoken about by many in Sailability clubs we had passed through previously. Born with phocomelia, Ame's lack of limbs hadn't stopped her from swimming, playing trumpet, operating a computer and winning State, National and International awards for sailing prowess. I had the pleasure of meeting Ame that evening, just before she went to town with her brother and sister. She was a delightful, openly normal girl who was capable of great achievements. Talking about her with Barny that evening it became more evident how the most successful Sailability clubs operated: their sailors were simply not treated as though they were disabled. 'You have to look on the bright side,' Barny said. 'She's never going to shut her fingers in a door, and despite her condition she still lives life to the full.' I offered a donation to Sailability Narooma but Barny wouldn't accept it, instead he tried to convince us to spend another day at Clark Bay. It was an offer I found harder to turn down than any other that had been made since Perth, but unfortunately we had to push on.

* * *

Three hundred and fifty-nine kilometres to the world record. I dreamed about a giant hand picking me up and plonking me down in Perth, just in time to start the journey over again – but this time I knew what was coming. Nightmares don't come more terrifying than that. The next two days were hell, continuing along Highway One through Bateman's Bay and Ulladulla. I discovered a seven-foot red kangaroo lying in the middle of the road early one morning, an enormous creature that posed a clear safety threat to traffic. I had no choice but to pull it off the road by the tail, its warmth signalling recent life, matter spilling from a head wound, the sweat of shock leaving a dark stain where it had lain.

Blisters on the ball and Achilles region of my right foot and also blistering over the new scar on my left heel leave me with pain at every push. I've been lucky for much of this journey, skating through muscle fatigue and pretty minor blisters but avoiding repeats of the horrific damage and infection that plagued the UK journey. Prevention is always better than cure when it comes to a journey with little rest-time built into the schedule, but as BoardFree Australia rolled into its fourth month my body was struggling to deal with the strain. My immune system was shot; the ulcer on my lower lip still present after more than four weeks, and I knew there was little chance my feet would heal completely before the journey was out. Team spirits were in limbo. We hadn't had a proper rest since Adelaide and everyone was completely whacked, going through the motions everyday with barely any energy to carry out an argument, let alone solve any lingering issues. The girls were astounding, like machines; fundraising and feeding was their forte and they haven't stopped for weeks. Thousands of dollars were being accumulated on and off the road, drooping eyelids were symptoms but not excuses, the early wake-up calls were taking their toll on everyone but the adrenaline was pumping now.

Six days out from Cann River I had skated 381km. We spent the night in the Entrance Tourist Park beside Lake Conjola, a mob of eight kangaroos emerging from the bush after a heavy rain shower, bright red parrots feeding from the team's hands. An almost eerie calm had descended despite the gusting wind, which bends trees sideways beyond our veranda, and Kate and I discuss the latest crisis to hit BoardFree. There was a problem with the production company. Pat had cornered Kate and berated her for the way she was dealing with the media, accusing her of promising them free footage. It was an attack made all the more frustrating because it was groundless, typical of the irrationalism that had had been growing since Pat's arrival in Melbourne. Tapes of footage had been handed to the media throughout the journey, extra minutes of stunning imagery shot on the Nullarbor that had encouraged local and national news reports to up the priority of the BoardFree coverage. It was a journey for charity and the more coverage we got the better, but now, as our profile was growing, dollar signs formed blinkers for Dom and Pat and they had started requesting a fee for the tapes behind my back. A fee, for publicising a not-for-profit charitable project; it was flabbergasting.

During our break in Sydney I'd spoken to Pat about Dom's behaviour but he just said that they were under pressure, that funds were haemorrhaging back home. It wasn't talk I wanted to hear and it certainly didn't put me at ease with their operation. The sands were shifting. Dom had continued to distance himself from me; they had scripted a new contract that if signed would ensure that I no longer had shared rights to the footage of the journey; and doubts had been expressed by both that I should be allowed free access to the film shot on this, my journey. The situation had been spiralling, commandeering my thoughts on the road day after day, and now that Pat had brought Kate into it my patience was wearing thin. She had been doing a remarkable job. With no prior PR experience Kate had been the main cog in sending the BoardFree story around the world and now, as the project neared a world record, my journey had never been so newsworthy. For hours on end she worked on obtaining coverage, and at the same time she carried out her duty as Cheech's second driver when Dan needed a break. The pressures each individual faced from their personal tasks was more than enough for them to cope with, and when professional issues with the production company began to arise I did my utmost to keep them out of everyone's eye line. By doing that, though, even more of my energy was consumed. Those were the formative stages of a long, ugly battle, and it was destroying me mentally, adding more strain to Kate and I, plundering our personal time and turning relaxation into emotional turmoil. God, the skateboarding was an afterthought most of the time, let's just get to Sydney, I told myself, and we can have a break there. Goodness knows everyone needs it.

When moods were low Kate often suggested that problems arose because of my poor communication, and she was right. In truth, I was so exhausted that dealing with issues was the last thing I wanted to do. I pushed people away, blocked them out, hid myself in a quiet place and tried to escape. My exhaustion grew as the days and weeks continued. Tiny, often insignificant things bloated in my mind, swelled as I pushed along the roads, tears in my eyes, angry shouted words echoing through the trees beside me. Everything was magnified. I wasn't in a position to deal with much so I escaped for everyone's sake, and as a consequence the person who took the brunt of my pain, anger and fatigue was Kate, for she was the only one to seek me out when I was low.

*   *   *

On the eighth day from Cann River I pushed 67km into northern Wollongong, where a Channel 9 television crew was waiting at the roadside. It was a last-minute ambush that even Kate hadn't known about, so breathlessly I gave a quick interview and skated around a bit for the camera off the main road. An hour later I was driving into town with Holly, Dan and Kate, three interviews and a visit to the Post Office on the schedule. I was in agony, the skin on my right heel having finally given way after 4,726km of skating. As had happened that mid-May evening earlier in the year, I had removed my shoes to find that the small blisters on the heel, encouraged by a lack of rest and by ever increasing humidity as the summer heat grew stronger, had finally corrupted, the friction of the day leaving behind open, raw flesh. The pain of this and dealing with swelling on my right foot, which I'd been suffering from for several days, merged with fatigue and flipped me over the edge. Kate was suffering too, frustrated with my inability to move quickly and, no doubt, with the tone of my voice. We began to fight, sniping at each other as I gave Dan directions through town. We had half an hour until the first interview but Kate wasn't happy for me to pick up our parcels before then. 'The Post Office is right there, it won't take long.' She followed me as I left Danny at the roadside, just wanting to be done with it all, wishing I could be lying still, asleep in bed. And then something snapped. 'Fuck off Kate, just fuck off,' I said sharply.

'What do you mean, fuck off, what do you mean? I don't understand.' She was getting hysterical.

'Please, I can't do this anymore, just fuck off.'

She was crying now and stopped as I walked on, disappearing into the Post Office, leaving her behind. Holly was with me, and we waited for a couple of minutes. They had the parcels, three of them filled with new shoes. The woman was messing around and I turned, looking out for Kate. She was lingering by the doorway. The woman was ready, I signed the confirmation receipt and lifted two of the boxes, Holly took the third. Kate stood in my way. 'Talk to me, Dave,' she pleaded. I wouldn't. I couldn't. I'd lost sight of how it had even started, all I knew is I was in a silent rage and didn't want to say anything else. I regretted it all so much but I was shaking with emotion, not ready to resolve anything, not being able to if I had tried. Kate cried out loud, tears streaming down her cheeks. I opened the boot, shoved the boxes in and slammed it shut. Danny was holding her and I remember thinking, If anyone should look after her, it's Danny. I stood nearby, my heart fractured, hating myself for doing this to her, not knowing why it was happening.

'Just go, Dave,' said Dan, and I went. Holly walked with me; I was just blank.

We reached the offices for the first interview. They were abandoned and a note hung on the door bearing a new address.

'Fuck! FUCK!' I shouted, 'Why is it never fucking simple!' I sat on the doorstep of the empty offices and called the number Kate had given me, it didn't work. I was fuming, with myself, with Kate, with the newspaper for moving offices. Holly asked directions from a passer-by and I managed to get through on another number. We walked around in circles without a map, completely lost.

'She has to leave me,' I told Holly as we paced towards the newspaper offices. 'I don't know why I'm treating her like this, but it's not fair. I'm sure she's going to leave me this time.'

'She won't leave you,' said Holly, 'she loves you too much.' And although that made me feel better, I knew it didn't excuse anything. I briefly put on my media face as we found the newspaper offices and quickly called Becki to see if she could pick us up in Kylie. We were cutting it fine to get to the second interview on time and needed a lift. I apologised to the reporter and explained that we had another to go to. The interview went quickly, a keen, sharp journalist. He kept apologising as the photographer asked for more and more poses. 'It's cool, mate, we've got a bit of time,' I told him. 'Thanks for understanding.'

Becs, Bev and Laura turned up in Kylie and dropped Holly and me off at the ABC studios. I was shaking, horrified at what had happened between Kate and I. Got the interview out of the way, actually skating into the studio before a nice, quick chat, an interested presenter. Another interview afterwards, this time on the phone down a back alley, and then, finally, back to the caravan site. This was a fairly usual scenario, a now regular afternoon. Except for my temper, which had finally boiled far beyond my control. I spent the rest of the afternoon and evening in floods of tears, uncontrollably sobbing. Someone had called my cousin and she rang saying she'd heard things weren't easy. After ten seconds I fell apart again and had to apologise. I hung up, inconsolable. Some members of the team came in to see how I was; I waved them away. Kate sat down beside me and put her arms around me. I asked her for a bit more time, I needed to be alone. I breathed through my fingers, realising that all of this was destroying me. In five months I'd had barely any time to myself and now, the fatigue of distance travelled and the stress of worry about how the documentary was going to play out accumulated into a soup of heightened emotion. I was lost and unhappy. Even two amazing visitors, Len Snowdon from Sailability Illawarra and Carmen, an old friend of mine who lived nearby, couldn't pull me out of my slump. Shortly before I went to bed Dom approached with the minicam. 'It'd be cool if we could get how you're feeling tonight,' he said, tactful to the end.

'I'd quite like my life back, now,' I told him.

* * *

I felt better in the morning, stronger, more rested. The world can be falling apart around your ears and still a good sleep can shed a new light on things.

Kate was beside me and her kisses told me she wasn't leaving. My feet looked and felt like they'd landed a lead role in a slasher movie, but I could still walk. Sydney's outskirts were within reach and Danny had Christmas'd up the vehicles with lengths of tinsel tied around the bumpers. The news reports last night had done their job and cars passed with raised thumbs poked through the windows and horns tunefully honked. Fifteen kilometres north of Wollongong I descended along the Sea Cliff Bridge between Clifton and Coalcliff, a 665-metre stretch of smooth, declining road that had reconnected the two towns after the old road had fallen foul of consistent landslides and wear and tear. Usually I would have flown over the bridge but a strong headwind whipped around the coast and stopped me dead. In order to freewheel at all I literally had to sit on my board, and even then I trundled along at a snail's pace.

We drove back to repeat the Bridge for the sake of the cameras, and afterwards pushed uphill for an hour between Coalcliff and Stanwell Tops, Laura briefly running alongside me only to fall foul of the prickly vegetation that filled the sewage gutter she was jogging in! I was then joined by my friend Carmen, who cycled with me to the freeway before saying goodbye. Carmen has travelled more than anyone I know and despite her fair share of challenges she continues to see life as a chance, not a chore. When we first met I was fresh from school and finding my own feet, she was touring East Africa solo and needed a spare bed; my friends and I had one and we've remained in touch ever since.

From there it was easy going, skating along a wide cycle lane big enough so Cheech could drive squarely behind me. As passing traffic continued to show its support the Welcome to Sydney sign appeared 40km or so south of the city centre. It crept up almost too quickly. Passing underneath it – my attention drawn by Holly and Dom's positioning in the middle of the lane I was skating along – I glanced up at the last minute and saw three words that made my day. Then through Waterfall, Heathcote and finally to Engadine, our stop for the night. Sydney's centre was only 30km away. We were put up in two motel rooms by Juergen and Colin, our sponsors from The Magic Touch who had provided the team with reflective jackets, t-shirts and other printed accessories to wear and sell on in exchange for charitable donations. This was the first time I had met either of them – Juergen had actually flown over from Amsterdam to find us on the route – and the BBQ they laid on for us was gratefully received.

There were four other guests, as well. Two hours after I had pushed into Engadine a rented campervan backed into the motel lot and out popped the first two, my brother Andy and his girlfriend Maddy, who had been travelling along the east coast for a couple of weeks. And then, once the van had squeezed into a slot that was far too small for its bulk, my parents appeared. 'Well done chum,' said my dad, hugging me and patting my back. And then my mum, tears streaming down her cheeks, stood there with her arms outstretched, trembling with emotion, her lips shaking as she kissed me and held me close.

'I can't believe I'm here,' she whispered, 'I'm so proud of you Dave, you've come so far.'

* * *

Simon had developed a new habit. A new milestone was on all of our minds, this time not a mere celebration of zeros but this time a real target. Jack Smith's world record, the 4,830 kilometres he had skated across the United States in 2003, was now in sight. By the time I reached Engadine I had totalled 4,770km. With a celebration parade scheduled just two days later I bid the team goodnight. 'World Record!' Simon mouthed at me before I left the room, 'World Record!' Next door, I walked out of the bathroom and stared at my brother, who swung his legs from a bunk. 'World Record!' he mouthed, doing Simon's dirty work no doubt by request.

We were up at 5 a.m. the next day. Andy and Maddy sat in Cheech with Kate and Dan as I sped up the freeway into Sydney. I hoped to skate 59km to the starting point of tomorrow's 2km parade, which would see the long-distance skating record broken. Sydney Olympic Park, where the parade was due to take place, was only about 30km away, though, so an awful lot of meandering through the city suburbs had to be done to amass the kilometres needed. The skies opened as I trawled through back streets and along riverside cycle paths, finding myself facedown in a puddle at one point after Elsa got stuck in the mud created by the falling rain.

An old woman strolling along with music playing in her ear glanced sideways at me as I skated past. 'Got a deathwish have you?' she snorted, not giving me a second look. Her naivety stuck with me all day, last-minute paranoia hanging in the air as I thought of the potential consequences of finishing the day a kilometre short of Jack's record.

Spirits were high despite the rain in the early afternoon and I decided to let the team into a little secret. I spoke into my walkie-talkie and told them about the night north of Norseman four months earlier when I woke up having wet myself. I turned and burst into laughter as Kate held her hand to her mouth. It was such a random place – we were simply skating through an industrial neighbourhood in Sydney – to let loose such an unusual piece of information, yet for some reason I felt like I had to get it off my chest. Two hours later I was

closing in on our 59km target and then took a wrong turn. I skated through
Rookwood Cemetery, trying to keep the noise of my scraping wheels down as
I passed by religion-marked sections of land. Some graves were decorated with
flowers, some left to the elements. 'Got a deathwish, have you?' The old
woman's words from earlier haunted me, and I realised then and there that I
didn't ever want to be lying in a grave. I want to be remembered for what I did
and who I was rather than where I lay when it was all over. 'I'd hate to be slowly
forgotten,' I told myself, hoping someone somewhere would hear me. 'I'd hate
to be stuck in a grave which no one ever visited.'

Outside Rookwood Cemetery Cheech pulled up alongside. Kate looked
stressed. 'Any luck with the news channels?' I asked. She'd been drumming up
attention for tomorrow's event.

'Looks like we've got Seven and Ten,' she said, 'but Pat's trying to get some
money for the footage so I'm not sure if that's going to bugger things up.'

I could feel the rage building again. 'Has Penny been involved at all?' Penny
was our contact at the Monster Skate Park in Sydney Olympic Park, and had
been involved in the organisation of the next day's festivities.

'Well, she arranged Channel Ten but says they're not going to pay for
footage, it doesn't work that way in Australia.'

'No shit! Why is Pat still fucking around?'

'I actually asked Penny if she'd speak to Pat and she said she wasn't
interested in talking to him.'

I couldn't believe this, I growled, 'if we lose any coverage because of this
there's going to be hell to pay.'

Right then, George pulled up with Simon and Holly. I checked the map with
Danny, worked out the final route leading to the gates of Bicentennial Park, and
set off. Those final 5km were filled with complete frustration. I was at my wits
end. I didn't know how the production company could even consider asking for
a fee at this point. How many times did I have to make my views clear? Were
they ever going to listen? My mood wasn't helped when, rounding a bend into
the park, a white van driver punched his horn right beside me and shouted, 'Get
the fuck of the road you little prick.' We were slap-bang in the middle of rush
hour and cars were end to end. It was a horrible time to be on the road, and
although a few people were applauding and shouting encouragement from their
cars I just wanted to finish the day without causing any more obstruction. I
didn't care much for the attitude of the white van driver, but even so I didn't
want BoardFree to leave a bad taste in anyone's mouth and rush-hour
frustrations always raised the mercury on the streets. I took pavements where I

could, sending Cheech on ahead to the next junction, and before I knew it I was crossing a main road into Sydney Olympic Park.

The Park was empty and the roads were smooth. It was a ghost town in mid-afternoon, an Olympic Village typically faded from the bustle of the event it was built for in 2000. But the empty roads were a relief after the chicken-run approach and I enjoyed the easy roll past all manner of sports pitches. The hockey centre lay dormant to my right along the final straight, and I wondered whether Bev had seen it: she'd be delighted to see a hockey field, even if no one was playing. And just as that thought was ending, I pulled up at the gates of the Bicentennial Park, sat on a concrete block and shook my brother's hand as he jogged over from Cheech.

'Well done mate,' he said, 'nearly there.'

And I was. The meandering nature of the day, the poor weather, more frustrations with Dom and Pat and even the imminence of an enormous achievement had absolutely exhausted me. The 59km from Engadine had sent my total distance travelled up to 4,829km. The next day I would skate just 2km; the first would see me equal Jack Smith's record of 4,830km, and the second would see me break it by one whole kilometre. By this time tomorrow, I thought, I will have travelled further on a skateboard in one journey than anyone else in history. And then Bev brought me down to earth with a bump.

'We're going to have to wrap you up in cotton wool until tomorrow,' she said, 'it'd be awful if you got run over or shot tonight and never broke the record.'

'I think it's time to go and get some rest,' I said. And we did.

The girls had managed to find two cabins about half an hour's drive west, along the early, built-up stages of the Hume Highway. As always following a skate, I sat up front and aired my feet, throwing shoes and socks into the foot well before plucking toe-caps and tearing off dressings from the heel and ball of my right foot. My phone rang, it was Pat. He wanted to talk about the footage for the networks tomorrow, saying he'd been trying to get a small fee from Channel 10, who had claimed they'd been promised it for free. He was being pushy and tried to tell me it was Kate who had told 10 the footage was theirs to have. I'd heard this story before and really wasn't in the mood. I told Pat what was going to happen. Kate was sat behind me and I didn't want to be talking about her without clearing it first, but it had been a long time since I had felt articulate enough to put my foot down and the chance wasn't going to go begging. First though, as I started to talk, I turned and winked, giving her a thumbs-up.

'Listen Pat, you have to stop blaming Kate for the networks wanting footage for free. Of course they want it for free! I've been with her when she's been talking to them and she has never promised anything. We've been through this before and I honestly can't believe it's still such an issue. You're not providing a unique service here, if you and Dom hadn't been with us they would still have been given vision tapes and we wouldn't have dreamed of charging for them.' There was silence on the other end of the line, so I carried on before losing the flow. 'BoardFree is a charity project and we need this coverage Pat, you have to understand that you'll benefit afterwards: the more people who see this on TV will know about the journey, and then they'll buy the DVD. For the time being get on our side, give the vision to the networks and don't ask for anything. If we lose coverage because you're asking for money I'm going to be fucking pissed off.'

There. Said it. Jesus that felt good. Pat was clearly drained by the whole thing too, and didn't say much before the conversation ended. I hoped that that would be the end of it.

'What was he saying about me?' asked Kate.

'The usual shit.' I turned to her. 'He's trying to make out that you've been making promises to the TV people.'

'I'm so fucking angry,' she said. And her face was so red, I knew she was telling the truth. I reached out for her hand.

'Please don't worry any more babes,' I said. 'I think I've just dealt with it.'

* * *

At 3 p.m. on Saturday 16 December I stood outside the Bicentennial Gates in Sydney Olympic Park with a group of skaters. Also present were my cousin Kate, and Kelly, Lisa and Jackie from Sailability. Two camera crews from Channels 7 and 10 stood by, as did an AAP photographer and a man named Mark who had heard about my journey a month earlier and bought a red rollsrolls board because of it. Juergen and Colin represented The Magic Touch and all of the other sponsors who had made this journey possible. Hagen from the Monster Skate Park assembled the skaters and read them the riot act. Alex Gardiner was there with Connor, who was going to ride on a tricycle despite his Lowe Syndrome. My parents were there, my brother and Maddy, and my team who had helped me to this point, my team who were mostly strangers a year ago. And Kate, who was so much more than just a team member – my personal lifejacket who put up with more than any woman should.

Guided by Park officials we set off and skated down Australia Avenue. TV cameramen sat in the boot of their car, leading the way. The team walked, Kelly rolled in her wheelchair, Connor pedaled hard. Bev and Laura pushed their rollsrolls boards and wore bright orange vests: they were my marshals. Left at the end of the road and straight for a few hundred metres, left again for the final time, onto Olympic Boulevard. I stopped to let the skaters surge ahead to the finish line, and then skated with the team, each of us linked, arms on shoulders. I looked right and left, taking in the faces that had been with me since the beginning. 'We did this together guys,' I told them before they pushed me ahead into a funnel of people, across the line. I'd skated 4,831km from Perth. Laura screamed, Holly cried, my parents smiled. I embraced Kate, finally finding her through the crowd. I'm sure, even though I didn't see him instantly, that Simon mouthed two simple words, 'World Record.'

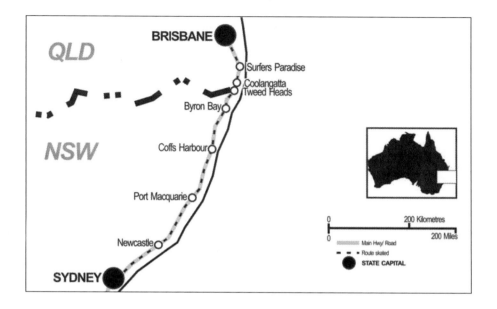

22 The Final Stretch

17 December – 22 January 2007

'Shit! Shut the windows, QUICK!' Dan seizes up, pointing through the windscreen. I instantly think something has gone wrong with the vehicle; we're pelting south along the Pacific Highway towards Newcastle and all of a sudden Danny isn't his usual calm and composed self. 'Huntsman!' he growls. 'Quick!' A large pile of legs and fur scuttles towards us along the bonnet of Cheech. It stops short of the windscreen and maintains its grip despite our 60kmph progress. Not far off the size of an adult hand, this arachnid has a glint in each of its eight eyes and although I don't have a big problem with spiders I don't fancy wrestling with this one. It inches towards the edge of the bonnet and then makes a dash for the passenger side window, which I'd pulled shut seconds earlier.

I can see three of its hairy legs strutting out from behind the wing mirror. On the walkie-talkie I tell the other two vans about our present plight. They pull alongside on the three-lane highway and I see Becki and Bev screeching. On the far side of Kylie, the vehicle they drive, I see Laura looking in completely the opposite direction with a hand covering her eyes as an extra precaution: she isn't a spider fan. The spider decides to make a dash for our roof and chooses the front windscreen as the most direct path. Kate screams her usual on-off scream, 'Ahhhhhhh, ahhhhhh, ahhhhhhh!' Dan clenches his teeth, one eye on the road and another on the six-inch critter, which is currently displaying its ugly grey underbody to the unhappy occupants of Cheech the Jackaroo. Simon pulls alongside in George and I see him mouth 'oh my God' as he watches the spider climb onto the roof, out of our view. Dan has flicked a switch and the windscreen wipers are swinging furiously but its too late, our little friend has ascended too far.

'If that thing gets in here I'm going to crash the car,' said Dan, matter-of-factly.

'Pull over then mate, I'll get it off,' I told him, with a calm sense of urgency. Dan obliged, finding a dusty verge with enough space for three vehicles. 'We're pulling over,' I talk into the radio.

The Huntsman had plonked itself right in the middle of the roof, out of reach from either side of the jeep. Simon jumped out behind us and ran across, minicam in hand. 'Dan, tell us your thoughts, what's just happened?' he asks our arachnophobic driver, at the same time as positioning him close to the car so the spider, which had by now ventured out onto a side windscreen, was in the background of the shot. Dan relayed the story, always keeping a worried eye on the Huntsman, which by now I was preparing to sweep off the vehicle with the only implement of choice, a metal salad fork courtesy of Bev's mad scramble in the back of Kylie.

'Well that's going to do a whole lot of good,' I said as she passed it to me. 'I'd be quite happy to be the spider right now.'

And then it was all too late. Before Dan had finished talking to the camera and as I edged closer with my culinary sword the spider sprinted into the rear wheel well, disappearing for good. Suddenly, we all became aware of just how many potential spider entrances there are in an old car. The gaps in between doors and frames looked mammoth and God knows how many underground passages there were emerging from the chassis. Kate, Dan and I got back in, slamming all doors shut. Kate pulled her knees up to her chin, Dan looked at me with a blank face. 'If that thing gets in here I'm going to crash,' he reassuringly told me one last time before starting up the engine and driving us back to Sydney, it was time for a holiday break.

Diary Entry: Saturday 30 December 2006

I had skated my final kilometres of 2006, the year of my life. There were two other years in my past that I can look back on and say, 'yep, just had a real goodun'. 1999 shook my body free of school and introduced me to adulthood, to travel and to self-belief. 2001 led me back to Uganda, to a strange few months of waking up under canvas to the rumblings of baby vervet monkeys using my tent as a slide. It was a time when I realised the values I'd take with me through life – some were selfish and dedicated to freedom and happiness, others led me to believe that whatever you were doing and wherever you were, things can end instantly. Five and a half years ago I had long hair to my shoulders and was at my best when a parrot sat on my shoulder, but for all my hippyish actions and appearance I was totally businesslike in my approach to life. Commonsense came first, and logic dictated that if a chance came along and I didn't take it, then I'd be kicking myself too hard not to regret missed opportunities. I wasn't going to grow old with regrets, I wasn't going to rely on the school-university-training-work cycle of life to send me forwards. I'd behave, I'd have ambition, I'd take the little chances that came along and sooner or later something would smack me in the face so hard I'd be an absolute fool not to sit up and take notice.

As a kid I'd daydream about drawing cartoons and making comics. Once in a while I'd take up a pencil and the resulting drawings looked like I'd taken ten dogs for a walk at a time. I couldn't draw. I loved football, I played until I was sore and aching, until I could barely walk home from the park. I dreamt about making it pro: I wasn't good enough. I started to write in '99, a daily diary I kept in Uganda about falling in love with a country and a girl. Later that year and into the next I wrote a book called River Road, based on the area in Nairobi that the guidebooks warned travellers about. I loved River Road, stayed there every time I visited Nairobi. The book was about following your own instincts, about positivity breeding positivity. It wasn't preachy, it was just a story that I fell in love with. I didn't back up my computer, I had only printed out a handful of pages, I got home and nothing worked. No retrieval possible, it was gone. Hundreds of hours, tens of thousands of words. It hit hard. I didn't write anything longer than a newspaper article until my first longboard turned up in the post four years later. It wasn't so much that I couldn't write, it was that I'd lost a little bit of my spirit. I'd simply had nothing to write about.

The hills I used to walk became new again. For two weeks I looked around from the passenger seat of a car or through the window of a train, thinking 'skating that road would be amazing, every road out there is skateable'. I pushed along getting stronger and stronger, physically and mentally. This was it. I woke up, I love this thing. I want to skate all day. I left the job. I decided to skate all day. I skated. I planned.

And in 2006 I skated all year long. The length of Britain. Never been done before. 900 miles of hills and cars and blisters and new friends. No regrets. The skin on my right heel would never be strong again. So what! No Regrets! I'd just found something that very few people ever did and it made me dizzy with happiness! Why the hell should I be the only one to benefit from this, EVERYONE should get a board and try this. It might not work for everyone but it HAS to work for someone.

This is brand new, this is amazing. This isn't a crazy dream, this is unusual reality and that's why it's special. What do you mean you're going to skateboard across Australia? You're never going to make it, YOU'RE NEVER GONNA MAKE IT. It's huge! Do you know how big Australia is? Do you know how hot it gets? Have you heard of the Nullarbor? It means no trees, and that means no shelter. With your pale skin we're taking bets on how many hours you'll make it out of Perth. Do you know what a kangaroo looks like after a road train hits it. Forty metres of red stain on the road. That's you if you try this. That's you.

People wrote these things. Strangers said I would die. Friends said I would fail. Who denies a dream! I'm fucking doing this!

So I did. I crossed Australia on a skateboard this year. I skated across the Nullarbor, through Adelaide, along the Great Ocean Road, through Melbourne, across the hills and mountains, up the coast. Into Sydney. Across Australia. People came with me. People I didn't know a year ago. Some who I did. A select band of people who believe in dreams and wanted to see this one through. Sure, it was my dream, but dreams are infectious. Jobs were left, lives were halted. Income stopped. This new word entered the vocabulary. BoardFree. What does it mean? Subtract Board, add your dream. That's what it means. Just be free. It always takes a risk, but if you make it count then it's worth it. Every time I step onto Elsa, my board, I BoardFree.

Diary Entry: Tuesday 2 January 2007

The new year started with a bang. The BoardFree team stood side by side within a calm Rushcutters Bay crowd, staring wide eyed as fireworks jumped from Sydney Harbour Bridge and leapt up from the top of the centre's high rises across the harbour, dancing flashes of colour reflecting off the water and the glass walls of the city, smoke filling the air as over 100,000 firecrackers were released to celebrate the Bridge's 75th anniversary.

2006 was over, and just as quickly 2007 began. I, being the elder statesman of the team, decided to retire soon after, my lack of staying power during late night social occasions now part of the programme. At 27 years old my legs ache after I walk across a room and I vanished to bed only after Si drunkenly wrapped a long arm around my shoulders and came up with an inventive metaphor for BoardFree. 'Dave,' he stumbled, 'you are Jack . . .' He paused, raising his free arm high into the air (I couldn't help but stare at the sloshing plastic cup at the end of it) to really drive home the point, '. . . you are Jack . . .' he repeated, breathed in deeply, and then, only when the drunken pause got to the stage where it really was just a drunken pause, he let the punch line go '. . . and BoardFree, my friend, is the beanstalk. It started off as a little seed . . .' he paused one final time, he loves a ramble does Si, and finished predictably '. . . and it just continues to grow, higher and higher, higher and higher, higher and high . . .' I walked off, because it was going to take a while.

Three days after the New Year began I found myself back on the Pacific Highway, finishing what I'd started after a decent break over Christmas, which shared the dual purposes of giving the team a good, final break and letting the large volumes of holiday traffic dissipate from the roads. On my penultimate day of skating in 2006 I passed a distance signpost, the first to feature the capital of Queensland, and couldn't help but exclaim, 'Holy crap! Brisbane is only seven hundred and seventy-five kilometres away!' It was only later, talking about it with Kate, that I realised just how that might have sounded to anyone not directly involved with BoardFree. It was still quite a distance, after all, but to Elsa and me, more than 5,000km beneath our wheels already, and to the team who were celebrating so vociferously in Cheech that the poor Jackaroo was swaying about like a feather in the wind, we were ever so close.

I pushed north through Bulahdela, Taree and Port Macquarie, the dry heat of summer now more potent than ever before, those moments of doubt about being able to push beyond Sydney now packed down in my memory. We were on our way.

Diary Entry: Saturday 6 January 2007

I start with an email just received from an old friend named Kara. 'Dave, G'DAY MATE! You flamin' galah, I just wanted to tell you how much you have delighted me/reduced me to tears over the last few months – I feel like I have been there with you in spirit every step of your incredible adventure, sans metal spike in my foot . . . You write BEAUTIFULLY. I was so proud when you made it into the London Metro and I almost told a whole (grumpy in the morning) tube carriage THAT'S MY FRIEND! Just wanted to say your adventures have made me laugh, made me cry, have been my best book of 2006.'

I read Kara's message while sat in McDonald's, Kempsey NSW, surrounded by people who chomp on Big Macs and slurp down vats of Coke, and I feel the tears welling up, rising and blurring my vision, dripping down my cheeks. Simple yet heartfelt, honest words from one of those few people who are able to be honest in everything. Enough to make me cry, even sob. I'm touched to the core and waste three minutes of Internet time trying to regain some control. I'm sure a fat man with a too-large-moustache is looking at me sideways. I wipe my eyes for the final time after crying in a fast food restaurant and realise I just learned more about myself in the last few minutes than I did during my 23rd year, when I didn't cry once. I'm 27 years old, in the middle of something wonderful, so physically and emotionally drained that I can barely hold myself together half of the time yet can blame this state on partaking in what many would consider to be an incredibly macho endeavour. I've skateboarded across Australia and I'm still able to cry like a girl when someone's overly nice to me, and what have I learnt? That I can deal with all of it, as long as some people care.

The first days of skating in 2007 have flown by. Every metre I travel on Elsa now extends the world distance skating record. Much of the weight has gone from my shoulders, the distance remaining falls away each day. A wave of support from passing motorists on the road pushes me towards Queensland, the last State, the place where it ends. Every other car honks its horn, passengers take photos, strangers hang out of their windows and shout at me;

'You're a legend!'
'You're the man, brother!'
'Keep going mate, almost there!'
'Yeaaaaaaaah!'

If you haven't been on the road with us it might be hard to imagine how it feels to be a part of the BoardFree team right now. I skated across a traffic light-controlled crossroads in Coffs Harbour and every car queuing on the other side — all ten of them — let their horns go. Awesome! After all it has put us through; Australia is willing us on, willing us to succeed.

In Nambucca Heads, at the Big 4 campsite which had kindly put us up for the night, Dan returns from the toilet to find five kids looking at the back of George. One of them, about seven years old, asks Dan what I do when I need to pee. Dan says something along the lines of 'well, he just stops and goes in the bush'. The child then had a think and trumped Dan with a blinder,

'OK, but what happens with Bush Teddies?'
'What are Bush Teddies?' asks Dan, confused.
'Poos in the bush!' the kid replied, as the others in the group laughed their heads off.

As time goes on and the road, which was once so long and seemingly endless, becomes shorter and more tangible, our thoughts turn more and more to life after BoardFree Australia. After 21 weeks on the road we have lived through Bev's song: 'when will we get to Brisbane, how long do we have to go? Through Adelaide, Melbourne and Sydney . . .' And now, we're closer to Brisbane than Sydney. The route map, studiously updated at the end of each day, is now home to a red line which leads all the way across Australia. The distance travelled is boggling, having skated it I am still struggling to fathom the achievement and I'm sure that none of us will quite get to grips with the last half year until we've had time to reflect. Some will go back to live with parents, others to the homes they left before flying to Australia. Jobs need to be found, debts cleared, and in many ways it may seem to some of the team like they're going back to square one, perhaps even further back than that. Of course, the memories are one thing, but the experience each team member has gained during this journey will stand them in good stead for progress in future careers. I'm quite sure, though, that at this time, when the journey's end approaches fast and worries supersede excitement that the potential career benefits are lost on most.

Personally, I'm starting to feel sadness when I think of Brisbane. 'Don't wish away the kilometres,' my cousin Kate tells me, and in all reality I don't. But saying that, I still have to skate them and every day another 50km or so is scrubbed from the remaining total, a figure that now seems tiny compared to the distance travelled already. I know I'll miss life on the road when it's over, but at the same time I'm sure that there are more journeys to come so I don't have much to worry about. I'm looking forward to not waking up with a grudge against the upcoming 70km day – the irony of my decision to embark on such an adventure because I'm not a man who likes rigidly imposed structure never escapes me. For more than a year I have been bound to attempting an achievement which can only be obtained by structure and discipline. A prisoner in my own ambition.

The heat was taking its toll on our vehicles, which at a far from sprightly age were breaking down on a consistent – and costly – basis. It was getting to the stage where contingency plans were being made to get everybody to Brisbane should one set of wheels permanently hang up their bearings. Elsa spent each and every day tutting at her larger, more fallible transport compatriots. She hadn't broken down once. The steady mid-thirties temperatures were also taking their toll on certain team members. Although Becki did have a part to play in more than her fair share of team conflicts she was a major cog in the BoardFree machine. In many ways her positives outweighed her negatives and her contribution to the team's daily running showed her dedication to the project. When things did go awry, the correlation between Becki's most fervent outbursts and Dom's contribution to her upset didn't go unnoticed. It was little surprise then, that when the heavens opened and more tears poured, that Dom had provided the cause and Becki was at the centre.

I returned to camp after two hours updating the website to find Holly lying down in a wide-open George doing a video blog with the minicam. I found it strange that she was being so open with her blog – they were almost always personal and recited away from others – and was therefore even more shocked to find that she was doing it on request from Dom, and was recounting her version of the events that led to the team flare-up in Nelson, Victoria. Becki, who had been pivotal in that disharmony two months earlier, was understandably upset at the issues being uprooted yet again. Cross at Holly, who really should have been more thoughtful, but more furious at Dom, whose timing I felt was terrible in trying to recoup lost elements of the story, I stormed into the cabin and confronted him. 'What the fuck do you think you're doing, bringing all of those emotions back up?' I said to him, my voice rising. 'We're all knackered and understandably Becki is going to be upset.'

'I didn't think it was a problem,' Dom answered, immediately walking out of the cabin. It was a typical reaction of his when he knew he was in the wrong but wasn't willing to face up to it, and I shouted after him,

'You need to start taking some responsibility, Dom!'

I spent the evening taking each person involved aside in an attempt to calm things down. Had anyone else been involved the situation would likely have been much less explosive, but Becki's personality coupled with Dom's unwillingness to be accountable meant our camp had escalated once again into a full-scale cold war. In all probability I wasn't at my best to mediate this dispute; several hundred kilometres on from Sydney my fatigue was returning and it was safe to say that I was at my wits end with both Becki and Dom. Months of hassle from the pair of them was making me yearn for Brisbane so

I wouldn't have to deal with them any more; without any tone of patience remaining in my voice, the conflict was never going to run dry before bedtime.

The next morning I stood the team in a circle and we talked it through. Again though, Dom refused to put his hands up and the meeting ended without a resolution. Preparing for another hard slog on the road and not looking forward to the grinding thoughts which would undoubtedly arise from the conflict, I approached Dom one final time before the off. 'I find it strange that you haven't asked me to do a video blog considering I was the one who brought Nelson to a conclusion,' I said to him.

'I'm the one making the documentary,' he said.

'Surely you're going to want it to be factual, then?' I said. 'I can tell you now you don't have my full reasons for leaving Nelson on my own on tape.'

'I've got what I need,' he said, defiantly. And it was then that I realised that the conversation I'd had with Pat in Hyde Park before BoardFree UK had lost its meaning. I realised that as far as the two of them were concerned, the documentary was now independent of the journey. Dom had been asking leading questions in interviews with other team members, searching for explosive answers that would back up the storylines he and Pat pursued. The situation had grown beyond repair because they were now working to an agenda that directly conflicted with the needs of BoardFree. My personal thoughts from Sydney onwards had been plagued by stress brought on by a fear that I wouldn't be able to have access to the journey's footage once the expedition was over. Sick to the stomach, I pushed on towards Queensland, with much more than just the road on my mind.

Diary Entry: Friday 11 January 2007

The Pacific Highway runs north from Sydney to Brisbane and beyond. It has been my main passage since mid-December when I skated out of the New South Wales capital as a world record holder, and today, a month on from that momentous day in Sydney Olympic Park, I found myself still pushing along the Pacific Highway with a green road sign drifting past to my left bearing the message, 'Brisbane 153'. Almost immediately, to my right, the driver of a truck heading in the opposite direction leant out of his cab, extended a fist of salute and yelled, 'You go, Davoooooooooooooooo.' His voice disappeared as he continued south and gave me some fresh mental fuel for the kilometres to come.

The tidal wave of support continues from passers by and motorists. Ash Grunwald, a cult Australian singer who I met when he supported the eclectic Xavier Rudd in Sydney on New Year's Day, pulled over on his way to a surf spot near Ballina and tried out his luck on Elsa. We talked a little and it didn't take long for him to make an offer: 'I've got a gig in Coolangatta on the 20th, come along and I'll interview you on stage, if there's room we'll have a skate! We'll donate $5 per CD to your charities and get the punters to put some in too.' He drove off, surf board in the back, leaving us all with huge grins. Some people can't help enough.

The donations continue. Becs, Bev and Laura are driving themselves into the ground, bringing in $200 or more dollars per day, which we'll distribute between Sailability, Link and Lowe. Contributions also come in from people who pass us on the road – often the van logos are enough to persuade some pocket-dipping, as Bev well knows after she became half of what must be the fastest donation in history when she accepted a $10 note from a motorcyclist as they both drove at 100kmph along the highway.

My fondest moment of the week involves Simon. Often the class clown, Si is a remarkably determined lad when he wants to be. To honour the section of the journey bought by his mother and sister in our Sponsor A Section donation game, Si decided to jump on one of our bicycles on a very hot day and pedal the 47km between Corindi and Grafton. By the end of the first hill he was gasping like a fish, the team chuckling to themselves having taken bets on how long he'd last. On the second hill he walked a bit, but by then I'd skated off and was waiting 15km up the road at a petrol station. But he pedaled on, reached us, and then cycled further. As one of the guys used to seeing me collapse in a ball of agony at the side of the road it made me immensely proud that Si was willing to go through that same barrier and join me on the road. 10km from Grafton little pieces started to fall off the bike (it's older than our vans) and poor old Si had to scoot on the pedals and walk the final 5km. But he wouldn't give up, much to the chagrin of his poor legs, which hurt so much he had to stay in the swimming pool all afternoon because he couldn't climb out.

Diary Entry: Monday 15 January 2007

Laura rushed in, cheeks aglow. 'I've just seen Alex Parks!' she gasped, 'I'm going to go back and find her again so she can have a wristband and leaflet.'

We looked at Laura, who funnily enough bares an uncanny resemblance to Alex Parks, the young singer who found minimal fame after huskily warbling her way to number one on the BBC's Fame Academy show. 'Alex Parks is in Byron Bay?' I asked, probably with too much cynicism considering this was indeed Byron Bay, home of the stars.

'Yes!' panted Laura, who was becoming more and more worn out by the thought of Alex Parks, rather than actually meeting her.

'Well,' I said, trying to tone down my enthusiasm in the hope that my calmness would stop Laura breaking down on the floor of the Internet café, 'you better go and find her then!'

'OK!' shrieked Laura, before dashing down the street looking everything like Alex Parks in a race.

Diary Entry: Saturday 20 January 2007

Western Australia, South Australia, Victoria, New South Wales and now Queensland. Two years ago I knew the names but not where their vast bulks sat in the giant Australian jigsaw. Now, thanks to an intimate five months skating across the world's sixth largest country, only a quick bout of Alzheimers would rid me of my love for this great, empty lump of land.

I crossed the last border of BoardFree Australia on Wednesday 17 January. Waking up in Tweed Heads, I had just 4km to skate before Tweed turns to Coolangatta and the clocks – rather confusingly considering Queensland is directly north of New South Wales – turned back an hour. Earlier that day, I had already spent three hours in Queensland, surfing with Real Wiiings' Chris Cleator, who has been sponsoring our surf lessons this journey. Bobbing up and down just out of reach of some sizeable waves that frankly scared the crap out of me, I gazed north at the glistening skyline of the skyscraper-clad Surfers Paradise, and couldn't help shivering with excitement. Long ago, two months before I flew to Perth, a friend sent me a photo taken of her standing beneath the famous Surfers Paradise arch. I had looked at the photo on my computer screen, then turned left to stare at the Australian map covering my wall. 'Dave,' I said to myself, 'it's going to take a bloody big effort to get over there mate.'

Two hours after the surf I rolled into Queensland and pushed into Surfers, the sky blocked out by towering high rises that line this section of the coast. Strangely, the place seemed just a little too empty for all this urbania. It seemed like everyone walking past held a surfboard under their arm. Of the few cars that passed, most honked a horn or waved. Many donated. 'Surfers Paradise is bloody close to Brisbane,' Simon had told me the day before, as if I didn't know. That thought settled nicely in my brain, closing out all the unnecessary noise that comes with travelling through a city – however empty it felt.

The phone is off the hook, Kate a picture of efficiency when our Knight Rider ringtone pierces the air. 'Hello, this is Kate from BoardFree speaking, how may I help you . . .?' The Sunday Times, Queensland's largest newspaper, send out a photographer as I skate north of Surfers. I interview with Lucy Carne, who spoke to me so long ago as I climbed Greenmount Hill on the way out of Perth. Several radio stations ask questions live on air and I'm becoming adept at fielding the ubiquitous cricket jokes. The Ashes have become a staple topic of conversation in this country and anyone with pommie links receives a regular earful from cocky locals. There have been few interviews since October which have passed clean through without a mention of the cricket, but I'm fond of turning the tables on the Aussies, asking presenters how many times an Australian has skated across his or her own country. Hong Kong calls, The Times and the Telegraph run stories in the UK. Richard and Judy want me on in February. It's all quite bizarre, but not nearly as much as the email received from a lady at ITV, who really wanted to cover the end of my cycle journey across Australia.

Two days of rest separated the Gold Coast from Brisbane. We stayed in Hope Island with Chris Cleator and his delightful family; Nat, Tyla, Kye and Jo who worked with Chris. Living with them, however briefly, I found myself feeling more at home than I'd felt in years. From there we rushed in and out – to a TV shoot with Channel 9, to the Wet n'Wild Water Park where the team were treated to a day out and I was the subject of a media call. Ever grateful for publicity – all which contributes to our growing charity total – I still find it strange seeing myself on the telly, especially when the focus of the piece isn't BoardFree or one of our charities. A 30-second NBN piece showing me plummeting down a ridiculously steep water slide with a face like jelly will always serve to add to the awareness of this journey – but I'll never quite get to grips with the way Australia has taken to BoardFree, and am happy to be the occasional light entertainment which brightens up the otherwise dismal news reports.

It was approaching evening as I pushed up a long, steep incline to Mount Gravatt. The mid-January humidity of a Queensland summer had created a sheen of sweat on my arms and hands, for a few weeks I'd struggled to hold onto my water bottles, several of them coming a cropper beneath the wheels of passing vehicles. People stood at the roadside taking pictures, the entire population of a nearby bar's outdoor deck rose arms aloft in a cheer as I passed by. This is it, I thought, we're so close. As the road levelled out I could see I'd skated my last uphill of BoardFree Australia, the brow of the hill revealing a dip in the land beyond, downwards towards Brisbane. I saw the city's skyline, hazy in the early dusk, rising from the horizon more majestically than any city I'd seen before. A moment that will stay with me forever.

I pulled the cars over and stood, staring, tears filling my eyes, memories of the beginning of the journey in Perth flashing into my head and then other images: heading onto the Great Eastern Highway, pushing along the Nullarbor's 90 Mile Straight, rolling through Adelaide, jumping on that signpost, the Great Ocean Road, everything I'd seen and done. There it is, after all this time, I had pushed out of Perth on Elsa and kept on going until now, five months later, I could see Brisbane. Two women, separate but meeting us seconds apart, arrive with donations. A man runs from a bottle shop and hands me a beer. 'Well done mate.' He shakes my hand. 'You're a legend.'

'Ah mate, thank you so much,' I reply, beaming, 'I'll save this one for later.'

It was time, now. Tears still squeezed between my glasses and my cheeks, my eyesight as blurry as the shimmering city below, and I breathed heavily as I pushed off down the hill. I was moving at around 40kmph when two uneven surfaces finally combined to dismount me from my trusty steed. I had skated more than 5,815km on Elsa since Perth without falling, 7,265km if you count the UK journey, and as Elsa's front left wheel struck a two-inch rise in the road and veered off at a right angle I gasped, knowing my time had come. I ran for three steps, weight moving forward more with each one, and then went down. I finished thirty metres further down the road, having rolled and scraped half the distance. Shaken, I sat up. My left ankle fired pain up my leg. My left side burned, my ribs screamed. The first thing I did was look around for Elsa and saw immediately that she'd happily wandered up a side road. Traffic hadn't been heavy that evening but even so I knew better than to stay in the middle of the road for too long. I heaved myself up, bent double in agony, and stumbled to a grassy verge at the roadside. I lay down, and closed my eyes.

When they opened, I was surrounded by people. Kate, Dan, Laura, Dom and his camera, Simon and his camera, Holly and her camera, snap snap snap. Chris Cleator was there, our host for the past two days, a friend now. Some strangers peered over the throng. Another man was by my side, a bearded man, a stranger. He spoke to me, 'Dave, I'm a physio, take it easy and I'll look you over . . .'

'How did you get here so fast?' I groaned.

'You skated past me back there, I drove home as fast as I could to get my camera and when I caught up with you . . . well, you were here.'

'Fair enough doc, do what you will.'

I lay there, eyes to the sky, chuckling to myself at the ridiculousness of it all. I've just managed to skate across Australia without falling off my board and here, now, minutes from the end and with Brisbane in sight, I fall, and fall badly. I'm grazed, bruised and scratched; my insides feel like they've been in a tumble dryer. I want to be sick. Feeling dizzy, pained, light-headed. All too quickly I'm on my feet, snow-white bandages covering my hand, elbow and shoulder. There's a small dent in my helmet, which ultimately ended my tumble. Thank God for the helmet. A man in his late sixties stood beside a bicycle dressed in a pink cyclist's top. He told me his name was Tom, he'd read about my journey in the morning newspaper and wanted to escort me into town. I agreed, got back on my board and set off downhill, more cautious than ever, counting my blessings, blood pumping.

For a brief minute a man jumps out of his car and skates alongside me, then vanishes just as quickly as he'd appeared. Ten minutes later, at 7 p.m., I rounded a bend and there it was, The Gabba, Brisbane's chief sporting arena, the home of Queensland cricket, towering large over Stanley Street as I rolled into the shadow of the stands. Another snapshot which I'll keep for life. I stopped opposite the entrance, walked across the road and sat on Elsa beneath the south-west lights. The irony of stopping here, the scene of recent British sporting failure in the Ashes, was not lost. Emotion overcame me – we'd made it. I cried tears of happiness, sadness, joy and fatigue as Pat and Dom interviewed me. Whatever happened tomorrow during the final 3km didn't really matter: I'd skated from Perth to Brisbane despite everything. The team came over and we embraced, clapped, smiled. I flinched at every hug as my recent injuries found their way through my adrenaline blanket, but I didn't care. I whispered 'thank you' into each ear. We'd made it.

We drove east to Bo and Elsa's house. We had met them on our last full day in Western Australia so many months ago, and Bo's regular emails ensured that we weren't going to miss out on the invite Elsa had extended to us in that hot, dusty rest stop 30km west of Eucla. They were outstanding hosts; funny and generous, the owners of well-stocked larders. Elsa shuffled about ensuring that everyone had food in front of them, a drink in hand. There was a floor or a bed for everyone and I retired early. One day to go.

* * *

By a quarter to seven *Knight Rider* had sounded seven times. Some calls bore good luck messages, most were from producers hoping to set up interviews for later. Kate had compiled a schedule of the calls for the morning; I identify one twenty-minute gap from 10 a.m. onwards when I could safely visit the toilet. Next door the team are spread out on mattresses like a parade of the homeless, and I wonder if their dreams are permeated with phone calls, because surely they can hear the ringtone through the wall, again and again and again. Coffee, cereal. Kate takes two calls when she's pouring her milk.

I give eight interviews before 11 a.m., and then we drive back to the point where I ended last night. It is the last performance of our ritual. I find myself talking to television cameras from channels 7, 9, 10 and ABC. Skaters turn up in small groups and Magic Touch reflective jackets are promptly dispatched. I put on my Circa shoes for the final time, my fourteenth pair this journey, the moment hungrily lapped up by the surrounding lenses. I issue instructions to the skaters, and check traffic plans with the police, who were providing two cars and two cyclists to accompany myself and the skaters on the final leg. Finally we get on the road and push slowly away from the Gabba, towards South Bank.

The traffic is heavy and one of the skaters falls backwards after a trick-gone-wrong. Laura is with me on another rollsrolls. She may not have been with us when the journey left Perth, but she is as much a team member as anyone could be. Dan waves in his mirror, doing his bit to lead me home. If Kate has been my strength, Danny has been my stalwart, keeping me safe across a vast country. He's my best mate and even now as he trundles along slower than even he is used to, we engage in a language of hand signals that has been refined by five months of silent communication. The driver and the skater; a unique relationship. Dom and Holly run alongside, doing their utmost to capture the final moments. The final 3km takes almost half an hour and I round the final corner at the Queensland Performing Arts Complex to whistles and screams. I can't believe the sight, hundreds of people lined up in a red, white and blue crescent, coloured by the British Consulate who have been so good to us throughout the journey. I keep my composure and stop at the roadside to let the skaters behind me overtake and join the crowds.

Simon is the last to speak to me, his minicam recording my last thoughts before the journey finishes. I hand him my vest, revealing a blue BoardFree t-shirt, the same colour as the one I wore when BFUK finished and when I broke the world record. It was time to go. I pushed off, once, twice, three times, a little carve and then straight for the line. There is brief confusion when my route is blocked by a pointing, wandering man. I don't understand what he is doing, what he's pointing at, but behind him I see a glimpse of the finishing line: red, white and blue held by members from the local Sailability club. In a split second I push through it arms aloft, the line breaks to cheers, applause, shouting, a cacophony of celebration. I stand Elsa on one end after kissing her. 'You beauty,' I whisper, and then rest on her, head down in a moment of self-thought, Dave mate, you've done it, it's over.

I stand and face the crowds, the cameras. The questions come in thick and fast and I answer passionately, stressing the need for donations, offering Elsa for a charity sale at the right price, discussing the hardest parts of the journey, the stresses, the tensions, the positives. Bruce Dickson from Sailability has flown in and addresses the crowd, and tells everyone he thinks I'm great because I'm Welsh. I laugh and shake my head but let it go, an Englishman who lives in Wales, it has confused everybody. Then I am led to the shores of the Brisbane River for photos with Getty, AP and another news agency from the UK. I pop a magnum of champagne for the cameras and sip a little, then some more for follow-up shots. I feel decidedly dizzy and fill up more glasses so I can clink them with the team. People said it couldn't be done, but we'd done it, all the same.

*   *   *

The following hours were a blur. Kate dealt magnificently with the media, the girls had managed to raise over $A300 at the finish line. We retired exhausted to Bo and Elsa's and collapsed. I spoke to another seventeen radio stations that evening, in between managing to watch four television reports on the main Australian channels. I spoke to Eamonn Holmes live on Sky News, BoardFree also made the BBC and ITV news back home. Most of the national newspapers in the UK ran a picture story, my ugly mug grinning with Elsa raised in one hand and a bottle of champagne in the other, the Brisbane skyline dominant beyond the river behind me. What a finalé, what an ending. When the time came to go to bed Simon was waiting and struck his by now usual pose; hand on hip, ready for amateur dramatics. 'Dave,' he said, 'do you know what you've just done? Perth to Brisbane on a skateboard. Perth, to Brisbane, on a skateboard!'

23 The Aftermath

Diary Entry: Monday 5 February 2007

Connor Gardiner is eleven and a half years old. He stands 4'1" in heels (please don't ask!), walks with his head tilted slightly to the side and wears spectacles holding lenses which, despite their thickness, will never be able to give him perfect eyesight. When he was born Connor, like all boys with Lowe Syndrome, had cataracts. As a consequence, the lens in both eyes were removed, and so began his life.

When we first met on the 3rd December at the BoardFree event in Rushcutters Bay, Sydney, he was in a strange place, surrounded by strangers and full of agitated energy. Out of his element, Connor clung to his dad, Alex, who cares for him almost full-time and often looked down to find his son wrapped around his waist.

The National Organisation for Rare Diseases defines Lowe with the following description: 'Lowe Syndrome, also known as oculo-cerebro-renal syndrome, is a rare inherited metabolic disease that affects males. This disorder is characterized by lack of muscle tone (hypotonia), multiple abnormalities of the eyes and bones, the presence at birth of clouding of the lenses of the eyes (cataracts), mental retardation, short stature, and kidney problems. Other findings may include protrusion of the eyeball from the eye socket (enophthalmos); failure to gain weight and grow at the expected rate; weak or absent deep tendon reflexes; and multiple kidney problems (e.g., renal tubular dysfunction, renal hyperaminoaciduria, etc.).'

Boys with Lowe and their families are often a forgotten lot. Relatively few sufferers of Lowe exist (between 300–400 registered boys to date) and this means that the disease often slips through the wide open cracks of the Welfare State. Support, therefore, is not always forthcoming, Alex and Connor are just one example.

Until arriving back in Sydney after rolling into Brisbane, I hadn't spent more than a couple of hours in the presence of Lowe Syndrome. Connor displays the consistent copybook traits of a lad with Lowe. He's affectionate, loving, has a wicked sense of humour. Looking at him, it's easy to forget he's not far off twelve years old. His size alone makes him appear six or seven and his behaviour bounces from shouting and violent to loving and kind. One thing is constant: he never stops. I watch him eat and he can't focus on his meal. At breakfast he takes a spoonful and wanders off, changing TV channels and repositioning his radio, before returning for another bite. He rarely finishes a bowl and I can't comprehend how he maintains his energy levels for eleven hours a day, but for all the constant attention he demands he is a pleasure to be around. When he finds something funny he tilts his head back and gurgles a giggle, now and then he'll sit down beside Kate or Si or Dan and just be still. His inquisitive nature never ceases seeking for information. 'Whadilly do today?' 'Where's Shiman [Simon]?' And sometimes he gives you love that you've never had before. On my first night in the house I was heading to bed. Connor held my hand as I walked upstairs and then, before I closed my door, he ran back in without a word, put his arms around me and kissed my hip, then ran away again.

Despite his affectionate, cheeky nature, he is hard work to live with, and I've just been here a week. His dad, Alex, loves him wholly and has the patience of a saint. Kate and I have tried to take some pressure off him, preparing Connor for school in the mornings, dressing him, getting breakfast down, standing hand in hand waiting for the bus. The bus arrives, Anton the driver gets out and leads Connor around to the sliding door. Other pupils are inside already, all suffering from some mental or physical disability. One of them, a girl wearing a black sunhat, waved to Kate, Si, Dan and me as we stood in the driveway bidding farewell to Connor. Connor was sat behind the girl and pounced on her arm. We all laughed. 'He doesn't want anyone else to wave,' Alex told us later. The next morning the same scenario, except Connor was now sat in front of the girl. She waves cautiously and then Connor turned, sensing some movement. Instantly the girl pulled her hand behind her head and feigned a scratch. She had learnt well! Connor stuck his arm out of the window and waggled it until the bus disappeared.

Kate offered to cook Alex and Connor dinner tonight. 'Let me ride in the Ude [Ute]!' Connor asked, his hundredth request to take a drive in Cheech, my once on-the-road support vehicle. This time, he got his wish. Little eyes just peeking over the dashboard, he directed Kate to the supermarket in Strathfield and helped her pick out a parking spot. Walking to the shops, every car was a new interest, 'what make is that one?' he pointed, then after passing a new car, he got cheeky, 'why would anyone buy your ude, it's old?!' Inside the supermarket, the fruit shelves gave Kate some headaches as Connor picked up each different fruit and veg, sniffed it (his poor eyesight means all new objects are sniffed to gain some familiarity) then offered a final assessment, either 'Yum' or 'Yuk!' A few grapes disappeared into his naughty little mouth, and Kate couldn't help but snigger when he grabbed a carrot, took a bite and then popped it back on the shelf!

I'd often wondered how I'd feel if I had a child with a disability. Completely removed from the realness of this – I'm not in the game of having kids just yet – I suppose the thought was based on an inate selfishness and love of freedom. How would I react at the birth? How would I deal with things? Would I put the child up for adoption? Seriously, I asked myself these questions from the safe vantage point of distance. Then, leaving Kate in bed to get some much needed sleep, I found myself dressing Connor, a half-hour process as he struggles and pretends to be a dog and cries and runs away. Right there and then, as Connor lay on his back and pounded the bed with fists and feet, it suddenly occurred to me that the questions I'd once asked myself were folly. Nothing really mattered, I realised. As I chuckled at Connor refusing to allow socks onto his feet, it struck me that if I had a child I would love he or she, no matter what. I love this kid with his thick glasses which he swaps for mine now and then, this lad who loves TV and has a brilliant fascination for his portable radio which he carries around the house and plugs in so people can listen to it. Admittedly, living with a boy with Lowe Syndrome probably isn't the best way to recuperate from a five-month skateboarding journey, but I wouldn't have had it any other way. I'm going to miss the little fella and his dad, and I'm looking forward to standing with Connor for one last time in the morning, holding his hand as the School Bus approaches over the hill, waiting to see what happens as everyone waves goodbye.

* * *

I was often asked what I would do after BoardFree was over, and with those questions there was almost always an insinuation that there would be a dip in fortune, or at least in spirit. 'I'll keep myself busy' I would reply, 'and it's likely that before I get to the end I'll have had so much time to think about what I'm going to do there will be hardly any transition at all.' In truth, things changed immediately. Two days of intense media attention after crossing the line at Brisbane ensured that there was an ear to my phone for almost 48 hours, the repetition exhausting, my head swimming with questions and answers. And then it stopped. There was silence. It was over.

* * *

I am adding the finishing touches to this book from a new home in London, six months to the day after our arrival in Brisbane. Not an hour has gone by without a flash of memory that whisks me back to Australia. I've once again become adept at pulling on socks and slipping on shoes without a twenty-minute bandaging session beforehand; I've slowly stopped reaching out to passing cars as I'm skating along, realising that I don't know the occupants and they're not there to pass me a new water bottle. The journey had seemed almost unreal, so separate from reality that for weeks afterwards I struggled to get a firm hold on the fact that as a team we had crossed a continent, or that individually I had actually skateboarded from Perth to Brisbane.

That first night after crossing the line I woke cramped in darkness, my entire body in spasm. My mind had shut down for the first time in almost two years and without that focus my stomach, thighs, arms, shoulders, back and calves jerked in fury, their job finally done. I slept little, my brain firmly whirring back into action with a disconcerting concoction of satisfaction and worry. It's still happening, I'm still dealing with everything. Writing this book has given me the catharsis I thought I'd never find in the confusion of those initial weeks back home. The rest of the team went their own way; having spent more than half a year volunteering for a hellishly stressful project the need for money started talking again; it always does.

My mind started to back away from BoardFree quicker than I could control. Imagine, five months without a break, the only time you spend alone is when you're pounding the road hard. For all the beauty of the journey between Perth and Brisbane, it wasn't what you could call quality personal time. A camera thrust in your face every time you stop and every time you have an argument with your girlfriend. The phone rings, another interview: whatever was happening at that time – whether it was mediation of a team incident, putting together a blog for the website, bandaging up blisters – didn't matter. The more people who hear about BoardFree the more people donate. It's a correlation that bolsters the foundations of this project; and so the media face arrives, the media voice, the positive, public side to BoardFree, never false but never letting slip what was happening behind the scenes.

It led me into turmoil. The physical and mental pressure of the expedition had manifested into a self-punishing monster that tore away at my basic character. The endurance and lack of privacy reduced me to a pile of emotions where life became so inconsistent I was unable to hold on to any stability. During the journey I had succumbed to emotion, subjecting Kate to endless, petty arguments, reducing her to tears too many times. I hated myself for what I had done, even as I was helplessly doing it, and failed to cope with that during the transition back to reality, whatever that had become. In utter confusion I pushed Kate away, our relationship, having soaked up so much strain during the journey now combusting as I found it impossible to achieve a compromise between the distance I craved and the closeness I needed. I became a walking, talking hypocrisy, unable to explain myself because for a brief while I simply wasn't sure who I had become. It took months for my fatigue to blow away, and by then it was too late. The damage had been done.

Physically I was ill for weeks. Stomach ache and headaches combined with a lack of appetite to compound the rib-revealing kilograms I had lost on the journey, but bit by bit I began to find some rhythm, some structure, some understanding. I'm not sure that I will ever quite accept the sheer amount of conflict that arose on BoardFree Australia and I have found myself wondering occasionally whether or not BoardFree had been a good thing; it was another by-product of my inability to extract distance from the big picture. Of course, yes it had been good. The core group of people who formed to create this dream, to believe in the ideas, the charities and the journey pulled together despite the hard times and made it through to the end, every one of them.

I have no doubt that Dom and Pat requested involvement in BoardFree because at the beginning they were truly passionate about the project. But as I write there still seems to be no sign of the documentary's release, on television or DVD, and a laborious struggle to gain direct access to much of the footage from the journey still hasn't borne fruit. Thus, in writing this book I have had to make do with still images, written notes and diaries to refresh my memory, while coping with the realisation that I may never see much of the film that was shot on the journey. It has been a heartbreaking, eye-opening learning curve, but inviting an independent production company to be part of the expedition remains my one major regret, not least because it was largely down to my naivety that the situation was allowed to develop so harmfully: all that stress, all those arguments, apparently for nothing.

As I mentioned, the team each went their separate ways. I fear that Becki has received more negative than positive press in this book, but the pressured environment in which we each survived affected us each in ways we could not control, and there should be no shame in that. Becki brought skills to the team that nobody else, except maybe Kate, could have. She was fearless in her pursuit of accommodation; she would walk up to strangers and ask them for shelter, for donations, for help. Without Becki BoardFree Australia would have been a very different journey and I'm sure a far less successful one. Bev and Laura deserve their praise, too. Both late but invaluable additions to BoardFree, they combined individual charm with talent and motivation and were the team entertainers, propping up morale and mucking in endlessly to fill donation buckets and dinner plates.

Holly's photography provided a unique looking glass into the world of long-distance skating and graced the pages of countless national publications. Once in a while you meet someone who is irrevocably attached to a particular vocation, and Holly has and will always be a fine photographer. I'm also grateful for her contribution to BoardFree UK as she gave up more than anyone to be a part of that journey, and I'm happy to say her enthusiastic response to being accepted onto the BoardFree team remains one of my most vivid highlights of this entire project: 'Hello, I'm Holly and I'm the photographer for BoardFree. OH MY GOD THAT FEELS SO GOOD TO SAY!'

I knew from the moment that Simon called me in November 2005 that he was a gem of a bloke, and from beginning to end he was an absolute pleasure to work with. He took hold of the opportunity to be part of BoardFree with both hands and never let go, showing an enviable ability to relish even the smallest moments, even though some of them led him to fear the inevitable end of the journey, even when there were thousands of kilometres to go. And of course Danny, who never got involved in any of the upset. He just got on with his role, carried it through as well as he could and stood by me to the end. I couldn't have asked for more.

And then, finally, Kate. I'm not sure I have the words left to sum up her contribution to BoardFree. Her personal support gave me the strength to complete both journeys and she never failed to act as the buffer between the team and I; a position described in no better way than with Simon's cheesecake analogy: Kate was BoardFree's biscuit base. She is the most loving, caring, genuine person I have ever met and her lust for life ensured that I never lost mine, not even during the lowest ebbs; for who she is and for what she gave me, I will always love her.

* * *

So where to from here? BoardFree continues to operate as an umbrella initiative encouraging people young and old to take up board sports and roll forever. The project has inspired many individuals to push for change and set out on their own long-distance skateboarding journeys. As I write Sam Benson pushes between Devon and Spain, the journey giving him his first ever taste of life outside the United Kingdom. Rob Thompson is currently skating a rollsrolls board from Switzerland to London in a practice run for what I'm sure will be a future attempt at the world record for distance skateboarded, the current accolade I am glad to announce was made official by the *Guinness Book of World Records* in May 2007, and advertised that Dave Cornthwaite did indeed travel 5,823km by skateboard between Perth and Brisbane. Other BoardFree journeys, from the width of Wales, London to Morocco, the length of New Zealand and Ben Stiff's upcoming 2008 attempt to become the youngest person to skate from John o'Groats to Land's End: all are current legacies of BoardFree's momentous first two years.

On completion of BoardFree Australia Peter Sanftenberg invited me to take the helm of marketing for rollsrolls, and I never cease to pinch myself when I visit www.rollsrolls.com and see that where Jack Smith's picture rested on my first eager visits to the website there is now a picture of myself and Elsa, hurrying downhill somewhere in South Australia. In other news, I recently joined forces with Rebecca Richardson, formerly of Kangaroo Poo clothing, and founded a company called Out Of Your Shell, which operates on the philosophy that if life is to be lived to the full, new challenges shouldn't be shirked. Among other things, incorporated into the company is our very own clothing brand; Chilled Turtle. I am currently brewing new long-distance ventures, some on a board but one of which will take place on a unique, and it has to be said, unusual device called an AquaSkipper, a human-powered hydrofoil that skips along in water and which forms the heart of a brand new project of mine, lovingly named BounceFree. I'm delighted to say quite emphatically that a return to the nine to five is not on the cards.

* * *

BoardFree has changed my life beyond compare, although aspects of the project have, admittedly, resulted in some frustration. Measuring the media coverage we gained against the amount of charitable funds we raised isn't a picture that fills me with glee. I'm saddened that we didn't raise more, but have to hold my hands up and take the rap for that. Yes, twenty thousand pounds is a substantial sum for an independent fundraising effort, but by selecting three charities to support I think I inadvertently made an error of judgement when considering our failure to raise the big bucks. Three charities meant a rushed description of each one during hallowed airtime, and I think perhaps it softened the charity message as far as potential donors were concerned. All said and done, though, the Lowe Syndrome Trust, Link Community Development and Sailability Australia were an integral part of my two journeys, and if I were asked to choose just one I wouldn't be able to and wouldn't want to.

Occasionally a letter arrives or an article is written which wags a finger at the team and I. What if we hadn't done the journey and instead stayed at home and donated £3,000 each to the charities? All in all the costs of the journey were very similar to the final total we raised, so what was the point? People actually write this to me and I'd be lying if the same thought hadn't crossed my mind a few times, but the answer is simple. BoardFree Australia wasn't just about raising money for charity. There is no calculation that can measure just how much awareness we raised for Link, Lowe and Sailability. It also promoted a niche sport, encouraging thousands to take up longboarding as a new form of exercise. As mentioned above some people, strangers to me several months ago, have been inspired by my pushes across the UK and Australia and are now embarking on their own board journeys for other charities like Water Aid and Corda and Everyman. Still think we should have stayed at home?

And then, of course, there's the human element, the ability to govern your own destiny and take a leap of faith, springing out from beneath the security blanket of a monthly paycheque to take on a new, far more fulfilling challenge than working for somebody else. BoardFree promoted positive thinking; the actuality that words can be turned into actions and that sometimes taking a risk leads to bigger and better things. Had I woken up that morning with Kiwa glaring down at me and not taken my dream further I may well have spent two years stagnating at my desk, rather than ploughing myself a new furrow. When people ask how I combated the boredom when I was skating across the Nullarbor I tell them that there was no boredom, that each time I glanced from Elsa to the bare empty plains and then ahead to an endless road I felt lucky to be alive. 'Where would you rather be?' I ask them in reply. 'Skating across a beautiful country or sat behind a desk from morning to night?'

I will never forget how lucky I was to reach my crossroads at a relatively young age, but I truly believe that limits are self-imposed and that you make your own luck; if this story doesn't outline that then I'm not sure what does! The friends I made along the way, the breathtaking places I travelled through, the battles that were overcome and the love I found and then, regrettably, lost in the aftermath. It all formed a remarkable, unforgettable story, one I hope that will long remain with everybody whose lives it touched along the road. I take from it a philosophy that will ensure I don't waste another minute of my life, and although I am sure there are more crossroads up ahead, I'm equally certain that the lessons I learnt from pushing Elsa previously inconceivable distances will prove to be worthwhile.

We can't skate across countries forever, but every now and then an opportunity comes along which gives us a chance to develop personally, and it won't always involve a longboard! Grasping that chance often means going against the grain, receiving criticism and learning to battle on even when heads are shaking all around you. But when you take that first push you realise that the doubters don't matter. What counts is your application, making sure you surround yourself with good people, and maintaining a constant belief that you can succeed and that as you do so others will benefit from your endeavours. There is nothing sweeter than exceeding expectations and I hope that at some point everyone has the chance to say 'I'll see you on the other side', because when they do they will find themselves the master of their own destiny, in the middle of their very own BoardFree.

Acknowledgements

Firstly, I'd like to offer an apology in advance to those who didn't make the list below, your absence is only reflective of the lack of a second book contract, as I'd need one to thank everybody who contributed, supported and had a hand in making BoardFree the success it was. People rarely achieve things completely on their own, and without this lot I'd still be pushing my way across the Nullarbor.

Writing this book has proven to be just as much of an adventure as the journeys themselves, but it wouldn't have been possible without the following. My ever-supportive editor Barbara Phelan at Anova, whose patience and generous praise gave me the confidence to complete this literary long distance journey. Also to those who persevered through the book in its varying stages and offered much-needed advice and thoughts, especially Verity Muir, Emilie Venables, Emily Stevens, Amanda Shipp, Alice Harding and Kara Fisher. Thanks also to Tom Bromley.

As 2005 went on and I learned to skate at the same time as planning the journeys, those who were closest to me did what all good friends do and provided support and encouragement even when they thought I was stark raving bonkers. Thanks especially to Rae Howells and Phil Poucher, Neil Dyer, Nick Bradley, William Clive, Bee Yazdani, Owen Morris, Gael Evans, Emma Hallet and Chris Harris.

I'd like to thank Lorraine, Andrew and Oscar Thomas at the Lowe Syndrome Trust, Steve Blunden and all the staff at Link Community Development, and everyone who supported us from Sailability Australia, especially Deirdre and Bob Schahinger, Chris Riordan, Rachael Cox, Tish Ennis, Len Snowdon, Melissa Richardson, Graeme Adam, Clem Barrack, Steven Churm, Dave Kinsey, John Price, Kelly Oriel, Lisa Quirk, Carol Henson and Jackie Kaye.

During both journeys countless people came out of the woodwork to make a difference to our progress, here are just a handful: Thanks to John, Margaret and Simon Brackenborough for their love and support. Ann, Mark and Connor Brennan, Alex and Connor Gardiner, Jo and Rick Halliday, Nat Halliday for his company on the road. Dave Roberts for all his help with the media. Sally Thurwell, Donald Smart, Dave Hulme, Sheryl Lawler at Kickback Cottages, Penny Warneford at the Monster Skate Park, Paul Kane, Lewis and Hopper at the Emperor's Crown, George at Traveller's Autobahn. Maddy Howarth and Simon Whittle for their support on the east coast, and everyone who attended the Ladies Guest Night at RAF Woodvale. Joe Rigg for extensive IT support. All those at Lake Conjola Entrance Tourist Park, Woollongong City Tourist Parks and Big4 Parks across Australia. Ken and Yvonne Bradford. Doug Thorne and his family and friends. Alan Fletcher, Jamez Looker, Xavier Rudd, Ash Grunwald, Sandy Nicomanis, Caroline Disney, Neil and Mary Thompson, Kerri Hall. Graeme, Ben and Sam, Emily Davies, Sonny Rolph, Matty Rogers and everyone else who sent us their music. Robbie Buck and Amelia Chappelow from Triple J. Clive Hunston, Megan Hunt and Samantha Kelliher at the British Consulate in Australia. Bosse and Elsa Estaberg for their hospitality in Brisbane, and Leigh Hurley from Crosshands Chiropractors near Swansea, for travelling to Australia to sort out our backs!

These people and companies morphed from strangers to sponsors, having decided to go with their hearts when their heads were surely telling them otherwise! In no particular order; Jason and Sue East (and their wonderful children) from the Mumbles Kiosk, Juergen Hagedorn, Jim Nicol, Colin Johnston and family at The Magic Touch, Alice Munro-Ferguson and Helen Najar from Clic Sunglasses, Dave Hulme at VWmagazine.co.uk, Paul and Tony at Screwloose, Mike Stride at Octane Sport, Mark at DogCamSport, Ian Gibbins at Playengine, Gavin Clarke at Holey Trucks, Nikki Barber at Garmin,

Scott Seelye at Sunriser, Iain and Gerry at Vapourised, Ed, Anthony and Raymond at Extreme Drinks, Sam Hale and Katrina Morphet at Advance Performance, Rich Auden at Lush Longboards, Niall O'Gorman at Iomega, Pam Custer and Jo Nisbet at Real Wiiings UK, Alistair Cole and Chris Webb at Lifesigns Group, James Barrett at Applied Satellite Technology, Samantha Fountain at Shewee, Tim Everett at C1rca Australia, Brad at Dijinus, Douglas Knight at Singapore Air, Eric Groenewoud from Catapult, Paul, Frances and everyone at Mincor, Paul Deans at Pro-tec, The Gadget Store, Bell, Khiro, Gower Graphics, Innocent Drinks, Eat Natural, Faltown Skateboards, Bustin Boards, Old Skool Boards, Bones Bearings, Bodycool UK.

I'll be forever indebted to Peter Sanftenberg, for designing a board that changed my life and for being the first person to see BoardFree's potential. Kate Goodanew, for making such a difference Down Under. Arthur Hendey for his timeless youth, Chris, Natalie, Tyla and Kye Cleator, our extended family in Queensland. Rebecca Richardson, Carole Gengler and Kevin Gentle at Out of Your Shell and Chilled Turtle, for being so patient with my absence as I wrote this book. The same must also apply to Duncan Macdonald at AquaskipperUK. And of course, I have endless reasons to thank my team, but however tough things got they remained loyal to BoardFree throughout, I couldn't have asked anymore. Thank you, Kate Brackenborough, Dan Loo, Simon Thorpe, Becki McKinlay, Holly Allen, Bev Blackburn and Laura Hatwell. Each of their families deserve a mention too, their support allowed BoardFree to succeed as it did.

I don't need to thank my family again, because as my Mum would say, 'of course I supported you, I'm your Mum.' But thanks anyway to Mum, Dad and Andy, with you on my side it didn't seem as hard as perhaps it should have.

Please visit
www.boardfree.co.uk

find us online

come and visit Portico Books
for all present and forthcoming titles at:

www.porticobooks.co.uk
and
www.anovabooks.com